WE ARE WHAT WE READ

A LIFE WITHIN AND WITHOUT BOOKS

Vybarr Cregan-Reid

\B^b\
Biteback Publishing

First published in Great Britain in 2024 by
Biteback Publishing Ltd, London
Copyright © Vybarr Cregan-Reid 2024

Vybarr Cregan-Reid has asserted his right under the Copyright, Designs and Patents Act 1988
to be identified as the author of this work.

'Nursery Rhyme of Innocence & Experience' from *Collected Poems 1951–2000* by Charles
Causley, published by Pan Macmillan; reproduced by permission of David Higham Associates.

'The World I Live In' by Mary Oliver reprinted by the permission of the Charlotte Sheedy
Literary Agency as agent for the author. Copyright © 2015, 2017 Mary Oliver with permission
of Bill Reichblum.

Every reasonable effort has been made to trace copyright holders of material reproduced in this
book, but if any have been inadvertently overlooked the publisher would be glad to hear from them.

ISBN 978-1-78590-818-7

10 9 8 7 6 5 4 3 2 1

A CIP catalogue record for this book is available from the British Library.

Set in Minion Pro and Dupincel VF

Printed and bound in Great Britain by
CPI Group (UK) Ltd, Croydon CR0 4YY

FSC
www.fsc.org
MIX
Paper | Supporting
responsible forestry
FSC® C171272

To those everywhere who have taught tertiary arts and humanities in the last decade, drawing on reserves of tenacity, patience and generosity. And to my mum, for all the same reasons.

'I am no novel reader—I seldom look into novels—Do not imagine that I often read novels—It is really very well for a novel.' Such is the common cant. 'And what are you reading, Miss—?' 'Oh! It is only a novel!' replies the young lady; while she lays down her book with affected indifference, or momentary shame. 'It is only *Cecilia*, or *Camilla*, or *Belinda*;' or, in short, only some work in which the greatest powers of the mind are displayed, in which the most thorough knowledge of human nature, the happiest delineation of its varieties, the liveliest effusions of wit and humour are conveyed to the world in the best-chosen language.

Jane Austen, *Northanger Abbey*

Only three or four things are worth living for; the rest is shit.

Carlos Ruiz Zafón, *The Shadow of the Wind*

I paid $120,000 for someone to tell me to go read Jane Austen! And then I didn't.

John Mulaney

Contents

1 This good-fellowship – camaraderie – usually occurring through similarity of pursuits, is unfortunately seldom superadded to love between the sexes, because men and women associate, not in their labours, but in their pleasures merely. Where, however, happy circumstance permits its development, the compounded feeling proves itself to be the only love which is **strong as death** – that love which many waters cannot quench, nor the floods drown, beside which the passion usually called by the name is evanescent as steam.
– Thomas Hardy, *Far from the Madding Crowd*

Books hold most of the secrets of the world, most of the thoughts that men and women have had. And when you are reading a book, you and the author are alone together—just the two of you. A library is a good place to go when you feel unhappy, for there, in a book, you may find encouragement and comfort ... Books are good company, in sad times and happy times, for books are people—people who have managed to stay alive by hiding between the covers of a book.

E. B. White's letter in *Letters to the Children of Troy*

It took thirty-seven years to finish the novel. Had I been writing it, perhaps that would have been an achievement. Instead, three-quarters of my life had been exhausted awaiting the completion of Thomas Hardy's *Far from the Madding Crowd*, finally getting to its closing pages and Hardy's conclusion that real love, love as 'strong as death', is that which is made of companionship and passion.

Across such a span of time, some people have families. They might rise through their careers, retrain and rise again in another, or they might spend their time travelling the world. Entire lives get lived in less than thirty-seven years; full ones, too: Jesus, Mrs Beeton, Bob Marley, Sylvia Plath, Keats, Kurt Cobain, Biggie and Tupac, Robespierre, Bruce Lee, Vincent van Gogh, and most of the Brontës, including the brother. Wars are won and lost, dictatorships rise and fall, empires are dismantled. And what had I done with my time? I'd finished a book I'd been set to read at school recounting the conjugal exploits of the spunky Bathsheba Everdene.

While I was well on my way through the book, I knew finishing it was going to be a big moment. It had to be, given how my life had played out since I'd first read those dozen or so chapters when I was fifteen years old. What I didn't expect was for it to be such a memory rush. The novel joined two disparate moments, which now sparked like live wires, flashing up thoughts and revelations about how far I'd come and how much reading had changed me, what it had done for me and, too, the ridiculous things that had been done to change how it's taught.

Back then, I was a feckless adolescent, as uninterested in school and study as you might expect. My only interest was music, and I mostly got my music by stealing it. I don't mean I illegally down-loaded it. No, I removed scores of LPs from shops, in bags, behind bags, stuffed up school jumpers or beneath conspicuously outsized coats. Theft was the antidote to the staggering boredom of hanging around shopping centres while skipping school. My side hustle was graffiti, a pathetic attempt to leave some sort of mark on the world, to prove I was in it and I existed.

And with every bad decision, my life got a little smaller. What was the point of going to school? I just failed at things: as ill-suited to scholarship as I was to friendship. What was the point of taking risks? What was the point of trying when I knew things didn't work out for people like me? Instead, it was easier to huddle into myself, limiting effort only to what worked, until one day I realised I'd become so small that no one even knew I was there any more. Then again, invisibility is a superpower to a thief.

i

Since those days, I have developed another superpower and I am more grateful for it than anything: I developed a hunger for stories. And if you're going to read, if you're going to spend thousands of pounds across your lifetime on reading glasses and hours of your life cleaning them, if you're going to learn to enjoy that exquisite pleasure of the gradual transition of a book's heft from your right hand to your left as you make your way through it... if you are going to read *a lot*, then Thomas Hardy, despite first impressions, is going to make his way, at some point, back on to that imaginary stage.

At first, *Far from the Madding Crowd* was tainted by association with school, but much later, I began to suspect the book might be quite good and hoarded it as an unexplored pleasure, deferred to the future.

You see, in those intervening thirty-seven years, I had fallen in love with literature so deeply, so unproblematically and so totally that I wasn't fit for much else. I had no choice but to become an English literature academic. That younger, indolent version of myself could not have foreseen the embarrassment that stung every time I had to admit, at conferences or in seminar rooms, to not having read the novel. 'Why embarrassment?' you might ask. It was because I specialised in, of all things, nineteenth-century literature, and worse, I taught an entire course, by choice, devoted to the work of said Thomas Hardy.

ii

The shiny new title of professor had been bestowed on me a few months before the chaos of the first Covid lockdown. After my fair share of challenges, I was finally living the good life. I'd made it to the summit of my career. That career, and its associated side gigs of publishing books, appearing at literary festivals, being on telly and radio and making radio series for the BBC to be broadcast all over the world, had also taken me all around the globe. In recent years, off the back of work, I had visited Japan, Singapore, Boston, Buffalo, Detroit, Seattle, San Francisco, Reykjavik, Sardinia, Groeningen, Brussels, Paris, Cyprus, Kenya, Venice, Rome and Berlin. It had taken decades, but I'd somehow made this work my job. Now, I was a professor too.

You're supposed to be cool and reserved as a professor. You're not supposed to like it too much, lest it seems you are unsuited to the station. But how could someone not feel grateful when data collected by the Royal Society in 2010 showed that less than half a per cent of students who complete doctorates go on to become professors?[1] Now, I was finally at the point where I wouldn't have to grind or level up any more. Instead, I could just get on with the work I loved doing and was good at.

What also made it so special was that, as a child, I hadn't once imagined such a future. No one else had either. One of our neighbours growing up was also, briefly, my maths teacher. When my mum told him the news (she told everyone she met), he was nonplussed: 'Vybarr? You mean, your son Vybarr... Really, Vybarr?'

I had done well in primary school, but awful, life-changing stuff rained down upon our family and after that I consistently ranked about twenty-sixth in classes of not much larger. What healed all that damage for me in the end was quite simple. Reading.

iii

I was able to exult in my new role of professor for only a matter of weeks before Covid struck. At that point, I became one of the billions whose livelihoods had been steered violently off course by the pandemic. Some were made redundant, some were furloughed, some were clenched in the purgatory of zero-hour contracts, some were overworked, many were just sacked. After a few weeks of enjoying my small success, it felt like I had stepped on the ninety-ninth square in a game of snakes and ladders. The pandemic was going to slide me all the way down the back of the serpent to the very beginning of my career. Everything gone. The news arrived that our department was to be cut by 50 per cent. I would likely be out.

It was all of this that drove me back to Hardy, where it had all begun. It was principally because it looked like the window of opportunity for me ever getting to teach *Far from the Madding Crowd* was closing. I was about to become one of the many casualties in the war on the humanities, which had been raging for decades. So, I set the novel on that year's Hardy course, not really considering what the impact of reading it might be.

iv

Being an academic with a heavy teaching load means that you don't so much read books as ram-raid them. You bungee into them, quickly grabbing only what you need before the elastic snaps back and you flee the scene, bound for your next crime against scholarship.

After I'd been rescued by books in my twenties, I read at home, on my way to work, at work, on my lunch break, on my way back home. I became an expert at negotiating people and street furniture as I walked with my head in a book, never once barging shoulders, missing my footing or disappearing down a manhole. I had the energy and hunger that only unsatisfactory work generates, and that work also kindly endowed me with the motivation to change, to study long and hard to get degrees, fellowships and a doctorate. Those changes came from my reading.

Now, in the present, my brain was mush from exhaustion. The

last two books I'd read for choice were both thrillers – carefully chosen in the hope that they might restore the compulsion to read. The experiment tanked. The first took me four weeks; the second took me six. Over two months of reading and all I had to show for it were two blown-out paperbacks in larger print than was necessary, with chapters a lot shorter than they ought to be and generous blank pages between to bulk out the sections.

v

On the day I started rereading The Hardy Novel, I had hundreds of emails to contend with, research impact statements to draft, references to write, meetings strewn across my calendar like an upturned box of drawing pins. I had lectures to record, tutorials to arrange with trainee doctors in the medical school and a pandemic to dodge. Nonetheless, I had previously worked out exactly how many days I would need to get the novel read in time for the class, and so I had to begin.

I shut my computer down. Heavy with work worries, I reclined into a protesting chair, but when I opened the book, I was suddenly back with my fifteen-year-old self. In a moment, I was in the plush armchair in the front room of our house, my legs curled up under me, sat in a single shaft of sunlight with dust motes drifting through it. I could remember the book's distinct orange binding, the colour of a Club biscuit, and the malformed geometry of the used paperback. Its dog-eared cover was cracked and torn but with a splodgy painting of some sheep, a gate, a forest and a golden sunset. This was not an enticing cover to a teenager more used to the Mardi Gras palette of *Asterix* and *The Adventures of Tintin*. But I'd made myself comfortable and even though it looked like there was a reasonable chance the novel might be about sheep, I was determined to read Thomas Hardy.

It had been a titanic effort on my part to commit to sitting still for several hours to do anything, let alone to read. My heart breaks to think of that kid, a kid that had learned to hate school and everything it represented. Yet, in an attempt to please, to do what I knew was good for me, what was right, I tried. I really tried. Nobody saw the effort; nobody valued it because it was just what was expected of me. It didn't matter that I couldn't do it.

Why is it that we are never fully present in these moments of great importance in our life? As I sat there, I failed to grasp that my future was in the balance. I didn't realise it but the portal to another world was open before me, yet I treated it like I was being forced to holiday with grandparents.

I leafed past the prelims. Chapter One. A long description of Gabriel Oak. Then, oh no! It *is* about sheep.

But I was determined. For hours I sat, eventually making it to page eighty-one. Later on in life, I might boast that I managed to read Margaret Atwood's *The Blind Assassin* on the same day as J. M. Coetzee's *Disgrace*, but on that day, I read far more than I had at any previous point in my life. The Hardy-esque irony, the tragedy in miniature that was awaiting the completion of my work, was the simple realisation that no one had told me you had to focus and try to follow the rill of the story. When I got up from the chair and realised that I couldn't recall any of what I'd read, I was a Sisyphus watching the stone roll down the hill but one who just could not be arsed to push it back up.

Why had no one told me that you had to concentrate when you read? I was outraged, properly angry. Then, acknowledging that it was all my own fault, I hit the ground like a safe. The outcome was that I turned my back on literature in a huff of such adolescent magnitude that it lasted for years. Looking back, it feels as though the very idea of 'school' was in the balance in that reading session.

School lost.

vi

Now, here I was in the present, chair at full tilt, feet on my desk, the living embodiment of the fact that my literary career hadn't terminated those decades ago when I started reading about Hardy's sheep and his 'oo-arrr' cast of locals.

What was odd was that it also felt a little like I was killing my reading career. Fulfilling this life goal of completing *Far from the Madding Crowd* was like admitting to myself that this really was the end. This wasn't just another book; *this was it*.

With days to go before the class, as we moved into the second lockdown, I was drawn once again into the landscapes of nineteenth-century Wessex, this time through this long-shelved novel. Locked in, I was reading about wide-open spaces; by lamplight I read about the qualities of sunlight; in the still air of grey rooms, I read about violent thunderstorms and swarms of bees that

swept the sky in a scattered and uniform haze, which now thickened to a nebulous centre: this glided on to a bough, and grew still denser, till it formed a solid black spot upon the light.

Some of the passages seemed so natural as to be unchosen – appearing not so much written as found. It was hypnotic. I was reading like I was falling asleep on the night bus: drifting unconsciously into it before being jolted awake by something teacherly that I had to note down. The 'strong as death' bit at the end of the book had registered at the time of reading but it drifted away on the breeze of inattention, lost in the commotion of a working day.

vii

A few days later I was out for a walk, trying to sluice my head of the day's accrued debris, when the 'strong as death' line resurfaced suddenly in my memory: 'Where, however, happy circumstance permits its development, the compounded feeling [of companionship and passion] proves itself to be the only love which is strong as death.' I *did* know it.

It was from a poem that we read at school at the same time I had started *Far from the Madding Crowd*. It was powerful stuff. I remembered being given the verses in class, and as I read them, I wanted to put my hands over the page. It was like the lines were emitting a bright light and I was worried others would see what was written there. I blushed the deceiver's crimson and sat rigid so as to remain undetected. My fingers splayed on the page, I tried my best to restrain the words from escape.

The poem was by the much underrated and prolific Cornish poet Charles Causley. The Blakean irony of the poem's title, 'Nursery Rhyme of Innocence and Experience', was lost on me at the time. And it does what Causley does best: musicality with complexity masked as simplicity, moving seamlessly from fairy tale to modern war story.

The poem begins with a boy on a quay, asking a sailor to bring him something exotic (a parakeet, an apricot tree) from across the seas. Refusing the proffered penny, the sailor happily consents. Then:

And he smiled and he kissed me
As strong as death
And I saw his red tongue
And I felt his sweet breath

'You may keep your penny
And your apricot tree
And I'll bring your presents
Back from sea.'

Years pass, and the ship returns, battered and with a hole in its hull. The boy stands on the quay and watches it dock.

'O where is the sailor
With bold red hair?
And what is that volley
On the bright air?

'O where are the other
Girls and boys?
And why have you brought me
Children's toys?'

In the cadence of what seems like a children's nursery rhyme, Causley captures the ordeals of war, the trauma of time passing, the loss of innocence and the grief of unfulfilled promises.

It was, though, that first erotic aside that punched me in the gut. ('Erotic'? Really? It is important to remember that adolescent boys are so primed for any kind of sexual experience that a change in the direction of the breeze can register as 'erotic'.) I had remembered the 'red tongue' but had long, long filed away the memory of how it had felt to read about a kiss 'as strong as death' when there were warnings about AIDS emblazoned across the newspapers.

The whole thing seemed written in Technicolor, but this was no Hollywood musical – more like an Elvis vehicle directed by Derek Jarman. The language is oversaturated, but the sentiment is not. The total effect is oneiric or hyperreal.

My teacher wanted a personal response to the poem. How could I have articulated to him or anyone how deeply the poem had struck me? I relished the exotic language of the 'apricot tree' and the 'parakeet'. I thought apricot was an Angel Delight flavour and I'd never heard of a parakeet. But the resonant nature of the language seemed inextricable from the homoeroticism of it.

Being a gay, closeted kid in the 1980s meant experiencing a queer phenomenology. In it, the very contours of reality were shown to be contingent upon one's point of view, age, body and desires – real to those experiencing them, imagined to those who only hear of them. In that world, the landscape was different; I saw different things in it, and I experienced those things often at one remove. And growing up in that hostile era has left me with an internalised homophobia embedded so deeply that even in my fifties I am still unable to pull it from its roots. Each time, like a tumour, it just grows back.

It wasn't that my school was such a terrible place, but as a gay teenager in the mid-1980s from a Catholic family, with Section 28 on the horizon, an AIDS epidemic in full sway, and the age of consent pushed pathologically all the way back to a remote twenty-one years, any and all kinds of sexual difference were in lockdown. I quickly learned it was better not to get too close to anyone, for the simple fact that they might see who you were.

But that poem was a glimpse into another world, an odd, queer, fantastical space, and registering the line from it in Hardy's novel brought the eroticism, the strangeness of it rushing back. And I felt it all again but fondly this time.

viii

I was not alone in seeking solace in other times, places and worlds in those peculiar months of finishing The Hardy Novel. Within days of those first lockdowns across the globe, many of us quickly worked out what our priorities were. It turned out that we really needed four things:

1. food
2. healthcare
3. connection
4. stories

In those first few weeks, book sales rocketed. As time wore on, Amazon's UK profits (from sales of all goods) leapt by 51 per cent. In the US they soared, rising 220 per cent with the company pocketing an extra $106 billion in net revenue.[2] In India, book sales spiked by around 60 per cent, with comparable rises in Japan, Canada, South Korea, Brazil and South Africa.[3] British readers spent an extra £100 million on fiction during the pandemic (a rise of 16 per cent).[4] Worldwide, the streaming services cashed in on their newly captive audiences. Thousands of hours across the globe were lost as we slowly, achingly punched our card details into the apps on our TVs to renew our subscriptions. The economics of all this creative output that fills up the streaming services, our gaming consoles, our bookshelves and our walls speaks for itself: creative industries generate £111 billion a year for the UK economy. In Australia it's A$90 billion; in the US it's $1.1 trillion.[5]

Within these numbers, buried so deeply that you need to drill down to the dimes and cents, are billions of individuals for whom stories were necessary sustenance.

In 2009, neuropsychologists at the University of Sussex ran a trial which concluded that reading for as little as six minutes can reduce stress levels by 68 per cent. More recent cognitive research has shown that certain kinds of fiction promote empathy in readers. It occurs when readers are exposed to a thing called free indirect discourse – a narrative technique that blends the voice of the narrator with the thoughts and expressions of a character. The effect blurs the line between quotation and indirect narration and it's often found in writers like Jane Austen and Gustave Flaubert.[6]

Reading fiction has been shown to quell some of the body's harmful and toxic responses to isolation and loneliness (reducing levels of cortisol). Losing oneself in stories has been a clinically proven way of alleviating the negative impacts of pain, anguish, depression and anxiety.

But no one is reading books because of the statistics or the health benefits, and the fact that we turn with such frequency to things like neuroscience to justify the habit is indicative of just how much trouble we are in. Mathematics is a means of understanding our world, not explaining the totality of it. People read because it is an act of faith, an act of love. Where Charles Dickens would have expended 900 pages making the point, the American poet Mary Oliver fits the whole idea into a few lines of verse in 'The World I Live In':

> I have refused to live
> locked in the orderly house of
> reasons and proofs.

The world I live in and believe in
is wider than that. And anyway,
what's wrong with *Maybe*?
You wouldn't believe what once or
twice I have seen. I'll just
tell you this:
only if there are angels in your head will you
ever, possibly, see one.[7]

Fact will only get you so far. We need fancy too.

Stories are so potent some even call them a technology, invented by humans not to teach us how to make a fire or build a skyscraper but how to deal with loss, how to understand others, how to forge connections, how to be. Toni Morrison's 1987 novel *Beloved*, about a family coping with grief and trauma, might, for example, be seen as a means for teaching its readers that trauma must not be buried but incorporated into our world view, acknowledged, otherwise we have no hope of flourishing in the future. Or Robert Louis Stevenson's *Strange Case of Dr Jekyll and Mr Hyde*: suppress sexual desire and the force of that suppression will emerge terrifying and uncontrollable. Or Rohinton Mistry's *A Fine Balance*: money and class status may buy you some advantage in life, but when it comes down to it, it's the resilient who survive.

Given what we've all been through in recent years and how much diversion we have all craved, it's no surprise that the turnover and profit of these creative industries is so impressive. Which makes what's happening to arts education globally as baffling as it is concerning.

'Creative industries' broadly refers to those in which the value of the outputs is symbolic: film, publishing, fashion, design, music, gaming, fine arts, architecture. These subjects are regularly offset against STEM subjects (for science, technology, engineering and mathematics, though the umbrella also includes medicine and healthcare).* In the education systems of the US, Australia and the UK, as well as those throughout south-east Asia and Europe, governments are flinging money at STEM subjects, stripping it from the arts. Those arts subjects are left to fend for themselves in a supposedly free market, when it's really one that's rigged against them.

This is not a new story. Governments all over the world have been clamping chloroform over these subjects for decades and my own discipline of English is no exception. Following a range of telegraphic policies that clearly signal intentions, the flow of students interested in taking arts subjects has been gradually staunched, leaving institutions scrabbling for the few remaining ones. In some parts of the world like Australia, policies have actively disincentivised students from selecting arts subjects, and the student fees are much lower for medicine than literature – even though the cost of the delivery of one is about a twentieth of the other. But while the efforts to stamp out the humanities continue, the students persist in choosing them nonetheless.[8] In the UK in particular, individual subjects such as English or History have been made exponentially more boring to endure at school (a subject I'll come back to in Chapter 5). Ivy League colleges in the US attempt to promote the value of English and the humanities as legitimate alternatives to STEM subjects, but the cost of studying them can in some cases exceed $300,000 across the four years of study.[9] In such a situation and with such expense, any student would be remiss if they didn't ask themselves, 'How am I going to pay this money back?'

UK students rack up the highest individual debt globally

---

* According to the Joint Council for Qualifications, STEM covers biology, chemistry, computing, design and technology, mathematics, physics and 'other sciences'. Humanities covers art and design subjects, classical subjects, drama, English language, English language and literature, English literature, French, law, German, history, music, Spanish, other modern languages, performing or expressive arts, political studies and religious studies.

(approximately £45,000 per borrower) but, compared to other countries, enjoy a relatively forgiving repayment system... at least, for now. In the US, the debt environment is more heavy-duty. There, the most common repayment plan lasts ten years, so with an interest rate of 6 per cent on $90,000 of debt you will have to find $1,000 every month in the decade after graduation – the time in your career when you are earning the least.

Some might argue that paying for your education is just like taking on another mortgage. Except, it's not. In the US and elsewhere (the UK, Switzerland, Australia, Israel, Italy, Japan, South Korea, the Netherlands, Canada, Chile, Austria and Hungary), student debt accrues interest at comparative to or faster rates than a mortgage. And with a mortgage, in leaner times you might choose to make some personal economies – perhaps to rent a bit of your house out or sell it and move to a cheaper area. But once you've bought your education, you can't sell it on. Education is treated in many ways like a commodity, like a raw material, but it's not. Once you have your Ivy League degree (which, if you are on the borrow, would cost about $2,755 a month), how are you going to pay that money back? You can't trade it. You love books, so you might think you could become an English teacher. It's an 'honourable' profession – but you know as soon as someone deploys that adjective, bad news is in train. As a teacher starting out in the US, you can expect to take home about $38,617; barely enough to cover your loan payments, never mind food, rent, childcare, travel, heating – and not forgetting the tax. It could be worse: some of the teacher starting salaries in Japan, Costa Rica, Czech Republic, Estonia, Colombia, Israel, Mexico, Greece, Poland, Hungary, Slovakia or Latvia currently are less than $30,000.[10]

Equally 'honourable' post-English degree careers might see you becoming a copyeditor, journalist, working in publishing or a museum. Looked at from this angle, it all seems a bit bleak. None are highly paid, but try to get a job in those industries and you'll see just how many people don't care about the salary; they are there because they are utterly in thrall to the work.

Unless you are specifically driven towards these careers, the story goes that you should steer clear of English because you'll end up an overqualified shelf stacker at a supermarket. (After all, isn't that the fate I am facing, with university redundancies on the horizon?) But there is a truth that no one wants you to know about the earnings of English graduates. It is a simple and beautiful fact, and you won't find it mentioned at parents' evenings or in the press: English graduates *aren't* badly paid.

ix

In the UK, the proportion of students studying the humanities has plummeted to 8 per cent from 28 per cent in the mid-twentieth century.[11] In the US, the number of those taking English majors has dropped about 50 per cent since the mid-'90s alone, whereas since 2009 the numbers studying computer science or electrical engineering have more than doubled.[12] Currently, there are about 530,000 studying business and management in the UK, compared with 15,000 studying English literature.[13] Despite humanities graduates having better employment rates, they typically earn a little less.[14] English graduates in the US earn a median of $44,600, a couple of thousand below the overall median.[15] While STEM graduates have a 3.2 per cent unemployment rate, it's only 1.2 per cent higher for English graduates.[16] The question arises: is a 1 per cent greater chance of your being unemployed a good enough reason for spending three to five years of your life and £60,000 studying something you hate?

I'm not sure it is. I'd easily take those odds if it meant I never had to do any chemistry ever again.

The answer doesn't sit in the numbers but in feelings. It's not that English won't get you a job, one that you will likely earn a decent wage from; none of the data suggests this. None of it. Anywhere. Instead, it's the loudly hailed, much repeated belief that this is the case that is making our younger generation think twice. Any parent considering their child's options has to work against waves of negative supposition – and most don't have the bandwidth to undertake the fairly deep research needed to find these figures. The belief that studying English leads to low pay is as pervasive as the mist in a steam room, where every molecule of water whispers its hollow mantra: 'But what job will you get?'

The message is telegraphed from all angles and repeated so often that everyone assumes it to be true. For example, one thing that corroborates, cajoles and creates the disdain with which the humanities are viewed in the UK is the share of central research funding that they receive.

The entire research budget for the UK is divided up across several central funding bodies, among them: nature and the environment, science and technology, medicine, economics and social studies, engineering and physical sciences, and biological sciences. There's also one for *all* the arts and humanities. I asked a few people to guess what share of the total budget these subjects might net in the UK. Most of the answers I got bobbed around in the late teens, with the lowest being 15 per cent. No. The total share of budget for over 100 arts and humanities subjects in the UK is 1.4 per cent.[17] And it's shrinking.

As academics, we are regularly prodded by management to chase a share of this money and in doing so, we become greyhounds released from the traps to ravage the hare we already know is a rubber chicken.

X

Around the time that I returned to *Far from the Madding Crowd*, what was most upsetting wasn't just my circumstances – facing devastating cuts to the department and the likely end of my career – but the fact that it was happening everywhere. All the time. The decades-long assault on the humanities had continued in the background with the persistency of tinnitus. You'd sometimes forget about it, but it was always there.

This particular cut was announced during the squally tenancy of the UK's then Education Secretary Gavin Williamson, the one with the look of a recently demoted prefect and who resigned before the investigation into the allegations that he had bullied colleagues could conclude.*[18] It was the confirmation that the government would, despite objections, be proceeding with more cuts to university funding across the arts. Among the subjects affected by the cuts were archaeology, art, drama and music. Each would have their teaching subsidies slashed by 50 per cent.

When the plans were first announced several months earlier, they received such backlash I naively thought that, unlike the plethora of other cutbacks, these ones might never see the light of day. It was part of the then government's playbook to make policy announcements and then backtrack. This one stuck, though, and the money saved wasn't being siphoned into some post-Covid relief fund. Like with other, similar policies, the money was being taken from the arts and humanities and given to STEM subjects. Williamson, who was called 'the most ignorant, clueless and incapable education secretary in the UK's history' by Labour politician David Lammy,

---

* Keir Starmer referred to him as 'a sad middle manager getting off on intimidating those beneath him' and a 'cartoon bully with a pet spider'.

explained, 'These changes will help ensure that increased grant funding is directed towards high-cost provision that supports key industries and the delivery of vital public services, reflecting priorities that have emerged in the light of the coronavirus pandemic.'[19]

The message to senior management in universities is clear: the government does not value these degrees. The message to parents: these degrees are frivolous. The message to students: do these degrees but only if you, or your parents, can afford the debt.

Williamson was eventually sacked as Education Secretary after a staggeringly long two years in post. A train of successors followed, whistling in and out of the revolving doors at the Department for Education. Each of Williamson's successors was as bemused, uninterested and unqualified as the one before. One of them lasted barely a day in post before resigning – this was enough for her to qualify both for severance pay (25 per cent of a Cabinet member's annual pay) and a ministerial pension on top of that for her few hours in public service, though she ultimately ended up rejecting both. At least she didn't make any mistakes during her tenure.

First up was Nadhim Zahawi, who lasted nearly an academic year, from September through to early July. Zahawi was later discovered to have been subject to an HMRC investigation into his tax affairs while he had been Chancellor of the Exchequer (i.e. in charge of the country's tax affairs), resulting in his having to pay a fine as part of a settlement somewhere in the millions.[20] Next up, James Cleverly managed to cling on to the education post for nearly two months. Kit Malthouse, Cleverly's successor, fared even worse: he only held on for seven weeks. This was clearly a government that did not take education seriously.

Worse still, in the most '2022' move of all, Williamson was rewarded with a knighthood – something that can only be interpreted as recompense for something big that the public was not privy to. After all, it cannot have been his performance in the role, which was awash with controversies like the A-level grading debacle, failing to provide guidance or equipment to schools that had to move online during the pandemic, or mistaking Maro Itoje for Marcus Rashford. Labour called the knighthood 'astonishing and disgraceful', the Liberal Democrats, 'an insult to every child, parent and teacher'.[21]

The message that so many of us are being tricked into broadcasting is that the only thing that matters is earnings, money, profit. Shareholders are king, and it is your boss who gets to say what it is that you need to learn, to know and, concomitantly, to think.

Luckily for all of us, not everyone is so easily duped. For example, instead of blasting off into space strapped to a kerosene-filled phallus, Dolly Parton has used her fortune to distribute nearly 200 million books for children. The economic benefits of Dolly Parton's charity 'Imagination Library' – active in Australia, Canada, Ireland, the UK and the US – has brought unquantifiable social, developmental, educational, personal and emotional succour to millions of children who are learning to love books.

xi

'Print is dead,' Egon Spengler claims in 1984's *Ghostbusters*. He says the line when the team's secretary tries to engage him in a conversation about reading. Uber-scientist that he is, he prefers to collect 'spores, moulds and fungus'.

Ink on paper may seem dead to some, but for others, the blacked-out space on a plain page is the stuff of sorcery. The seventeenth-century poet John Milton also spied alchemy therein, claiming:

Books are not absolutely dead things, but do contain a potency of life in them to be as active as that soul was whose progeny they are; nay, they do preserve as in a vial the purest efficacy and extraction of that living intellect that bred them. I know they are as lively, and as vigorously productive, as those fabulous dragon's teeth; and being sown up and down, may chance to spring up armed men.[22]

This is a 1644 version of Stephen King's wonderfully pithy assertion that books are 'portable magic'.[23] For Milton, books are a vial of distilled intellect; they contain the elixir of genius. The second part of the quotation refers to a scene in Ovid's *Metamorphoses* in which Cadmus scatters dragon's teeth onto the earth and watches armed men grow from these seeds. I love this image of books as tooled-up soldiers ready to fight their cause with their refined concentrate of wit. And it's also why it breaks my heart that books and ideas are being sidelined in national and international debates, reduced to something that people are free to do but only once they've earned the time and money to do it. Plays, drama, theatre and literature, the messages seem to say, are all things that you should be doing for fun, like jigsaws or collecting stamps. But they are not the trimmings of a life. They are life.

It breaks my heart because the thing that I love – all the more so because it got me through the worst parts of my life while also gifting me the best – this thing that has taught me more than I can articulate, this form (the novel) whose job it is to interpret our present, our place in the world, is now treated like it's being towed for scrap. It's being taken away from people who don't even know they need it yet.

I had not the worst but a tetchy start (partly because of what happened to me and my family and partly due to my own selfishness, stupidity and inexperience), but I eventually fell in love with English as a discipline. How that happened, where I started and what it did for me are all subjects of this book – and as such, all of those things are about what literature can do for anyone.

A life in literature has afforded me some terrific opportunities. It's taken me to corners of the world that I could never have seen without it. It's made me the person that, through it all, I wanted to be and hoped I might become. It's gifted me a kind of stability that I could only see elsewhere when I was growing up. It's taught me that reading isn't just a means of learning how to navigate the world but it's also about finding one's place in it. How many activities result in you getting to change your name… twice? From Mr to Dr, then Dr to Professor?

It has changed the way I see the world. It has changed the way in which I understand it. It has taught me to write, to think, to look and look again. Now, when I finish a good book, the loss I might feel at leaving that world is suddenly offset by the giddy excitement that I can, in a matter of seconds, go anywhere and anywhen. Inside the piles of books I have around me as I write are civilisations, cities, histories and futures, challenging you to look upon them and not despair, because you are never lonely when you are reading. The activity suspends you in a web of relations between your present and your past, between you and the voices of the page, between you and the bustling lives of those you meet there. Finally, reading sits at the centre of your being and, like a force, pushes itself into your thoughts, your actions and your life. It's as enigmatic as it is powerful.

Reading offers a kind of freedom that cannot be garnered any other way. Its value cannot be implied, only inferred; it cannot be instructed, only constructed; it cannot be given, only received; it cannot be shown, only made; it cannot be taught, only caught. No amount of computing power can download or process it for you; no one can be paid to do it for you. You can't copy it from someone else. No amount of money can buy it – its miracle is that it may only be acquired in the doing of it. Literature becomes you.

Now, are you sitting comfortably?

xii

What follows in this book is my own story of transformation through reading. When I had the idea, I originally wanted to write a paean to reading, but the assaults on its value and contribution took over. So, on our journey, I will burrow down into the specifics of the books that have mattered to or changed me most and what they continue to do for others. But it's not just about me: I present my reading story here alongside the story of the recession of the humanities and the study of English literature because I think it shows the future-changing power that reading has, as well as the things that it's able to do and to achieve.

We are going to disinter some of what has happened to English, from primary through to tertiary. I want to show you a little of what it is that people do when they 'do' English and a little of what it's like to be an academic – not too much though because it's mostly emails and meetings so stressful the participants' jugulars visibly throb. I want to tell you about what happens in universities, what they are trying to do and why it matters. I want to show you some of the artful and wrongheaded ways that English is being destroyed, and I want to do it by showing you what it did for me.

While reading might appear to be a solitary activity, it is in fact a companionable one. Books, as we will discover, can have similarly beneficial outcomes to our wellbeing as powerful as meeting up with friends. And, just like our friends, they change as we do. The best of them stay with us and, like an ageing face, their pages take on a certain pallor, they develop fine creases and wrinkles, but what they mean to us changes and matures, too. This is their magic.

In Hardy, there always has to be a little tragic irony. When I finished the novel, I felt like I had lost something, like a relation. In the past, the book was an open field to me. In my imagination, I would regularly breeze past it, the gate to it would be wide open, the grass would be winnowing in the breeze – there would likely be a few sheep in there too. Now, thirty-seven years on, it's all fenced up and cordoned off. *Far from the Madding Crowd* is finally back on the shelf with thousands of other books marked as 'read'.

There's a line in the book I came across while reading it: 'He had been held ... by a beautiful thread which it pained him to spoil by breaking.' I underlined it and reflected on the fact that I should have thought more deeply about closing the oxbow in time that that novel represented. While it also inspired me to reflect on where I had come from, for me *Far from the Madding Crowd* was, more than any other book, what 'English' was and what it stood for. Here I was, at the other end of my career, looking down over the balustrade at all that had been done in recent years to muffle its voice, to denigrate the creative and critical thought it fuels, to devalue the nuanced reading it stimulates, and ultimately to sideline its tremendous and transformative power for conveying a simple and organic truth: you are not alone. You never were.

2 There was no more work for him to do; and he did take up a lot of space. **"Where you going now?"** he said, slurping his tea noisily. "What are we going to do with him?' whispered Cem. "Just not fetch him any more," said Chas. "He's not bright enough to find his way here by himself." "I hope you're right," said Cem. So, as the night fell, they took John home for what they thought was the last time. – Robert Westall, *The Machine Gunners*

Experience was of no ethical value. It was merely the name men gave to their mistakes.

Oscar Wilde, *The Picture of Dorian Gray*

There are a couple of reasons that I wanted to write this book. One was that reading of Hardy. But there is another that emerged by coincidence around the same time. The story in my family goes that as a child, I was a lively, excitable, fun-loving, radiant and extrovert little squirt. I have always winced on hearing this because it's not how I remember it. If you asked one of my siblings for their side of all these stories, you would likely get a different version, chronological errors corrected etc. But theirs, like mine, will be just as inclined towards the fragmentary, and the weird glitch art that all familial memory is. Putting together a history for yourself is like trying to explain a dream that you know in the retelling was not as sense-making or causally linked as it sounds. I can only tell it like I remember it.

There is one photograph of me as a baby, but so bundled am I in christening skirts, I might just as easily be a loaf of bread. There are a handful of photos taken until I was about eight, then little beyond that. Home video was not yet invented. In my thirties, I was excited to discover an old roll of 8 mm film, but it turned out to be as blank as our memory of its first exposure. With my dad gone and our mum out working to provide for the four of us, recording the minutiae of our upbringings wasn't much of a priority.

With *Far from the Madding Crowd* sitting on the desk, I had finished teaching at the screen for the day and was idly scrolling social media. A friend had posted the opening credits from a children's TV programme, with a 'click "like" if you remember this!'

'Of course I remember it. I was on it,' I thought.

I watched and waited for the opening credits to finish to see which episode it was. Could it be?

It wasn't, so I emailed the YouTube channel and asked if they had access to more episodes of *Cheggers Plays Pop* from 1981. The response was almost instantaneous. They could get more; which school was I interested in?

A couple of days later, it arrived.

As a kid, I knew my music. I aced the school's pre-selection tests and made it onto the show's 'Hot Box': a quick-fire round of pop trivia. The other kids would have to demean themselves by racing across a bouncy castle assault course dressed as human spiders, with colanders strapped to their heads holding water-filled balloons.

It was a crushing disappointment to learn that Duran Duran had been into the studio earlier in the week to record one of their first-ever TV performances. In the studio, we watched the playback on a tiny TV dangling from the ceiling and then had to sell the lie of their presence by going wild in appreciation.

Nobody recorded the episode because nobody yet owned a VCR. It aired, and the transmitted signal was sent tumbling off into deep space, by now reaching the northern stars of Ursa Major.

i

I loaded up the video and sat down to watch. At the age of fifty-something, to see yourself at twenty-four frames a second, to hear your voice, to see how you held your frame, how your hair sat (how much of it you had!), to see how you conducted yourself, to hear the lilt of your accent, to see the pallor of your skin, how it moved – it is a remarkable thing. There's bathos in it, too – feelings lurch between wonder and laughter at the triviality of it all.

I thought I would recognise everyone who took part in the show but I'd forgotten most of the kids.

Then, the 'Hot Box' and there I was at the end of the desk. Four questions in all, and I was obviously unclear whether we were permitted to confer.

The other half of the team were played a snippet of a song to identify. I, meanwhile, could be heard off-camera singing the lyrics to myself. They managed to get the song title but got stuck on the artist. From the edge of the screen, I can be seen leaning over and mouthing the answer, but they didn't get it. Eventually, I gave up on the tradecraft and just said 'Graham Bonnet' aloud.

It was my turn next. Cheggers pronounces my name 'Veebar' – I mean, he could have rehearsed. I got asked how to spell the surname of New Wave princess Lene Lovich. I whispered the answer. And that was it.

What I found so uncanny was the difference in levels of confidence. The kids on my team were 'on it', every cell of them knowing they deserved to be there. They may have been unsure of the answers but not of themselves. Their self-possession is tangible. I, by contrast, am quiet, hunched, insular, mild – to such an extent, I look like I'm both nervous and bored. My hands are clamped between my legs and my shoulders rounded to make myself even smaller than I was. My expression is so meek that it seems like the only thing that could emerge from my mouth is, 'Please, sir. I want some more.'

I share the clip on my social media and people laugh because being eleven is just funny. Friends commented on how 'sweet' and 'shy' I seemed.

Until I reached my twenties, I believed that I was adept at hiding the fact that I couldn't cope with my home life, with being a gay kid, with being abused – but in two minutes of screen time, it seems obvious.

ii

It was only a couple of days later that I was talking to a friend, who told me that the police (his employer, he's not a perp) had sent him on a course.

'It's all about ACEs,' he said.

'What is?'

'ACEs. Adverse Childhood Experiences.'

He went on to explain that ACEs were predictors for offending, as well as various physical and mental health problems. He told me about an ACEs questionnaire. You fill it out and it gives you a score. I'm all over practically anything you fill out for a score, so off I went.

With data drawn from more than 17,000 people, an influential 2002 study explored 'The Relation Between Adverse Childhood Experiences and Adult Health'. The study was subtitled 'Turning Gold into Lead' and compared current adult health status to childhood experiences decades earlier.[1] Much of their focus was on people who scored as high as a '4' on the questionnaire. They discovered:

- 'A person with a midrange ACE score of 4 is 390% more likely to have COPD [chronic obstructive pulmonary disease] than is a person with an ACE score of 0.'
- 'A person with ACE score >4 was 460% more likely to be depressed than a person with ACE score of 0.'
- A 4 on the test was associated with a '1,220% historical increase in attempted suicide'.
- In groups with 'higher ACE scores, incidence of attempted suicide increases thirtyfold to fifty-one fold'.
- 'More than two thirds of suicide attempts could be attributed to adverse childhood experiences.'
- 'A male child with an ACE score of 6 has a 4,600% increase in the likelihood of later using intravenous drugs.'
- A 4 or higher also showed a strong relation to many later-life diseases, such as 'hepatitis, heart disease, fractures, diabetes, obesity, alcoholism, occupational health, and job performance'.

My questionnaire complete, I scored a 7.

iii

From before I was born, I was already competing with my siblings for attention. I was the last of four, with five years between me and the eldest. I had a nuchal cord: the umbilical cord was wrapped like a noose about my neck in utero. I arrived about two months early. Survival rates for such early arrivals were about fifty-fifty. Those who survive tend to be diminutive (check!) and asthmatic (check!).[2]

I am the only one of us born in Manchester. Before I came along, the family lived in Cheltenham, but I'm unsure why. One of the stories is that, as a chess master, my dad had wanted to live in 'the chess capital of Britain'. Perhaps it was Cheltenham's proximity to Government Communications Headquarters (GCHQ) which made it so. My father didn't work for the government. He was intelligent but not educated. He had been a policeman back in Ireland and had won a medal for bravery in the line of duty. He was a competent poet. He was often kind and indulgent but in the wrong mood could deliver a beating, the ferocity of which could be remembered for a lifetime.

iv

By the time I arrived, the family had already moved into a semi in a suburb of south Manchester. The house had a front garden about the size of a single bed. It had a shared driveway to a pair of garages at the back (one for us, one for the neighbour). We also had a back garden. It seemed big at the time but is laughably compact when I return to it now.

Even when our dad was around, our mum was no domestic drudge. He wanted her out working and earning. She tried to be there when we got home from school, but things like meals and bedtimes were always haphazard. Extra responsibility defaulted to my eldest sister. My brother and I shared a room and were quite similar as children. But we responded very differently to our changing world. As teenagers, we diverged about as much as is possible for two people who are related.

v

We were never much of a bookish house. We had a couple of shelves of chess books: *The Grünfeld Defence*, *French Defence: Tarrasch Variation* and *Logical Chess Move by Move*. There were some encyclopaedias, sources of essential information on things like venomous snakes or how long it takes to sink in quicksand. We had some classics – but just like Andrew Lloyd Webber is music for people who don't like music, our 'classics' were too ornate to be read. Gold leaf embossing, so delicate it perished on handling. Paper so thin as to resemble a hotel Bible. I now know that absolute bangers, like *Jane Eyre*, *Pride and Prejudice*, *The Woman in White* and a couple of dozen others were sitting right there on the shelf, at my fingertips. (I have an addictive personality, and in the case of the latter, I now know that it is so compelling a read I have to stay away from it unless I want the next four days written off.) But the worlds these books contained somehow took on the patina of their kitsch, faux-leather covers. They looked as ornamental as our Capodimonte.

The proximity of books, of all kinds, is important for children. In 2010, a longitudinal study that had been running for two decades published its results. It examined the long-term, comparative educational outcomes of children who grow up in households with books and those who don't.[3] It was previously believed that the strongest predictor of educational attainment in children was the educational level of their parents. This study, though, found that the children who grow up in bookish homes spend on average an extra 3.2 years in education. For a comparable educational outcome, both parents would need to have completed degrees. (An expensive attribute, nowadays.) The cut-off figure for what counted as a bibliophilic household in the study was 500 books. Given its role in encouraging engagement with literature and reading, and its consequent impact on all educational outcomes, English seems like it might be the most important subject of all. Once a child is hooked on reading, their future is practically set. They are ready to flourish at nearly anything they put their mind to. Yet still, English remains one of the most misunderstood subjects in the curriculum. (It strikes me that it might be a good idea for the government to mass-purchase books for every household with children, and if they do, can I go on the list?)

vi

If you want to confuse an English teacher, just ask them what exactly it is that they do. The ones educated in a rehearsed response will be easy to spot. The others, though, will look skyward and admit to never having really thought about it before. The reason that question can be so difficult is that the job they do is so very complicated. Historically, their role was undertaken by about seven specialists. Within their remit is: handwriting, the basics of the language, composition, comprehension, oracy, the ability to code switch and the exploration of forms and genres. Without a proficiency in your first language, the student cannot flourish in any other subject. They all employ sophisticated language and narrative, and without a proficiency in English, these cannot be passed on; neither can they be assessed.

This is also part of the problem of English – why it is in crisis in universities and schools alike. And the situation only worsens when we consider the nature of what it is that we do.

Geography is the study of places and their relationships to people. A geographer is one skilled in, or a student of, geography. Biology is the study of life and living organisms. A biologist is one skilled in, or a student of, biology. And so on. More obscure nomenclatures exist within the field of biology: melissopalynology is the study of pollen in honey and the pollen's source, melissopalynologist is the name for the expert or practitioner. Similarly, deltiology is the study and collection of postcards, practised by a deltiologist. There are hundreds of these examples. But English is the study of... what? Some books? The expert in or practitioner of English is a... what? There isn't even a word for what we do.

English has a PR problem. It's the only subject that I'm aware of in which the practice of it is nameless. It's the John Doe of education. But it's also the cornerstone of it, which is why so much of our timetables in school are given over to it. And while I might not remember much, or any, of the specifics of what I was taught in those lessons, I have no difficulty in remembering the stories.

vii

In the early '80s, when I was bound for secondary school, English as a distinct subject to be taught in schools was still less than a century old. This isn't so surprising when we understand that the entire school system was designed around a Victorian factory model: raw materials in, product out.

Anyone interested in the range of schooling available to children in the period doesn't need to read stodgy histories of the subject. Charlotte Brontë's *Jane Eyre*, Charles Dickens's *Nicholas Nickleby* and *David Copperfield* and Thomas Hughes's *Tom Brown's School Days* run the gamut of the educational landscape. Perhaps the only thing missing is the informality of dame schools, with children sent to a local spinster to be taught anything from needlework to the translating of Virgil. Literacy rates in the period varied greatly and it wasn't until the end of the Victorian period that this really changed.

In 1870, the Elementary Education Act toyed with real change by establishing school boards. An additional Elementary Education Act of 1880 made school compulsory for all children between the ages of five and ten.

'English' in the nineteenth century was concerned solely with syntax, analysis and comprehension. Reading, writing, composition and literature more generally were all treated separately. It wasn't until 1904 that the subject was elevated to compulsory status, and even then it was taught by several teachers and only rarely were they qualified.[4]

viii

It's a similar story in universities, most of which resisted taking English seriously as a subject. Not until the twentieth century did Oxbridge finally start to teach it. Before then, it had emerged in the late eighteenth century at Edinburgh. Thereafter, the subject found its way into places like University College London. What links the character of these universities is that they weren't for 'gentlemen'. English was taught at these schools to working folk who wanted to be able to pass as well-educated gentlemen. Britain was so class-ridden at the time that the study of English as a subject *for* working men meant that the subject was viewed, as one public school headmaster put it in 1918, with some suspicion:

> The lack then of a due balance of qualities and acquirements in so many authors ... is a cause ... of that belittlement of the literary side of education which are on the whole marked features of the English attitude to-day ... And it is only the lack, in so many of the greatest writers, and the neglect, in so many educators and educational systems, of that due balance of qualities and acquirements of which I spoke just now, which have induced in superficial minds a distrust and often a contempt of literature as a subject of education.[5]

'Contempt', 'belittlement' and 'distrust': a succinct summation of the status of English. How could it be other? Functional literacy was for the lower classes. Literature, and especially the reading of novels, was for girls – in the right families, their brothers would have been away at a public school learning their Latin and Greek and not getting stuck into either of the Shelleys.

In the early twentieth century, the newly literate working classes were free to enjoy fiction of all kinds. 'English literature', though, sought to distance itself from any notion of populism. As John Carey cynically notes in *The Intellectuals and the Masses*, modernism (epitomised by the likes of Virginia Woolf, T. S. Eliot and James Joyce) rejected the accessibility of the Victorian novel with a new literature aimed at a higher-educated elite. There is some truth to this.

English literature ramped up its status as a subject after figures like F. R. Leavis, who emerged in the 1930s, argued that teachers of the new subject were responsible for the wellbeing and vitality of the language itself, even for the dissemination of moral values. Leavisite standards for what stood for 'English' and its practice as a discipline persisted throughout most of the twentieth century. There were skirmishes as new critical trends emerged in the 1960s and '70s (structuralism, feminism, poststructuralism, deconstruction), but it was Leavisite criticism that dominated the teaching of the subject at secondary level.

ix

School-level English is not only the foundation of all subjects in the curriculum, but it's also the means of conducting one's life

– certainly on a practical level but also for processing our thoughts, feelings and interpreting the world.

Its remit as a subject only grows the more you think on it. It's about:

- the development of the whole person;
- helping students to understand and interpret their entire curriculum;
- helping students prepare for the world of work (learning to code switch in both verbal and written language);
- exposing students to, as Matthew Arnold put it, 'the best that has been thought and said';
- enabling the student to become an independent and critical thinker.

There are competing pressures in here. Some English teachers, understandably, don't like that their role is considered as servicing proficiency in other disciplines, rather than their own. Some despair at the instrumentalisation of English, when its value is seen only in terms of employability and the transferable skills that it inculcates in the student. In these terms, English is never seen as itself or for itself, only as a conduit to more serious disciplines or the world of work.

With so many competing forces, ideas, drivers and interests, it is a fair conclusion to draw that no two English teachers can be said to be the same. Many will be equally committed to their subject, but what exactly they see that subject to be will be as unique to them as their fingerprints. Bureaucrats don't like the fact that something might be amorphous, without limits, bound only by the imagination or up to a professionally qualified teacher to decide. It is precisely this sort of thing that makes governments decidedly twitchy.

X

The idea of a National Curriculum had been a long time coming by the 1980s. In 1976, Labour Prime Minister James Callaghan, in a now-famous speech given at Ruskin College, Oxford, remarked:

> The goals of our education, from nursery school through to adult education, are clear enough. They are to equip children to the best of their ability for a lively, constructive, place in society, and also to fit them to do a job of work. Not one or the other but both ... There is no virtue in producing socially well-adjusted members of society who are unemployed because they do not have the skills. Nor at the other extreme must they be technically efficient robots. Both of the basic purposes of education require the same essential tools. These are basic literacy, basic numeracy, the understanding of how to live and work together, respect for others, respect for the individual. This means requiring certain basic knowledge, and skills and reasoning ability. It means developing lively inquiring minds and an appetite for further knowledge that will last a lifetime.[6]

Twelve years later, after a change of government, we get the Education Reform Act of 1988 and the emergence of a National Curriculum. But we are getting ahead of ourselves. Let's get back to 1981.

xi

The 1970s was something of a golden age for children's fiction. Raymond Briggs, Maurice Sendak, Nina Bawden, and Susan Cooper were all at their best. So, when our teachers took it upon themselves to read a novel with or for us in English, they had a goldmine of books to choose from.

One such was *The Machine Gunners* by Robert Westall. Set in the Second World War, it tells the story of Chas McGill and his friends. Together, they liberate a machine gun from a crashed bomber and set it up in their fortified den, awaiting the Nazi invasion.

I related to a troop of kids making dens and keeping secrets from adults. My friends and I always aspired to a place that was our own. It didn't matter how mucky, untidy or exposed it was; if adults weren't able to fit in it, it was perfect.

The set-up sounds like the novel might play out as many before it, following the trope of children liberated from the watchful eye of parents (as in, well… take your pick: *Peter Pan*, *The Famous Five*, *The Secret Seven*, or *Swallows and Amazons*). But Westall's novel is tougher and more real, with higher stakes, in which friendships and loyalties are both tested and shift. The children swear, parents are killed in air raids. And there's a damaged character in the novel: John. He is put to work by the group and is, like George R. R. Martin's Hodor, simple, well-meaning, easily led and strong as a rhino. 'Where you going now?' is all he can say, and he repeats it throughout the novel. Where you going now? Where you going now? Where you going now?

Is there a more important question for a school kid? For years afterwards, kids repeated the question in lessons, in the corridors, the playgrounds. It became a greeting, a farewell. Never was a question of such gravity used so easily with so little sense of its import.

xii

Our English teacher had enjoyed sharing Robert Westall, and after she punctuated the classes with a few more comprehensions and write-this-in-your-own-words, we segued back to another novel: Gene Kemp's *The Turbulent Term of Tyke Tiler*.

On the one hand, it seems like a pretty standard tale of a misunderstood kid, warring with the competing loyalties of home, school and friendship, wondering which, if any, of these matter and trying to figure out who they want to be. The story baits its readers into thinking the protagonist is a boy, and it's only on a rereading of the book that one can see the efforts Tyke's friends and family go to to help her fit into the world in the wrong body.

It was a novel that taught me it was possible for the world to accommodate difference and as such mattered more than any number of comprehensions or lessons on parts of speech. I wanted more but there was none to be had. Our teacher was replaced by someone more curriculum-driven, and I lacked the self-possession to find the stories for myself. It should have been a lightbulb moment; it was my fault that the wattage was a little low.

It's since been suggested that one of the key reasons that exposure to fiction matters, particularly to children and adolescents, is that it is a means of presenting them with various simulations, experiences and worlds. Furthermore, it is one of the reasons why exposure to fiction in psychological studies positively predicts greater scores for both social ability and empathy.[7] Persistent and regular readers, whatever their age, have already spent their time in other people's heads, living other people's lives, multiple times.

The tragedy for non-readers, or even devotees of non-fiction, is that they are not free in the same way. Instead of sampling a hundred lives, they are confined to one.[8]

I wasn't brave like Tyke. I wasn't as tough, independent and single-minded as her, but, thanks to the novel, I understood what it was like to try to make a place for yourself in the world when you felt yourself to be at the peripheries of it. Stories mean something and matter because they help us to interpret the world by speaking to us and our circumstances.

xiii

What was stopping me from running to the school library and asking a kindly adult there what I should read next?

There were four of us kids, we were a single-parent family and Mum was out at work until all hours. My mum was keen for us to enjoy being children but also completely exhausted by us. I don't re-member how we heard about it but there was free swimming going. The supervisor at one of the local pools would let a few kids in to swim after hours for free. (I know! You're already caught up.)

It never escalated all that much. There was a lot of watching, vig-orous towelling, wrestling on crash mats in the gym. The gold of his wedding band twinkling between hairy knuckles on his fat fingers that were always tickling, probing and pushing in places they were not supposed to be. I feel ashamed complaining about it, as it would have been worse for some. I also feel ashamed for being complicit in it. Why, if I didn't like it, did I keep going back? For years, *years*? I didn't know what was happening at the beginning but I did towards the end. By then, I'd worked out that this was transactional: the swimming was free on entry; it was on your way out you had to pay. It's for that reason that I can't help but conclude there was a class component to it. Moreover, what I experienced is common enough as to be something resembling a rite of passage. A study conducted by the NSPCC in the UK found that about one in twenty children between the ages of eleven and seventeen reported experiencing child sexual abuse.[9]

Those probing digits of his also inveigled their way into our family. Once there, he established himself as indispensably kind, generous and charitable, someone who did something seemingly for nothing.

Years later, I worked up the courage to disclose to my mum what had been going on. Her reply was that he'd been very good to our family.

You can't live your life the same way after a betrayal like that. I was angry with her for years, maybe decades, until one day it dawned on me that it wasn't her fault. He'd groomed her too. In chess terms, he'd got us in check and any move would only place us in further jeopardy. In her paralysis to act, my mum was a different kind of victim but a victim all the same. It wasn't either of our faults that any of it happened. He was drawn to the vulnerability of our family. I suspect that if he'd known of the violence that my father was capable of, we would never have seen him again.

More than once, it had struck me that there was another version of this story. It was the one in which she did act, took me to the police station, made a complaint and so on. What then? This was the 1980s, the groomers' decade. There would have been investigations, cross-examinations probably more scarring than the abuse, and everywhere, people either not believing you or thinking you deserved or were complicit in it.

Instead, once I realised that nothing was going to happen to him, I decided I wouldn't let it bother me. But as I missed day after day after day of school, as I plummeted down the school's tiers of ability, as I failed reams of exams, as I stole my way into the possession of a record collection, as I became a ghost in classes, as I lost contact with practically everyone I knew from school, as shame and secrecy became so much a part of me that they were like the carbon on an old pan, as I stole money, as I repeatedly ran away from home, as I daubed cars with paint, collapsed brick walls, graffitied, set fires, I told myself it didn't bother me. It was only in writing this that now I'm thinking, maybe it did.

I'm not quite sure when the stealing started, but I can't not mention it because it was a big part of my teenage years. Early on, the odd bar of chocolate might find its way here and there into my pocket. Then I had gone with a friend to a supermarket, both smacking our lips, and we were collared as we left the shop. The police were called and my friend and I were taken away to the station, which was only next door. Parents were called. Evidence was gathered, amounting to two chocolate bars. The whole time I was thinking about the KitKat that I'd snuck into an arm pocket in my coat, worrying its discovery would mean more time in chokey. So, I scoffed the evidence right there in the cell.

After that first caution, things gradually escalated. A friend or two might come along for fun. Once, I went to a bookshop with my best mate from school. The place was deserted, so my mate put his dorky briefcase down on the floor, opening its jaws as wide as they would go. Then, with a sweep of his arm, he sent an entire shelf of books, tumbling one by one, into his greedy valise. He bent over and closed the case with a snap. Took the handle, dusted himself off and, with a nod, signalled he was ready to depart. My head swam with fear and excitement as we scuttled out of the shop, nervous energy finally detonating into helpless laughter.

xiv

It's one thing to have an overwrought parent when there are four of you to dissipate the attention. It's quite another when there's only one of you left. My eldest sister and brother both moved out in their mid-teens. My other sister, the academic one, was holding out for university and eventually departed to go there.

My mum wanted us to do well at school and there was a natural variation among the four of us in our commitment to this philosophy. Like most people, I can't be made to do anything I would rather not do. I'd be shut in my room for hours to do schoolwork. It's a mystery to me now what I spent my time doing. I can remember some drawing and re-reading a lot of *Tintin* and *Asterix* from the local library. I learned to do killer Dalek and Donald Duck impressions, but that's about it.

My sister would try to help occasionally. One day, I had several pages of equations to do for school. It was a couple of hours' work at most. My sister sat down and worked her alchemy with the letters and numbers, and then it was time for her and mum to go out for the day.

The moment they left, I looked at my exercise book and couldn't make sense of anything that she had done. At which point, I was mostly done thinking about maths for the day.

I was all churned up. It was nothing more than a crush, but I didn't understand it. I couldn't satiate the desire because I didn't know what it was. How long would it last? How long could I stand it? Who cared about the value of the Xs and the Ys? Looking at them made me feel sick, like I suffered from algebraic trypophobia.

Distraction was what I needed.

I got up from my chair and checked the TV. Wrestling on two channels and a war thing on the other. I should try to work. I sat back down, looked at those Xs once more, then shut the book.

I wanted someone to explain this to me. But who was I going to ask? A priest would probably tell. A teacher? I didn't talk to any. Was this gay? Had the swimming teacher made me gay? Again, I tried to work. It's the tragedy of adolescence that one needn't be able to understand something to feel it.

'Gay.' It wasn't the first time the thought had occurred to me.

I went to the bookshelf to look up homosexuality in our household medical dictionary. The book was leathery, the colour of bone. The outline of a human was embossed on the cover, and one of us children had at one point put a felt tip into the groove and followed it inexpertly round the body's profile.

Homosexuality was in there. It was a sickness, after all.

Ever since the term's invention in the nineteenth century (the term 'heterosexuality' was invented at the same time), the men in white coats have fought vehemently for dominance over the narrative as to what homosexuality is.

The three points of contention generally boil down to pathology, immaturity and normal variation. Twentieth-century medicine leant more towards pathology. This was disastrous for the many young men who were forced to endure aversion therapies and, in some extreme cases, underwent brain surgery in attempts to cure them of their illness. I don't know when our medical dictionary was published, but it was only in 1973 that the American Psychiatric Association removed the diagnosis of 'homosexuality' from its standard diagnostic manual. Psychiatrists could find it categorised under 'sociopathic personality disturbances' within the subheading of 'sexual deviations'. By that point, homosexuality was already enshrined as a mental illness.

The pathologizing of homosexuality persisted in other medical quarters too. It appeared in the 1952 edition of the World Health

Organization (WHO)'s *Diagnostic and Statistical Manual of Mental Disorders*. In the 1979 version it was still there, listed under 'sexual deviations and disorders', where it sat with its compatriots of paedophilia, bestiality, sadism, fetishism and exhibitionism. The WHO, which also listed homosexuality in its *International Statistical Classification of Diseases, Injuries, and Causes of Death*, only removed it from its roster of defects, ailments and abnormalities on 17 May 1990.[10]

If you were a kid seeking information about homosexuality, what little you could find would most likely scare the shit out of you. And then there was AIDS.

XV

It might have been before the time when 'gay' was the go-to schoolboy synonym for everything rubbish, but queer baiting in national debate and in the newspapers had already reached 'blood sport' levels of ferocity by the mid-1980s. Homophobia was an allowable discourse, and stories with ludicrous headlines would appear in the papers. 'Gays in Fear. They Dread Revenge' might be left on the bus; you might unwrap your chips and find 'I'd Shoot My Son if he has AIDS, Says Vicar'; a pass-the-parcel layer might read 'AIDS may be a timely blessing, says doctor' (that article begins, 'AIDS could be the best thing that has happened since the Black Death'); or a glue-dripping shred used for papier mâché might read 'Perverts are to blame for killer plague'.[11] And it went on and on and on: 'Homosexuals who have brought this plague upon us should be locked up ... Burning is too good for them. Bury them in a pit and pour on quick lime'.[12] The oft-repeated joke 'I suppose you know what GAY stands for – got AIDS yet?' did not come from one of the tabloids but the satirical magazine *Private Eye*. Another cartoon (of many) from the same publication has an adviser talking to God, who is looking at a list entitled 'Plagues'. God is addressing the adviser: 'OK. That's sorted out the homosexuals, now let's have a go at the estate agents.'[13]

Our police chief constable in Greater Manchester was also famous for claiming that God had been speaking through him when he said that homosexuals were 'swirling around in a cesspool of their own making'.[14] He was later knighted.

When I opened up our medical dictionary searching for help, I was already contending with all mainstream media, but not only that, there were the eternal fires of hell to consider. And beyond that, the opprobrium of friends, family and anyone who had ever known or met me.

Fortunately for me, our dictionary was at the more liberal end. Out of the three approaches – pathology, immaturity and normal variation – the latter was too much to hope for. Instead, our dictionary went for the 'immaturity' approach.

The entry riffed on a few ideas from popular culture that had no basis in science or medicine. Homosexuality was common among boys who had too strong an attachment to their mother. Ergo, it was also common in single-parent families. So, I put a tick in that box. It was more common in boys that didn't like physical games and pursuits: a cross went into that box. Then it delivered possibly the most damaging hammer blow, information that would set me back for years: homosexuality was a phase. It is unclear to me why I believed this at the time. I thought of my brother. There was no way he'd been through this. I thought of my friends and couldn't imagine this had happened to them, either.

Instead of diagnosis, it sowed only confusion. Nonetheless, I clung to the idea of the phase like it was the last plank of a wrecked ship, and I held on for years.

xvi

Night fell. I'd spent hours channel hopping, peppered in between with time curled up on the chair in the front room, wallowing in self-pitying angst. I went back to my books. I looked at the arrows my sister had drawn, changing pluses to minuses. It still didn't make any sense.

I heard the car pull up. Then their voices as they walked around the side of the house to come in the back door. They'd had a good day. There were chirrups of praise as they were evidently impressed to see me still at the table with my books. My mum went about her business and my sister sat down to see how I was getting on. She worked out in a snap that I'd done nothing. With conspiratorial loyalty, though, she did not let on what she'd discovered, and given there were much better things for her to be doing with her time, there was no anger either.

'I don't understand what you don't understand.' A pause. 'What don't you understand?'

I stared at the page like I was attempting numerical telekinesis to move the numbers for me.

'Here.' She took the pen and the exercise book. 'We can't solve this as it is. So, let's just focus on what we can do with it.' I watched the cuneiform sorcery unfold before me as she worked and turned numbers from multiplication to division and back again.

'Do you see?'

No reply. Why would someone even want to move numbers around like that?

'Do you see? Come on, it's not that hard.'

A tear dripped onto the pad. I wiped another from my face, but then more came.

'I'm sorry, no, it's OK. We can take a break.'

It was too late. The lock on the canal was open: the frustration, the isolation, the fear, all of it transformed to lipids, mucus, sodium and water, gushing from my eyes.

'It's my fault. I'm sorry; I didn't think you'd find it so hard.'

I cried and cried. I cried at the holy water I'd drunk in the hope it would cure me. And then I cried some more because I knew it wouldn't. I cried because I was making my sister think it was her fault. I cried because I needed her to be misdirected in this way. Then I cried at the thought she might believe all of it, any of it, was in any way connected to quadratic equations.

xvii

As the years progressed, I had tumbled down the school's ability-tiered classes and was now floundering. In one particularly excruciating school report, I was awarded a 'B' for effort but only an 'E' for attainment. It was brutal.

With only one child at home, things were a little easier for my mum. With eighteen months to go before final exams, we both decided a smaller school might be the thing.

We went along for an interview. The headmaster looked like a werewolf with his big white teeth, beard, and chest hair so exuberant it reached over his tie and collar in thick brown curls. He called in the English teacher at one point, who asked what I liked reading. I panicked and said, '*Return of the Jedi*.' His face visibly sank. (If you think this is bad, I have a friend who, when asked the same question at his interview for one of the Cambridge colleges, replied '*Charlie and the Chocolate Factory*'.)

I aced the interview, it seemed, by turning up. I went from a year of about 300 to being one of sixteen, in which most of the kids had been together since the age of five. Where I'd been to five schools, they had been to one. It wasn't small because it was exclusive but because it was going out of business.

First lesson, across the corridor. The only available seat is at the front of the class.

French. With no concession to the nascence of my arrival, the teacher made much fun of the fact that I'd mistaken the gender of one of the nouns.

'Well, I suppose it might be right if you were… a bit like that,' she said as she made the infamous teapot gesture with her hand.

Such an insult at the new boy's expense would normally ignite flames of laughter in a class. But nothing happened. My inference was that the other kids already knew how horrible she was and were just grateful it wasn't them being ridiculed.

History. Our history teacher seemed about a hundred and ninety years old – wizened, teeth missing, with the disposition of a dyspeptic polecat. As short of sight as she was of breath. She was deputy head of the school, the werewolf's enforcer. In assemblies, to accompany the hymns, she would hammer away at the piano, banging out chords – or discords – with all the precision of a drunken Les Dawson playing in a pair of boxing gloves.

She was a terrible teacher. She would talk – something about Parliament in the seventeenth century – then would repeat it all, this time dictating so we could copy it all down. That was it. Then she would test us. I would cheat, but even then, I don't think I did all that well in the tests.

Computer science. I would sit at the back of the class with my hands supporting my head about my ears. I presented as attentive, but my hands masked headphones pumping electro into my ears.

xviii

English. This was a different chapter, same story. The teacher looked like a D. H. Lawrence impersonator fallen on hard times. He handed round a poem and told us to 'do' it. I had no idea what 'doing it' was. How do you 'do' a poem?

I read it.

> I will arise and go now, and go to Innisfree,
> And a small cabin build there, of clay and wattles made;
> Nine bean-rows will I have there, a hive for the honey-bee,
> And live alone in the bee-loud glade.

I read it again.

I looked about the room to find everyone eagerly scribbling. I looked back down at the poem, looking for the key that would unlock a similar flood of writing. All I could think about was the fact that my middle name was Innes and I wanted to be free. The irony was I wasn't, and I struggled to write an analysis of someone else that wasn't either.

It was the mid-1980s and there were so many ways to die. Everyone smoked. The petrol was leaded. At the height of the Cold War, Russia had 45,000 nuclear warheads, all pointed west. And if they didn't kill you, then AIDS probably would. Meanwhile, what were we reading? John Steinbeck's *Of Mice and Men* and *Romeo and Juliet*, the latter recounting in impenetrable language the story of two feuding families of the Veronese aristocracy. It runs for four hours and doesn't end well for anyone, including its reader.

Then things got worse. I began to strategically skip the bad timetable days. Given there were so few of us, I'm surprised no one really noticed that I'd stopped attending.

There was one exception. We had a part-time teacher for biology. She was the only one who remarked on how often I seemed to be absent but she never took it further. She was stern but I now realise cared deeply about her students. To me then, being noticed was equivalent to being caught, but I can now see that her spotting me meant she was concerned. During one of the half-terms, she invited a few of us that were falling behind to her house for one-to-one lessons. She wasn't paid for this. I wince at the memory, but when she opened the door for my first lesson, she noted I was an hour late. 'You do realise that I'm doing this for you?' Silence. She might have added, 'Have bad things happened to you, or are you just an awful person?' I was too embarrassed to speak, to apologise. Nonetheless, she invited me in, made me tea, gave me the lesson, and we agreed I'd return in a couple of days for another. I never went back.

It was the strategy with the least friction to avoid failure, reducing exposure to observation and judgement, and risk. I pressed myself against the wall of my life, flat as a shadow.

xix

Skipping school is tremendously boring. Without any money, you can't bob into the cinema and stay for the day. There are libraries, but people notice you if you spend too much time in one place.

I would idle around shopping centres, as wan and directionless as the confused pigeons that had accidentally found themselves on the wrong side of the automatic doors.

I loved music, so would hang around at record shops, riffling through the crates of LPs. It didn't take long before I wanted to have a go at stealing a record. It seemed like a feat, to shoplift an awkward, outsized, inflexible disc and walk right out the door with it. The next day, I made sure I had a bag large enough that I could drop a 12' of New Order's *Confusion* behind it. I went in. Found the record where I'd left it the previous day. Checked the coast was clear and dropped it behind my bag rather than in it (the wrestling of which would attract attention). I browsed a bit more to see if anyone was suspicious, then I walked out.

My new life had begun.

I mainly stole records but my boredom became so acute I was even willing to give reading a go. The boys at school had been talk-ing about James Herbert's *The Rats*. Books were easy to steal and presented practically no challenge, so I nabbed a copy for myself – a white cover with a giant rat beneath the gold-embossed lettering of the author's name. I took it to a park bench to read – nobody bothers you if you're reading, I discovered.

The story opened with the tale of a pathetic gay man who has an affair with an underage work colleague. When gossip gets out, the gay man is ridiculed, then shunted out of his job, becomes homeless and is then eaten by rats. End of first chapter.

I shoved the book into the stuffed mouth of a bin and left.

After a couple of weeks, I had a few records to show for my efforts. After a couple of months, I had a collection. I would occasionally sell some on to Sifters record store in Burnage in Manchester – later immortalised in Oasis songs. I'd then use the money to buy ciga-rettes. I stole more books (which I didn't read) as well as anything I liked the look of, from stationery to a personal stereo.

XX

This went on for months. It was so easy, I barely bothered taking precautions. I was in my favoured big store, dropped an album behind my bag and slipped out the fire exit onto the stairs. A few seconds later, I heard the clatter of the fire exit door open again and a chase ensued that went on for about a mile.

To this day, I am at a loss to understand how I was caught. I used to breakdance for hours every day. My friends and I got so good at it that Nike sponsored us with free gear to wear. I probably had about 8 per cent body fat. I was all fast-twitch muscle. Yet still, the guy that worked behind the counter in the store ran me down. Manager's office. Police car. Cell.

Once I was in the cell, I was at last overwhelmed by the desire to do some reading.

More cautions. I returned to school but there were now only weeks left before our final exams. You have to worry about a student who approaches exams with relief at the fact that there are no lessons to attend, that sees them as a break. Once exams were over, school came to an uneventful end. I was grateful I'd never have to go back, and I imagine they felt the same way.

xxi

The results were in. My mum, keen to know the outcome of my efforts (or maybe they were her efforts), drove me to school. I thought it a good idea to offer a fellow pupil a lift. I wanted someone along for the ride because I suspected I was going to need a buffer. He was a nice lad – the cleverest in the school and, with some nominative determinism thrown in, his surname was Sage.

We marched into the school, collected our brown envelopes and brought them back to the car. His transcript was one of uniform 'A's.

I rictus smiled for him. I opened mine to find so many 'U's it looked like a list of Disney movies.

I was crushed; quite why I don't know. My mum later said that it was hard for her to watch. She wasn't in the least angry. Her response was an uncharacteristic, 'Ah well, love. Don't worry.'

xxii

I spent no time considering my next step. Too immature to start work (I'd not long since been sacked from a paper round because it was too complicated for me to cope with and getting up early was too much like hard work), I decided to retake. I signed up for a college near the centre of Manchester, famous for the riots that took place there in 1981.

Over the summer, I took up with some friends. My best mate, who lived just up the road from me, and two boys from one of the secondaries I'd been to: Pat and Wes. We consulted on what we would do next. Pat's dad was an academic, so he had an enormous house we could disappear into. We spent weeks smoking and playing snooker in the attic. Wes lived too far away for us to drop in and my mum wouldn't let anyone in at all, so when we weren't potting balls, we hung out on street corners because there was nothing else to do. In the evenings, we'd get stoned when we could or go to a pub in the village, buy four halves and nurse them all evening. These were proximity friendships, so we never talked much about anything that mattered.

When September finally came and we went off to sixth form, it became clear there were two tiers of ability at the college: some were there to advance, others to redo.

Within weeks, I was hanging out in the subterranean smokers' common room rather than attending the lessons. The teachers were just like those at school, all parroting things about self-discipline and commitment that I didn't understand. There were two exceptions. I rarely missed French, mainly because he was a superb teacher and seemed to like his job – he was also gay. He spoke to and treated us like adults. (Coincidentally, the college's other French teacher, Raymond, was gay too. Raymond was a language savant, fluent in most European languages as well as Russian.)

The revelation, though, was English. I never missed a class. Our teacher was a not-very-ex hippy who insisted on being addressed by her first name, Margery. She swished about the class, offering advice and encouragement in equal measure. I couldn't believe it when she suggested I might like to use my personal stereo while I worked, 'if it helped?'

One day in class, someone was talking about a project about pop culture. I can't remember what I contributed, but Margery turned to me and said with a smile, 'Is there anything you don't know about?'

She and the class quickly moved on, but for me, it was like there was a group of muscles, clenched so long I mistook them for my body. When they released, I felt new.

xxiii

A few months into my retake year, I agreed to visit my sister who had since left to attend university in Sheffield. In the matter of a few days, the whole world changed because of E. M. Forster.

Universities and students were very different in the 1980s to how they are now, but in many ways the same tune was being played. Any reader of David Lodge's campus novels will know that such were the cuts taking place, entire departments were sharing a single phone line while also being tasked by management with entrepreneurial labour in order to find income any- and everywhere. (If academics were entrepreneurially talented, they'd just be doing that, surely?)

As the swingeing cuts took effect, there were concerns as early as 1982 that some universities were about to declare themselves bankrupt, while also being pressured that they 'should become technological'.[15] (This is also the case today.)

In the 1980s, about 15 per cent of school-leavers made the cut for university. Between then and now, many governments made pushes towards widening participation in higher education, and now almost 40 per cent of school-leavers attend university. As this scaling up has taken place, much of the extra funds needed to teach the students were found through economies: more students could be taught in the same class, fewer one-to-one tutorials and more seminars and lectures etc.

The students of the early 1980s enjoyed a relatively generous funding environment. Few took on additional work during their studies. Unless they were homeowners, there were no rates or council tax for them to pay. Their tuition fees were paid, and they received grants equivalent to about 50 per cent of a low-paid job. There were no student loans but banks offered favourable overdraft facilities. In the vacations, students were able to sign on for unemployment payments. Most students at graduation that I knew at the time could expect to be running an overdraft with their bank of £1,000–3,000; meagre in comparison to today's debt of £50,000–60,000 or more.

xxiv

'He's not a man. He's sixteen,' was the tenor of the argument, but the porters at my sister's halls of residence were having none of it.

No men were allowed to stay. Instead of staying in her room, an old sleeping bag was unfurled from a box for me. I would spend the next couple of nights sleeping on the parquet floor of the dining room.

That night, I was taken to a nightclub. Smuggled in, I went to a student night at the legendary Leadmill. I recognised The Smiths, The Housemartins, Art of Noise and New Order from *Top of the Pops*, but apart from that it was all new to me. I didn't really know how to do normal dancing. I'd spent most of my teenage years as an early adopter of the extraordinary and acrobatic kind. I found doing the kind of dancing meant to deter people's attention completely beyond me and instead bounced around like a misfiring child's toy.

A last dance to Nina Simone, then we were turfed out at two in the morning into the sodium-lit streets of Sheffield. My ears were ringing. My clothes were sweat-soaked.

Even the way the cool kids walked was different. They telegraphed their independence by not huddling together, as school kids do around a football, but spreading out, diverting and diverging as their will dictated. A few hours ago I had been a child, but now I could feel the growing pains of transformation.

As we approached the halls of residence, one of the group invited everyone to her room. We stayed up all night talking. We left when it was time to return to the refectory for breakfast.

As we ate our toast and cereal in the corner of the dining room, I noticed the zip on my unused sleeping bag was open slightly. It looked like it was smiling at me.

By lunch, we had met with the friends once again. We would be going to the cinema that night. I feared it might not feature any kung fu. I'd done a good job of pretending to know the music I'd heard last night; now I would attempt to look as if I enjoyed films for people over the age of twelve. We made our way into the busy cinema screen and sat in the second or third row. The trailers were promising. Plenty of aliens trying to get along on earth, trucks crashing through barricades etc. The lights went down and orchestral music began, then a soprano voice – slow, meandering, romantic. The kind of music that no one I'd ever met listened to. This was going to be terrible, all bickering, parasols and teacups.

Within the first few moments of screen time the gibbering commenced. Something about a girl wanting a room with a view but not having a room with a view. Then being offered a room with a view by a man that had a view. He didn't want the view because he's a man, so she should have the view because she's a woman. But she doesn't want the view because it would put her in debt to the man to accept it. Without a view, though, how could she experience the beauty of Florence. I put my head in my hands and reflected that there was to be two hours of this. Whomever this E. M. Forster person was, I never wanted to see another of his films. I maintained that position up until a lightning bolt struck.

We had already met Lucy, the protagonist, in some preceding scenes, in which she established herself as quiet, prim and starchy. But here, in the supposed solitude of the hotel's lobby, she is absolutely thrashing out the final chords of Beethoven's 'Piano Sonata No. 21 in C major, Op. 53', the 'Waldstein' (as I would later discover). The piece goes spinning through C major, C minor, A flat major and F minor chords before the final, dramatic diminuendo. Unbeknownst to Lucy, another hotel guest, the Reverend Mr Beebe, is listening in on the performance and speaks to her from the darkness: 'If Miss Honeychurch ever takes to live as she plays, it will be very exciting both for us and for her.'

Someone also hiding who she really is? I was rapt.

As the story unfolds, our heroine appears to be searching for something deeper. She plunges into it when she thrashes out some Beethoven but returns to the surface of polite society, irritable and peevish at all she had to surrender to exist there. She wants to please, to be what people want her to be, but how much of herself has she to concede to survive in polite society? And if she surrenders so much, will she even be herself any more?

In Florence, she encounters George, a mysterious, pushy but likeable man at odds with societal norms – it was he and his father, Mr Emerson, that wanted to forfeit their rooms with views for Lucy and her chaperone. Later, the group go on a trip searching for another view. The couple stumble upon one another in a field of barley overlooking the city and George kisses her. To avoid any further scandal, Lucy and her chaperone instantly depart for Rome.

We pick the story back up in England. Lucy has become engaged to Cecil, an appalling and monstrous creation – educated, yes, but an effete snob. So uptight he shits coal – no, diamonds! He is an ideal match for Lucy's public face. Meanwhile, she conceals her past with George. Amid a blizzard of lies, Lucy's true feelings emerge when prompted by another of George's surreptitious kisses. It is George's father who finally wrings the truth from the girl, resulting in her breaking her engagement and instead marrying George. The couple honeymoon in the same hotel in Florence, and there we learn of the societal resistance to their union, with friends and family (particularly the men) struggling to accept the unconventional pairing.

XXV

Even though I felt the significance of the film when I saw it, it wasn't until later that I understood it and the impact it had had on me. Many years later, after I'd read everything by Forster (even some of the odd biographies, like those of his great aunt), I was alone, staying at King's College, Cambridge (where Forster had both studied and worked). I was there researching a dissertation I was writing, and I was working my way through his handwritten diaries and commonplace books that the library held. In them, Forster complains about how difficult his mother was to live with (he lived with her throughout his thirties). He also wrote about how impatient he had become with writing about heterosexuality and a world that he could only observe but never inhabit. It was then that the thought struck me: *A Room with a View* is a closeted gay man's coming out fantasy. Very little of the plot, beyond Lucy's gender, needs to be changed to make everything fit: society's opprobrium, the mother's understanding, the frosty rigidity of the men that everyone knows will eventually thaw. It was the best coming out that a man of that era could hope for, and he turned it into his first bestseller.

It's a tragedy in miniature that *A Room with a View* has only just made it onto the GCSE syllabus. Its themes seem those that kids of that age can relate to: calling out the hypocrisy and sanctimony of adults who put themselves in charge, fighting against pressures to conform, understanding the need to live your own life and not someone else's. It's a novel that resolutely asserts: be who you are and those that really matter won't mind.

As we left the screening, it was clear that everyone had enjoyed it. We discussed the plot, the nudity of the men's bathing scene, the actors, Helena Bonham Carter. She seemed wooden (it was her first role). And now that I know the film better, I can understand why she was cast. That woodenness is perfect for Lucy. The awkwardness of her manner speaks to her character, which requires her always to be improvising a performance, in real time and without rehearsed lines.

From that day in Sheffield to this, I have loved E. M. Forster.

Throughout the 1980s, the Merchant Ivory film production partnership often came in for a drubbing for producing weightless films, heritage cinema, a celluloid wrap of Tory ideals in a Laura Ashley tote bag. It was cinema for *Telegraph* readers.

Heritage cinema. It's such a damning name for a genre. One of the things that's interesting about it, though, is it is one of the few genres named by its opponents. It's a little like renaming the metaphysicals to the unintelligibles, the modernists to the snobs or the Romantics to the narcissists. Suspicions, though, that the audiences for these films were superannuated, cruise-booking fat cats, more attuned to the harvesting of interior design ideas than any sense of politics or drama, are not borne out by the fact that people like this don't go to the cinema. Young people do. Thanks to the research of people like Claire Monk, we know that the audience that was attracted by these films was a predominantly young one.[16]

In Merchant Ivory films, often written off as costume dramas, there is always something else going on beneath the starchy attire. The costume's role is to conceal it; that's the point. It's what makes the best of them engrossing because the costume is a metaphor for the personae we adopt when others want or need us to be something or someone else.

xxvi

With a compilation tape jammed into my personal stereo, I rode the National Express bus home to Manchester with a dead feeling in my stomach. People don't change like they do in the movies, within the bounds of a single scene. Change is the flap of the butterfly's wing – undetected and nonlinear but slightly altering all that follows.

I'd grown up more in three days than I had in as many years. It was my first sight of what a life could be. On screen, Lucy had got there. It wasn't an altogether happy ending. Her honesty had come at a cost – but an affordable one.

With Bauhaus, Clock DVA, Cocteau Twins, The Cramps, the Psychedelic Furs and Sex Pistols playing in my ears, I watched the Pennines sweep by, the scenery gradually turning greyer as we hit the outskirts of Manchester. I listened to a new band called The Chameleons, who I went on to love more than any other because, hailing from Manchester, their music sounded like rain. Mark Burgess, their lead singer, wasn't like Morrissey riffing on Keats and Yeats by the cemetery gates. No A-levels were necessary in gaining access to these songs. Like I'd later discover with Joni Mitchell or Kate Bush, in songs by The Chameleons there was never a single wasted word to pad a phrase or line.

The dance music I'd loved for years was primal, meant to stir the body into response. All these bands tried to do that but added another stratum: words. Sometimes long and difficult words that were supposed to make you think as well as feel. They would send me careering to a dictionary in the hope that a supplied definition would provide the key to interpretation. Sporadically it did. Others were like Bauhaus's 'The Spy in the Cab', which took dozens of listens before the penny dropped that it was about the encroachment of technology and surveillance into everyday life.

Once I was home, the Human League and Duran Duran ceded space on my stippled bedroom wall to The Chameleons, Sisters of Mercy, and a greyscale picture of a soldier taking one in the back below a single interrogative in bold type: 'Why?'

The Mr Men lampshade had been up so long it failed to register and survived the transition unscathed. I think it might still be there.

xxvii

I returned to my sixth form wanting to succeed, but I was all conviction and no commitment, wanting the plunder not the pursuit.

I listened to music all the time, so often and so loudly that I still have tinnitus four decades on. The ringing I can hear in my head as I write this is a scar from the years I spent trying to blast my thoughts and feelings to smithereens.

In English, we were undertaking an experimental course of study called a 'CEE'. They were killing themselves with that name. I never really worked out what it was, but given it sounded so similar to the more middling 'CSE', I assumed it was about the same. We didn't do Steinbeck or Shakespeare; instead, Margery would sweep about the class in her long black skirts, encouraging us to 'Write, create!'

She set us prompts like 'the environment'. For that one, I wrote the kind of poem you might imagine an angst-ridden, barely post-pubescent tyke writing. She liked it. She liked it so much that she went to the head of the college and demanded our work be exhibited at the main entrance. For weeks, I blushed with pride as I walked past and saw staff and students looking at the display with my poem at its centre.

xxviii

It was exam time once again. Nothing for English, which instead consisted of a compilation of coursework. On results day, our gang of four convened to discuss our progress. My mate from up the road had done OK. I don't remember how Pat fared, but he always seemed steady and competent, awaiting the thing that would one day excite him. Wes had failed – he was disappointed, as he'd had his heart set on something to do with marine biology.

And me, had I changed? My transcript was less uniform, there were no Us, but I still hadn't actually passed anything.

I was still unsure of what the English 'CEE' was, but I'd been awarded an 'I' for it, whatever that meant. I presumed it was either an 'I' for 'indifferent' or a lowercase 'L' for 'lacklustre'. But not passing anything made me feel like I'd failed my teachers, who seemed to have invested so much in all of us. I'd failed myself, too. Being seen to try and then to fail seemed so much worse than the sustained carelessness of my first round.

To commiserate, I took my friends to our house. My mum must have been out for the day; otherwise, I wouldn't have dared. There was always bread in the house, so I lit the grill and began making tea and toast for everyone. As I watched the bread slowly turning terracotta beneath the blue flame, the desire suddenly struck me that I should burn my transcript. I took it from my pocket, unfurled it and carefully pushed the end in between the bread and flames until it ignited. Once it was going, I made some theatre of walking through the kitchen with it, opening the back door and waiting for the results slip to burn down to embers, before lifting the lid of the bin and dropping it in.

It was a piece of adolescent drama. 'Look at me, so cool! Not caring about anything!' I went back to the grill, finished up the toast and we sat and ate. Wes finished first and went out the back door for a cigarette. We talked about nothing as he pulled on his fag. He held it like a soldier in the war, pinched between thumb and forefinger with the glowing coal hidden in his palm, as if trying not to disclose his position to a sniper. Once finished, he extinguished it on the ground, picked it up from the floor and went to discard the butt in the bin. As he lifted the lid, suddenly drunk from the influx of oxygen, fire roared upwards like the exhaust of a rocket bound for the centre of the Earth. Flames snapped at his face like serpents. He leapt backwards. I quickly grabbed a washing-up bowl full of grimy water and threw it into the flames. The serpents hissed as steam and smoke billowed into the air.

The waste bin was (or had been, at least) plastic. In the smouldering heat, it had melted on one side and begun to collapse. Someone mentioned that we should probably call the fire brigade, and it was then that it dawned on me why my mum didn't want anyone in the house.

It was OK, though. I had a plan. Our neighbours, with whom we shared a driveway, were… difficult, and they had two perfectly functional bins. So, I exchanged one of theirs for ours. Job done. And Wes's eyebrows would eventually grow back just fine.

xxix

The next day, my mum and I were discussing my options over a cup of tea. She became distracted when she noticed a commotion outside. She opened the door to find our neighbour trying to swap one of her damaged bins for ours.

Relations were already strained, and my mum practically convulsed with glee at having caught her nemesis in the act of trying to pull one over on her. She spoke like a villain in a comic, all exposition and exclamation marks: 'Ha, I've caught you! You thought you'd catch me out, but I was too clever for you!' It was then that I noticed the melted and deformed lettering on the side of the bin that said 'No Hot Ashes'. It looked like blackened mozzarella being torn from a hot pizza.

My mum and the neighbour argued over the provenance of the bin, pushing it one way, then the other.

The neighbour eventually submitted. Putting her finger to her temple and grinding it like a key in a lock, she said, 'You're crazy. Craaaazzzeeee!' My mum laughed in victory.

Returning triumphant, she uttered to me, 'She's the crazy one.'

'Yeah, Mum. I agree.'

The resulting feud, more bitter than Bette Davis vs Joan Crawford, ran without interruption for over a decade until the neighbours eventually moved, leaving behind them the bin that looked like an extra from a David Cronenberg film.

xxx

The educational landscape was shifting and with it, the LGBT one. In 1987, at the Tory Party conference, Margaret Thatcher bemoaned the fact that 'children who need to be taught to respect traditional moral values are being taught that they have an inalienable right to be gay'. What is often forgotten in the recollection of this speech, this display of public homophobia, is what she says only six lines later:

> I believe that government must take the primary responsibility for setting standards for the education of our children. And that's why we are establishing a national curriculum for basic subjects.[17]

Odd to think that with standardisation of English and maths, the standardisation of heterosexuality was also being served as a side dish.

The shutters of Section 28 came crashing down soon after (as part of the Local Government Act 1988). Also known as Clause 28, it stated that a local authority 'shall not intentionally promote homosexuality or publish material with the intention of promoting homosexuality' or 'promote the teaching in any maintained school of the acceptability of homosexuality as a pretended family relationship'.[18] It would be the first anti-gay legislation since the Criminal Law Amendment Act of 1885 – the one that did for Oscar Wilde. Section 28 was indiscriminate and barbaric, and I can't do justice to the damage it did to the (does some back-of-an-envelope arithmetic) approximately 2 million queer kids that went through the system with that weight hanging over them.

xxxi

The nationwide, common programme of study, known as the National Curriculum, has now become a fact of educational life internationally (they have something similar in France, Hungary, Ireland, Italy, Japan, South Korea, the Netherlands, New Zealand, Norway, Portugal, Singapore and Spain). There are exceptions – the US doesn't have one, for example. In the UK, it systematically introduced the basics of attainment at four 'Key Stages' across a child's educational career. Key Stages 1 (ages five to seven) and 2 (ages seven to eleven) took children through their primary education and the basics of reading, writing and arithmetic. Key Stage 3 (eleven to fourteen) assessed children throughout their lower-secondary education. That education completed with Key Stage 4 (fourteen to sixteen). Students would take national tests at each level, meaning the school was being examined as much as the pupil was.

Standardising the minutiae of what a child should and should not learn seems, on the one hand, to be the fairest approach to those suffering at the hands of idiosyncratic schools, teachers or Local Education Authorities. On the other, the establishment of a curriculum on which the basis of all further study might be pursued is too tempting a toy for governments or, worse, for overconfident and shamelessly incompetent ministers eager to make their mark.

With the new National Curriculum in place, what our children might be taught, might know, might deem to be valuable was now in the hands of a government minister. In rankings of the least trusted professions, bailiffs come tenth, paparazzi sixth, bankers fifth, car salesmen are third, and politicians come first.[19] These are the people who are often flushed with pathological levels of self-confidence, with the toxic mix of the lack of patience and tenacity to familiarise themselves with the gravity of their undertaking, yet are entrusted with running education. Perhaps if they do well, they might get given the Treasury brief next. Why would we trust these people with a National Curriculum when they can't even keep our school buildings intact, when secondaries can only open four-and-a-half days a week because they can't afford their energy bills?[20] Meanwhile, we are £66 billion into the construction of a high-speed railway, most of which has already been cancelled.[21]

xxxii

After failing my retakes, I was figuring out what I was going to do next when news arrived that a chain restaurant was opening up in town. At the job centre, I read about the role. 'No qualifications necessary,' the card said. I was perfect for it. I further distinguished myself from the field of applicants by turning up late for the interview, bed-headed, in crumpled and dirty clothes. Despite my efforts to self-sabotage, I was taken on part-time. Initially, I thought I would sign up for a second year of retakes, then see where I was. I was like a bird that had just flown into a window, the severity of the impact erasing the memory of the pain of it, and in a daze, I was midway through repeating the mishap. I saw myself many years later, aged and wizened, sitting at the back of French and leaving the class to collect my pension.

The day after being offered the job, I asked to transfer to full-time.

At first I felt only relief, then a kind of resignation. My years of idleness and my lack of commitment to anything unravelled as easily as a ball of wool tumbling down a flight of stairs.

My destiny was to occupy a fire-retardant sailor-themed uniform with a paper hat, asking everyone I met if they would like fries with that for £1.45 an hour.

xxxiii

I still think about that fire, though. That little slip of paper turned the ignition on a decade-long feud and, weasel-like, I quietly congratulated myself for getting away with it all so easily. There were a couple of bumps, but hadn't I basically got away with everything? I got caught stealing but had escaped punishment. I'd made it to the end of school and was now out of reach of all of them. None of them could mark me any more or make snide remarks at my lack of ability. And no one knew my secret. It was buried so deep that I don't think I did either. Society had failed to exact its revenge. On the one hand, I felt like I'd won, but there was the other hand too.

The years, doleful and lazy, disappeared just as the transcript had turned to ash. The ink may have burned like it had been drenched in accelerant, but the grades hadn't. I couldn't bear to consider it.

As the embers smouldered to a white heat, like some indestructible holy relic, the grades were preserved. It was a slow realisation that I wouldn't be able to erase my grades with the same easy negligence with which they'd been acquired. This would prove an expensive mistake, I thought. I was going to be paying for those grades for decades, maybe for ever.

xxxiv

About a year later, at a house party, I bumped into Margery Kim, my college English teacher. She seemed disappointed with what I was doing and was sure I could have done better. I took the opportunity to ask her about the CEE, what it was, what it meant, and what that 'I' symbol was on my results.

'No, that wasn't an "I",' she said. 'That was a one. You can't achieve a higher grade than that.'

'But what does that mean?' I asked.

'I'd say it's the equivalent of an A-level.'

The remark should have floored me. Instead, it ricocheted from me like a pinging bullet from Superman's pecs. The 'I'd say' couched the grade in foggy terms that quickly calibrated down to zero to my ears. I chose not to interpret it as a simple turn of phrase or linguistic filler in an informal chat; instead, I defaulted to the harshest inference and dismissed what she'd said as speculative guesswork. Or worse, maybe she was just being nice.

I shunted the conversation on and we talked fondly of our time together. She asked if I was still writing poetry. I said I wasn't. She urged me to reconsider. She told me that Raymond, the gay teacher in languages, had suddenly died of AIDS. I only barely knew him but I registered the news with a jolt, like I'd missed a step on the stairs. She asked what I was going to do next. I didn't have an answer. Soon after, we parted. I never saw her again. I little thought it would be nearly forty years before I fact-checked what she had told me about the CEE and discovered it was all true and correct. At the time, her words floated away and I submitted to gravity's pull, evoking the old self that did well at nothing worth doing and cared even less about the outcome.

I drifted out into the twilit garden, buoyed by the chatter of guests and the clinks of glasses. I soon forgot about Margery, my grade and poetry and instead looked for my friends. I found them out at the end of the garden, huddled down in a tide of cow parsley, the scent of which mixed with the smoke as it roiled in the warm air. I was just in time for the last pull of a joint.

3 Thquire, thake handth, firtht and latht! Don't be croth with uth poor vagabondth. **People mutht be amuthed.** They can't be alwayth a learning, nor yet they can't be alwayth a working, they an't made for it. You mutht have uth, Thquire. Do the withe thing and the kind thing too, and make the betht of uth; not the wurtht!
– Charles Dickens, *Hard Times*

The last trumpet ever to be sounded shall blow even algebra to wreck.

Charles Dickens, *Hard Times*

I demonstrated the same agency over my working life as I had over my schooling. I left home but not really, only exchanging one parent for another – most of us kids had. Our situation seems almost inexplicable now, after everything my father had done. We lived siloed in the same house. He rented the ground floor with my brother. My eldest sister was on the first floor at the front of the house. She could afford a big room because she disappeared every day to work a counter at a department store. I took a shoebox at the back of the house. The room cost £12 a week, more than a third of my wages. My toothbrush sat in a stained tea mug on the draining board beneath a geyser that I couldn't afford the gas for. My dish-cloth doubled as a washcloth. The carpet was so worn in places it looked like someone had spilt tar.

My girlfriend was nice, but I felt bad about lying to her – just not enough to tell her. The pair of us had been shunted together by friends at college and I thought I might be able to make it work. But with every month that passed, I knew it was wrong.

To straight people, being closeted might sound like it's something that has to be managed every once in a while. To pass as straight, all you need to do is not kiss boys or appear too enthusiastic about a new Kylie single. Gay people, though, know you're always in draft mode, editing your behaviour on the fly. And I sowed lies like seeds strewn about me and they turned into a forest of thorns, impenetrable to even the most handsome prince. All this while you wake every day in the knowledge, belief, (no) hope, that today you might start telling the truth. The impulse is strong at first but weakens throughout the day. Each morning, you look over the edge of the precipice, and slowly as the sun rises you back away from it into the ever-vigilance you know so well. So, with the dawn of every day, I zipped myself tightly into my straight suit. I attenuated my gestures to just the right volume, joined in with the occasionally homophobic banter, didn't talk too much about anything that mattered. All the while you'd be thinking 'just say it. Go on, say it. Say it!' The thought would then recline, only to lurch forward once again minutes later.

Meanwhile, I had graduated from Hamburger University (as they called it, without irony) and I was asked if I might like to go to Edinburgh to assist in the haemorrhaging of fast food into communities there. It was an opportunity for a new start.

i

From the station, I had to make my way to a slightly edgy-looking B&B out in Leith. All the new arrivals were put there. I had moved my whole life, left the city I'd grown up in. This was my chance; I was already feeling the relief of it. I booked in to my room, then got a knock on the door. A similar new arrival invited me down to the bar where 'a few of us are having some drinks'. By the time I'd won the night's beer-mat flipping competition (forty-six in total) it was as if the train had left the station and I'd missed it. The opportunity for starting fresh seemed to have passed at some unidentifiable moment of the evening and I woke the next morning to find I'd accidentally gone to sleep in my straight suit and now it was so tight I couldn't get it off.

The work may have been dreadful, grossly underpaid, boring and stressful, but there was always fun to be had because we were young.

We had the bomb squad in one day, who had to shut down Edinburgh's main shopping street to perform a controlled detonation of what turned out to be a forgotten Dundee cake.

Events that punctuated the boredom weren't always good ones. I was in charge one quiet night when the building was set alight. I tried to extinguish the fire, got lost in the smoke and thought I was going to die until I was pulled free. By the time I was assaulted by drunks wielding a half-eaten cheeseburger, I concluded that I could handle the bad pay, the poor diet, the rules and regs – it was the disdain that got me. Stained with ketchup, a pickle stuck to my clip-on tie, the job, I concluded, was no different to going to the zoo and allowing the chimpanzees to fling their shit at you.

In the weeks that followed, I'd grown sick of the food that gave me spots at one end and haemorrhoids at the other. There was a break room, but it was always rowdy with arguments over whose turn it was on the CD player or whose mess hadn't been cleaned up. So, I'd taken to buying a sandwich on my break and sitting in Princes Street Gardens. In the cold autumn sun, with the smell of fermenting yeast in the air from the city's breweries, I'd look up at the towering basalt upon which Edinburgh Castle had been built.

I'd watch the purposeful going back and forth in their smart clothes, seemingly getting on in their lives. Day after day I'd sit there in silence, wondering if this was it for me.

What was the difference between them and me? Was it that they knew they could get more from life, whereas I only wanted it? Was it that they only had to work hard to be rewarded? If I worked harder, I might earn an extra £10 a week, but my career debt would only deepen as I invested more energy in a life I didn't want.

Through all of this, I suspected that stories held something for me and that if I followed them, something might change. At the very least, my 'now' would be improved by them.

One day, instead of heading for the park beneath the castle to Eeyore my way through lunch, I found myself wandering into Waterstones. There was only one author I really knew about, so I went to Fiction / F / Forster and defaulted to the slimmest volume. It had tiny font and the whole thing was only about 6 mm thick. It was beautiful – an Italian scene on the cover, framed by a fascia the colour of willow. It was his first novel, from 1905, *Where Angels Fear to Tread*.

Back on my bench in the park, I peeled open the book and read:

They were all at Charing Cross to see Lilia off—Philip, Harriet, Irma, Mrs. Herriton herself. Even Mrs. Theobald, squired by Mr. Kingcroft, had braved the journey from Yorkshire to bid her only daughter good-bye. Miss Abbott was likewise attended by numerous relatives.

If you're not counting, that's eight characters introduced in forty words and five in the first sentence. How did people do this? The students that I constantly rubbed shoulders with because they comprised the majority of our part-time staff didn't seem especially capable. How did they find this so easy? I envied them so much! I envied their freedom, their interpretation of shift start times as being like party invites: 'seven for seven thirty'. Their laxness and lateness both conveyed that the job was only a fraction of otherwise busy lives. I envied their knowledge that the thing I was clinging to was for them a mere stopgap. Many of them didn't stay long, resigning after a few weeks, moving on to productive and fulfilled lives. Their freedom made me as sick as their potential did. While many were house-trained, a proportion shared the same contempt for the work as our loutish customers did. That contempt extended to me too, standing as the exemplar of everything they were frightened of becoming if they failed.

Perhaps if I'd asked one of them about the Forster book, I might have learned that the opening of the novel is just terrible. It's the literary equivalent of being introduced to an entire room of people at a party, except their faces are covered up and they aren't allowed to speak. In my copy, I quickly took to writing the characters' names in biro on the flyleaf. And the fact I was having to concentrate so much on following the story meant there was little chance of my getting lost in it. And anyway, my forty minutes was up, and it was time to head back in.

ii

Two fellow staff and I lived in a two-bed flat on the outskirts of Edinburgh, furnished with kitsch ornaments, a ketchup carpet, which hid the stains, and mustard walls, which didn't.

On days or evenings off, I'd sometimes go to the local pub. I'd tell myself that it was just to get out of the flat but it was also because

I fancied the bar manager. I'd sit there, writing stuff like lyrics or trying to read with a pint. I couldn't steer my way through a narrative sober; why I thought I might fare better reading while over the limit, I wasn't certain.

The pub was medium-sized, freestanding and absurd-looking. It stood on the bank of the Water of Leith, a river, which, given the grey surroundings, a busy B-road and the proximity to a notorious housing estate, made the pub look like a failed attempt at gentrification. It was thickly carpeted and had vinyl tables and flimsy cushioned stools, seemingly designed so they would break easily when smashed over someone's head.

One quiet afternoon, I went in for a drink and came out with a job. The bar manager that had attracted me in there had been sacked by the boss.

I walked back to my flat, the ferric taste of daytime drink on my breath. I was going to be a pub landlord. I was going to be a man. I was going to be a straight pub landlord. It sounded grown-up. A man of property. Respected by the local community. I saw my future and my future had my name written over the door. I was so desperate to get away from colliding shifts (the kind that overran to such an extent, they met your next) and the clearing of druggies from the loos that I never really thought about what I was going into, and I fizzed out of the burger joint as fast as a lit fuse. I soon discovered, though, that the chimps in the zoo only got worse. This time, the chimps got drunk.

iii

Just try being a little gay Englishman with the vocal authority of Joe Pasquale in a Scottish football pub.

Once I'd arrived there was a mutiny among the bar staff, most of whom left rather than work with someone so clueless. New staff were brought in who were less equipped at detecting my incompetence.

Daytime hours would be filled with folk sitting up at the bar to enjoy a little banter to the soundtrack of Deacon Blue, Hue and Cry and Runrig that always seemed to be playing on the jukebox. Sometimes the jokes and stories would be harmless, other times horrific.

One particularly homophobic story involved a friend of a friend of a regular who worked at the hospital and had seen a gay man as a patient. The regular then recounted a hideous story involving penetrative sex and traces of semen found in colostomy bags, all to prove, with the nodding ascent of the regulars, how disgusting, desperate and perverted gay people were.

The boss, Frank, was imposing, impressive and fearsome, with asbestos fingers that could pinch the fuse on the most drunken piece of dynamite. I would later try to parrot some of the lines he would deploy in sticky situations, like refusing to serve a drunken bare-chested stevedore that had girders for biceps. Instead of confronting the man with an 'I won't', he'd say, 'I daren't'. And it seemed to confuse them so, it worked. When I had a go, it was as hopeless as giving me some of Meryl Streep's lines and expecting me to deliver a comparable performance.

People would rock up on payday and get crimson drunk. We had to hire bouncers. Two men, pink-faced. One the size of a two-seater sofa, the other could have sat three.

One Saturday, with the crowd three or four deep at the bar, dozens already pissed on their whiskey and Irn Brus, the hormonal stink of a fight hit me. The bouncers would be on it in a second; the priority was to get round there and separate the men. I dug through the crowd. The man I reached first was very much the punchee, but he was the only one at hand, so I grabbed and swung him like a hammer throw at the Olympics. He disappeared in the melee. Still no bouncers. The guy doing the hitting didn't care who he was punching, as long as it was skin, bone and weaker than him, so he grabbed me by the tie. (Why had I always made fun of clip-on ties?!) He yanked it so hard I lost my footing and tumbled onto my bum, leaving me sitting upright wedged against the bar, a circle of onlookers around me. 'The bouncers will save me,' I thought. With my tie still in one hand, Thumper cocked his other fist, poised to land a life-changing punch. I closed my eyes, awaiting impact. A beat. A whole second. Two. No punch. I opened one eye.

Looking up, I saw Thumper had been grabbed. He was being held by the hair by one pair of hands while being punched in the head by many others. I noticed the hands were slender, bejewelled. The cavalry had arrived but it wasn't bouncers or squaddies; it was the new bar staff. I crawled out from underneath Thumper and fled. By the time I was back behind the bar, he had disappeared into the crowd. There was still no sign of the bouncers and the music played on. I thanked the staff. No one knew who was in the fight, who wasn't or where they'd gone, and in the four rows of braying punters nobody cared; they wanted to be served.

A little later, it was time for a loo break. There had been word that the toilets weren't in good shape, so I took a pair of rubber gloves with me. News about the state of the toilets turned out to be under-reported. They weren't 'bad'; they were agricultural. The urinal trough had overflowed hours since. The floor was now a glimmering lake of piss-water. Someone had vomited in the drain and it had settled like cold stew. None of which had deterred those that had been pissing in it for hours. I pulled my gloves from my back pocket, snapped them over my wrists and as Yazz's 'The Only

Way is Up' thudded in the bar, I got to work gouging, not for the first or last time.

iv

I settled into the job. I had been terrible at first, getting a round of applause every shift because I would break glasses. But now I got on with most of the regulars, and the fights had cemented something between me and the other staff. I landlorded for the landlord when he and his family went away. I landlorded about the region for others too. I did my best to keep up with the regulars' football talk. Once they got to know me, they did their best to include me in it. And I did my best to resist the temptation to say things like, 'Hey, I saw a wonderful film last night, called *Maurice*. You must watch it, guys. It's so brave.'

I looked up the pub recently on Google Maps. I couldn't remember the address, so started my route at the flat where we lived at the time. I clicked on a little arrow represented on screen as if it were painted on the road. A click and the whole picture distorted into a zoom as it shot me down the road. At the junction I turned right, past the door in a high stone wall that once, while drunk, I had tumbled into, breaking it open to reveal a flight of stairs that I tumbled down, clattering into some bins. Under the railway arches, each click seemed like I was travelling through time. I turned left at the lights but couldn't see the pub. A couple more clicks, then rotating the image to the right to find nothing. Where the pub had once been was now a pile of rubble. There was no trace of any signage, the painted exterior wall, the roof. Everything was reduced to grey lumps of concrete. Only the bones of the place were sufficiently substantial to endure.

v

Back then, I sometimes couldn't get out of bed in the mornings because I didn't see the point. In the afternoons, I'd sometimes think that everything would be easier if I wasn't there any more. I'd been drifting in and out of feeling hopeless, worthless, a liar, a coward. I drank so much and so frequently at work that I would sometimes wake in my clothes with no keys, having climbed through the bedroom window – terrifying my roommate. Occasionally, I wouldn't make it home at all and would nod off for a few hours in the street. I drank bottles of Newcastle Brown because it tasted of sadness.

After tumbling down those garden stairs that night, I had to go to A&E between shifts the next day. Other nights out might find me passing out in the loos of a club and waking up to find myself securely locked in the building, not wearing a shirt for some reason. I woke up cold, in such dark I thought I'd gone blind. Then, climbing atop the toilet stalls, I anti-burgled my way out of the building by smashing my way through the asbestos roof and jumping from it into an alley. As shopkeepers rolled their awnings down that morning, I sprinted by, topless in the morning sun, my torso scratched and scraped with exit wounds, wearing one shoe.

vi

One of my flatmates was going to visit a university friend on the Isle of Man. I had some holiday owed. I was usually so hard up I'd take holiday time as extra pay, but this time it felt different, so I went along with him. In 1989, same-sex sexual activity was still a criminal offence on the island. I don't remember the root of it, but I recall looking at the head-smashing waves crashing against the hull of the ship and thinking 'what a sorry mess I've made of things'. I'd opened up so many avenues of lies and deceit I was now lost in a metropolis of them. What if I jumped? All of the duplicity, the loss, the failure, the deception, the fear of ignominy, all of it clung to me like a leaden weight every day and I was completely exhausted by it. I couldn't go on any longer. A leap over this waist-high rail and it would all be gone. And I wouldn't be here to mind its going. There might be a few days away from my life on the island we were bound for, but then I'd be back in my life same as before. Time just went on. I didn't want to carry on and berated myself for doing so. I had nothing to show for my time. The water was cold and rough; I'd most likely drown rapidly or die of hypothermia. I would at least be taking decisive action. It wasn't the first time that I'd thought about it.

None of this was out of the ordinary for someone like me. Figures published by the LGBT rights charity Stonewall in 2018 reported that half (52 per cent) of LGBT people had experienced depression in the last year, one in eight LGBT people aged eighteen to twenty-four (13 per cent) had attempted to take their own life in the last year, and one in six LGBT people (16 per cent) said they drank alcohol almost every day over the last year.[1]

I was lucky – that moment, like the ones before it, passed. My friend came along, touched me on my arm, asked me something like what was I listening to. My line of thought was disrupted. We exchanged a few words and before I knew it, the ferry ported and we disembarked. It sounds daft to say it now, but back then I refused to buy things like concert tickets for the simple reason that deep down, I couldn't be sure that I'd be around in three months' time to see the show.

vii

On a quiet October day in 1989, the public phone in the bar rang. One of the regulars would get up to answer it, as they were always nearest. It was for me.

From the bar, a few of them saw me wince. I dropped to my haunches. 'No, no, no!' I blenched, hung up the phone and stood for a moment in disbelief. I walked back behind the bar, ashen-faced.

'Wa's up, son? Has yer hen chucked ya?'

The others laughed.

'My dad's dead.'

In the days that followed, I kept forgetting my father had died. For me, it was the defining emotion of the experience. I'd be sat in the bath, a few moments would pass and I'd remember. I'd be walking down the street, take a few footsteps and remember. I'd be on the train heading home for the funeral when I'd forget, then remember. Others I saw had cried storms. For me, it was a philosophical oddity.

It was like becoming famous. I doubted that I'd changed, but the people around me suddenly did. They'd start telling me how I felt, telling me what stage of grief I was at and which I might expect next. I think any normal grief for a person you loved probably does proceed through phases in that way. But there was little that was normal about mine and our family's relationship with Dad. I certainly didn't love him, whatever that meant.

He had been seriously ill for over a decade at this point. His death wasn't unexpected. The dadless world was phenomenologically different, though. It had a quality to it. What I was experiencing wasn't grief. It was more like I'd slipped into an alternative universe where the only thing that was different was that my dad wasn't anywhere in it.

viii

The day of the funeral came around quickly. Early winter, crisp sun, the grass damp underfoot. I read from one of my dad's poems at the service: 'My Dream of a Happy Death'. It's not his best. The rhymes land too heavily and are mangled into place. There are hints of Yeats in it, if he had been more religious. The poem opens with the speaker meeting Death while he walks in a sun-dappled wood 'strewn with moss, bluebells and lichen'.

> In silent whispers I repent
> For evil done with clear intent
> I plead for love and humbly pray
> To Jesus waiting on the way.
> [...]
> Let those who on my body gaze.
> Remember me for happy days.
> There is now no more than a disused pad
> That's launched its final shot to God!

My father didn't die in a sylvan glade; he died in a hospital after about a dozen strokes and heart attacks. He died in penury, with nothing to leave but a ring, a watch and a chess set. There was no glut of mourners. Among us, we could only find four pallbearers: me, my brother and two others I didn't know.

My brother is tall. I am not. The other guys were a little-and-large act too. We went short at the front, tall at the back. My dad was a large man. Coffins are made of hardwood. Individually, both are heavy. Together, they were unbearable.

The coffin, on a slant, was slipping forwards every time we took a step, pulling at the fabric of my jacket, my shirt and the skin beneath them. The sharp edge of the corner dug through my muscles and into my bones. We progressed what seemed like a long way, from the church to the graveside. My mother stood at the back of what wasn't a crowd. Heaving the coffin up to our shoulders from waist height in the church had been easy. Now, with an audience, we had to place it ceremoniously on the wet ground by the graveside.

My brother and the other man at the back shifted the heft of it up from their shoulders to their hands. The centre of gravity suddenly changed, and the shiny box began to tilt forwards like it had crossed the event horizon of a black hole. I felt the coffin's inertia release. The weight of it sunk so deeply into me, the edge of it began to grind my collarbone. The pain was unbearable and I felt my knees start to quiver. Then, stealing the little grip that we had of it, the dead weight inside the coffin shifted. Finally, the coffin was tumbling, out of control, into the grave. It fell, colliding with the edge of the pit. With a crack, the lid broke open an inch. Inside, it was trimmed in bright white satin, but there was a darkness around it. The body wanted to submit to gravity. Another crack, and the lid was suddenly free. My father pitched out. His slack jaw caught the edge of the hole and the impact knocked his dentures free. Then, the grey corpse, suddenly unsecured, was sent flailing as it disappeared into the ditch. I saw the sextons jumping in after him, trying to heave his uncooperative corpse up out of the mud. Everyone was watching as my father's head appeared above the crest of the hole, as he was dragged free and his mud-stained corpse was folded back into the box.

Fortunately, before any of this happened, as the coffin first slipped forwards on my shoulders, I felt its momentum being caught by one or both of the taller pair behind, and we managed to recover our balance.

We laid it, with only a slight wobble, neatly at the graveside. And I did all this while trying to suppress a smile at the image only I'd foreseen.

At the graveside, the priest said a few more words. I tried to summon tears but none came. It was then the turn of the family to throw handfuls of dirt into the ditch. When it was my turn, I threw the poem in too.

And then he was gone. All the violence, the chaos, the lies, the boiling anger, all gone with him. He seemed to have lived such a big life, but from the age of about fifty he was reduced to someone that couldn't even say someone's name unless they were called John (his own). The only other thing he could manage was a stream of expletives that would shock a sailor, delivered with such efficiency they must have been sourced in an undamaged part of the brain.

ix

On the train back to Edinburgh, I continued reading my, by now dog-eared and creased, copy of *Where Angels Fear to Tread*. I underlined a sentence: 'For the dead, who seem to take away so much, really take with them nothing that is ours. The passion they have aroused lives after them, easy to transmute or to transfer, but well-nigh impossible to destroy.'[2] My father's life was one dominated by passion in all its shades. Whatever he wanted he got – if only temporarily, before bailiffs took it from him and us. After he was gone, though, the fires he set continued to burn and the consequences of his abuse lasted decades beyond his death.

Once a parent dies, something you feel among the flurry of emotions is the fact that in the universal order of things, you're next.

The second sentence I underlined was one that I now know appears twice in the novel. A character utters it early in the story and when I'd read that instance of it, it had passed by me unnoticed. When a character repeats the comment back towards the end of the novel, my usually darting eyes stopped scanning the page and instead read and reread the sentence like it was a mantra: 'I and my life must be where I live'.[3]

x

Edinburgh was a failure. With little friction, I found a job and handed in my notice to a disappointed Frank, who always thought I'd be a failure, he said, and told me how sad he was to have his doubts about me confirmed. I picked up my last little pay packet, a tiny envelope stuffed with notes and coins, and went home into 1990 – a world of answering machines, bypass protesters, pagers, Sunny D, Paula Yates and Princess Diana. Boys wore curtains and the girls wore Wonderbras.

I was going to be working in a grand old dame of a cinema. Like Dickens's Mrs Gamp – a 'lady' but gone wrong, dirty, scruffy and a bit smelly – the cinema had seen better days. As winter set in, I kept thinking about how cold my father's body would be in the coffin, under the hard earth. When the grave was filled in, a simple wooden cross was erected. We were told that we should wait six months for the soil to settle properly before a gravestone was made. When the bill arrived, it was a week's salary and I resented every penny. I couldn't navigate to the grave today even if I wanted to.

xi

The least familiar aspect of working at the cinema was that there was nothing to do for hours every day. From 11 a.m., once the place was prepped, all you needed to do was be on site. Some managers would sit in their office and listen to the cricket, some would knit, others liked to watch football.

It was sheer chance that Manchester's largest bookshop was just across the street. Eventually, the emptiness of those hours only seemed to lengthen, so it was more boredom than curiosity that drove me in there. I noticed a very imposing book in the window. It was piled every which way, the display looking like a tractor had unloaded into it. It was Umberto Eco's *Foucault's Pendulum* and it was so heavy that the third little pig might have selected it as hardy construction materials.

Inside the shop I recognised the Penguin Classics, spotting those forbidding black spines with a scarlet stripe at the top. For me, they were associated with my sister's desk at home and her copies of school-set *Northanger Abbey* and *Jane Eyre*. I headed for 'F' and the familiarity of Forster. I wasn't ready for anything novel length like *The Longest Journey* or *Howards End* (his shortest novel had, after all, taken me months to get through). I opted for his 'other' collection of short stories.

Published posthumously in 1972, *The Life to Come: And Other Stories* gathers together many of the tales that Forster had written across his career but felt that the public was not ready for. Given the hostility of the critical backlash against the collection, he was right to have held them back.

Forster is one of the most important writers of the twentieth century, yet readers today are still presented with two collections: a 'straight' one and a 'gay' one. Oliver Stallybrass was the editor of several of the standard Abinger editions of Forster's works, and he wrote in the introduction to *The Life to Come* that 'not every reader will find it easy to assess coolly a group of stories in which buggery is an almost unvarying feature'.[4] Most of Forster's posthumous fiction was received with similar or greater hostility. The general tenor of it was that Forster's reputation was being destroyed by such fiction: 'We will read you, but please don't talk about who you are because that's embarrassing.' It's infuriating criticism to read.

I can't recall when I first learned that Forster himself was gay, but I do remember feeling offended. Wasn't this the single most important fact about him? It seemed so to me at the time. Why had the sexuality of one of the most influential writers of the period been deliberately suppressed? We congratulate ourselves on the acquisition of knowledge, but culpability for our ignorance always seems to lay elsewhere.

It wasn't that we didn't study any gay fiction at school. It was the fact that the genre simply did not exist. Back at school, the authors were an array of straight, white males. In the poetry anthology we studied, of the forty-five authors, two were women. Everyone, to my knowledge, was straight. Everyone was white too. Section 28 didn't result in the emptying of libraries and the burning of books. Instead, the stage was already set by a prudish, reserved canon. Section 28 would later play a role in the 'straightification' of the canon, but it also came indirectly by means of an emergent centralising power, predefining what a subject should be, what should be read, what the agreed standards ought to be.

While I was browsing that bookshop, the entire canon, the entire curriculum, was being carefully constructed, paragraph by paragraph, behind closed doors. Classics were being made but classics were also being erased.

The new educational syllabus that every child would follow, straight or gay, cis or trans, would be called the National Curriculum,

which Thatcher had first announced in that rousing party conference speech in 1987.

I spoke to a friend of mine, Dr Clive Johnson, to find out more
about what it was like to be an English teacher at the time the National Curriculum was being debated, drafted and rolled out.

xii

Dr Johnson is a former secondary English teacher and assistant head
teacher, who has also taught in further education and at university
level. He taught English at secondary school between 1992 and 2008.
Johnson explained to me that after the initial announcement, many
teachers at the time dreaded the imposition of a National Curriculum. By the time the Cox Report arrived in 1989, there was some
relief.[5] Penned under the chairmancy of Brian Cox (not that one, or
the other one – this one was the pro-vice-chancellor and a professor
of English Literature at Manchester University), he was regarded by
some as 'an ogre of the Right'.[6] *English for Ages 5 to 16*, later known
as the Cox Report, is a substantial document that focuses on the
mechanics of delivering the new curriculum.

Johnson explained:

> I think that the original National Curriculum was quite a humane
> document ... It wasn't too bad in the circumstances and came out
> being reasonably positive ... I think many English teachers felt
> they could sign up to it, maybe less so the assessment elements
> of it but certainly the content. [There was a sense that] in the '60s
> and '70s, teachers had become too free in terms of what they were
> teaching and they weren't delivering competent, workforce-ready

young people, that educational standards had slipped and that we needed to be getting back to basics.

The belief was that English was too skills-based, focusing on competencies in composition and creativity. According to Johnson, teachers feared that there was going to be a strong pushback, an attempt by the government to turn English into a content subject. This is an important distinction and one we will revisit, as it's a point of particular tension in debates over how English can and should be taught and assessed.

Other subjects do not have the same challenges to overcome. If we look at the post-Gove curricula for other subjects, it's easy to teach and assess that pupils should be taught to 'understand and use place value for decimals, measures and integers of any size'.[7] Without any specialist knowledge in maths or education, even I could assess whether a pupil understands this and even write a test that would look for and expose these abilities. Likewise, with only a modicum of a refresher, even I could draft a test and assess whether a pupil understands the 'differences between atoms, elements and compounds'.[8]

If we have a look at the post-Gove English curriculum, learning outcomes are rather more complicated. I'm not sure I would know how to test and assess a pupil's agility in expressing and 'knowing how language, including figurative language, vocabulary choice, grammar, text structure and organisational features, presents meaning'.[9] Who would? And what qualifications would they need to mark it? It seems on a different level altogether.

For clarity, these are all attainment targets for Key Stage 3 (pupils aged eleven to fourteen) from the 2013 curricula. The problem isn't so much that the level of attainment is hard in English but that it is a fundamentally different kind of subject that is being forced into behaving like all the other content-based ones. The reason the English curriculum is difficult to assess is that it is ontologically different to those of other subjects.

Johnson explains: 'English is a skills subject. In English, you might do a Shakespeare play, you might not, but you can still write an essay, or you could still deliver a talk, or still read a complex text. It's not content dependent.' In a content model, the child's mind becomes a deposit box into which information is lodged.

xiii

The Cox Report was indeed a humane document, one that sought to address some of these issues as best it could, one aligned with many English teachers' values. It explained the role of English:

> To foster in pupils a love of literature, to encourage their awareness of its unique relationship to human experience and to promote in them a sense of excitement in the power and potential of language can be one of the greatest joys of the English teacher. It is also one of the greatest challenges.[10]

And:

> We do not wish to underestimate the straightforward pleasure that reading can afford. An identification of books with enjoyment and a positive readiness to devote leisure time to reading seem to us wholly desirable outcomes of primary and secondary school experience. But we would nevertheless hope that by the end of their school careers as many pupils as possible will have

been able to 'grow' through literature – both emotionally and aesthetically, both morally and socially – by virtue of coming into contact with the 'range of possible thought and feeling' identified above. An active involvement with literature enables pupils to share the experience of others. They will encounter and come to understand a wide range of feelings and relationships by entering vicariously the worlds of others, and in consequence they are likely to understand more of themselves.[11]

Sounds amazing! The Cox Report was not the National Curriculum, though – it only informed it.

The proposals were viewed as too liberal for the then Education Secretary. One of the drivers behind the idea of a National Curriculum was the eradication of bad grammar. There is a problem with this recurrent concern: linguists cannot agree what constitutes *good* grammar. Where does regional variation sit in our idea of correct grammar, when every dialect has its own syntactical rules? Whose grammar is to be taught in this project of nationalisation?[12] Moreover, the history of English over the past few hundred years is peppered with the dates on which grammar moved into and out of fashion in educational circles.[13]

After the Cox Report, the National Curriculum Council – responsible for interpreting the report and introducing it to schools – took the ominous step of adding grammar in several places in the curriculum. There were two drivers for this. One was the dubious belief that there is a 'correct' English to be taught, learned, acquired, then spoken and written. But the other issue is assessing the pupils.

Johnson explains:

It's very difficult to assess an eleven-year-old writing an essay about what they did over the summer. That can only be assessed by an English teacher saying, 'Well, that's really good, because you've used a variety of sentences. You've got good vocabulary. You've structured it well. You set it up well. You've come to a conclusion that comes right back to the beginning and, you've done all that really well. That's an A.' Michael Gove might look at that and might agree that it's an 'A' but he'd think how can we logically assess that? How can we dependably assess that? Of course we can't, you've got to trust English teachers.

Once you agree on a set of prescribed rules like grammar, English becomes more content-ready. Speech and writing can be marked 'right' or 'wrong'. Section 28, introduced alongside the National Curriculum, did a similar thing for adolescents' sexualities.

For over two decades, the National Curriculum held sway over the sensibilities of the country's teaching workforce and of troubled school kids looking for stories that would help them understand their identity. Clause 28 ensured that there was no one left to tell them about the contributions of queer writers and thinkers.

xiv

Given the prevalence of HIV, I wasn't interested in one-night stands. I can't tell you how I went about finding someone because we were always a bit cagey about how we met. It was neither interesting nor scandalous, though – just a little out of the ordinary. He lived 200 miles away and soon we were speaking every day on the phone. On my way home from work at eleven or twelve at night, I'd scuttle into the red phone box 100 yards from our house, call him with my ten pence piece, and when that ran out he'd call me back and we'd talk for half an hour about our day. He was twelve years older than I, a lot when you're twenty. He was already settled in his career but not in life. It all felt dangerous and exciting but when we were together, surprisingly normal. And soon, my days were merely the punctuation around the time we spent either speaking to or being with each other. About six weeks later, with the earth still shifting and settling on my father's grave, I was ready.

XV

In March 1990, I went for a follow-up HIV test. I waited the Schrödingerian three weeks for the results, in which two alternative lives are lived; one negative, one positive. I was clear.

I decided I would tell my sister, who after Sheffield was now working in London and was up visiting me in Edinburgh. I thought my whole world would fall in, but it turned out to be easy. With the door cracked open, I could feel a rush of life flowing through it. It was as if I'd worked a fingernail under the wallpaper and now wanted to strip it all away. Mum next. When I got home, I couldn't wait, so told her while she was doing some housework. She had never ironed a dress with such vehemence. She batted away the news with something along the lines of that sort of thing being fashionable and that's why I was drawn to it. Then she retreated to asserting it was a phase and maintained that position for about a decade.

I had felt like some giant in a fairy tale held down by threads and suddenly I was free of them. Next, my other sister. There was no one I wasn't ready to tell. The stalemate broken, I moved on to some friends. I overcooked the first and met a gasp of relief: 'I thought you were going to tell me you had cancer or something.' But one of the responses I quickly grew tired of was 'I don't mind'. Correlation is not causation, but there's so much wrong with it. It's permission-granting, parental, like your identity is somehow within their gift. All the people who used the expression, I've since lost touch with. One heard the news from a third party, so I phoned them. All they kept saying was 'I don't mind' and from there retreated to 'It's just so weird'. They repeated it over and over with a peevish snigger. We haven't spoken since.

Coming out, at least for people of my generation, also meant trading most of your network for a little authenticity. I'm sure there are numerous exceptions, but none of the gay men that I know are close friends with people they know from school. Not many are still in touch with the friends they grew up with, and when they are, they tend not to be close. This is the quiet death of coming out and it's slow to mature. It's not until years later that you realise it has happened. There is an emotional cost to this, making people more vulnerable, lonely even. But there's also a fiscal element to it, too.

For the last two decades, if you were to compare, across numerous datasets and different countries, the wages of gay and straight men, with similar levels of expertise, education, skills, job responsibilities etc., you would discover that gay men consistently earned 5–10 per cent less than their straight counterparts – though the situation has now, happily, improved.[14] The results had previously been laid at the door of prejudice against LGBT+ people. While this will be true, I can't help but feel that the demographic is also less statistically likely to have a longstanding network to draw upon when looking for work or being out on the grift. In the '80s and '90s, so many would have been Jimmy Somerville's 'Smalltown Boys', cutting ties and moving to bigger cities to begin again without connections. Clinging on to the bottom rung is an expensive place to be.

xvi

Once I knew who I was, I could decide where and what I wanted to be. I handed my notice in at work and had to get through a couple of weeks of anger from everyone for wasting their time, which, in fairness, they'd mostly spent watching the cricket.

My mum took little time in coming round and, except for wanting it kept secret, was as supportive as she could be. I wish I'd known then, that when I later got married, she'd insist at the last possible moment on giving an unscripted speech at the wedding – and slayed it. And, in the weeks, months and years that followed, kept repeating that it was one of the best days of her life.

Gay, queer, trans kids, this is the most likely long-term consequence of coming out. It can take years (even decades) for your world to get a little traction, but it catches up with you eventually.

It was a warm spring in 1990 when I left, bound for a flat by the sea in Brighton.

Brighton is normally where people's stories end, not begin. Something to do with proximity to the sea, but it makes sense that the people who want out will go as far as geography will permit.

My boyfriend and I were a legal couple since I'd turned twenty-one. Our first-floor flat, rented from a friend of his, was a hundred yards from the sea. In heavy storms, pebbles from the beach would blow all the way up the street.

Our time together was our own. The demographics of Brighton and Hove at the time were dominated by retirees and LGBT+ people. My jaw would drop when we'd walk about the town and see gay couples holding hands. But it wasn't all pride and rainbows. We'd only been there a couple of weeks when, stood at our front windows one evening, a rock the size of a fist was hurled at us from below, shattering glass over the living room.

I signed on the dole for about a fortnight while registering with agencies for temp work: 'No, I don't have any qualifications.'

Early on, we got a visit from one of his friends. She had stumbled into a job as a PA at a publishing house. She arrived bearing gifts. Two books, one the recently published autobiography of George Blake, glossy and Russian red. It had caused a furore because it was the first time he'd been heard of since he'd dramatically escaped from prison in 1966. In 1961, Blake had been sentenced to forty-two years in prison for passing secrets to the Russians. He did this while working in Berlin and Eastern Europe during the Cold War. To escape to Russia, Blake climbed out of a window of Wormwood Scrubs while the inmates and guards were engrossed in a film. Some collusion provided him with a rope ladder to scale the wall.

The other book was shiny, icy blue, lustrous and pristine, with a weight to it. It was, as an object, impeccable: too polished to soil with a thumbprint. I knew I wasn't interested in Blake – 300 pages of non-fiction about someone who had fled the country before I was born. But the novel looked serious and aspirational. I recognised it as the one whose display had replaced *Foucault's Pendulum* in the window of that Manchester bookshop opposite the old cinema. The book was Ian McEwan's *The Innocent*. We set the books aside and settled into our evening of getting to know each other.

The next morning, I gingerly opened the front board and read the novel's blurb. I leafed past the royal blue endpapers and heard the spine emit a tiny 'crack' as the dried glue gave way for the first time. The paper smelt of ripe fruit. I leafed through a few pages, which whispered as I turned them. I passed the ornate colophon. I turned to page one and read, with high expectations, the opening line: 'It was Lieutenant Lofting who dominated the meeting.'

'Oh', I thought. 'Sounds boring.' I snapped the book shut and lay it aside, where it sat for weeks on the table, throbbing with the future.

xvii

We didn't have a bookshelf because we didn't own any books. So, George Blake and Ian McEwan lay on the table as we dined and breakfasted around them.

Meanwhile, I was working as a temp. I worked at several places until one of them became permanent. I found myself doing a 'computer job', with no knowledge of computers (I'd worn a personal stereo during those lessons). In between data-entry sessions, there seemed hours to fill. Going to and from work – on breaks, on lunch. When I got home, there were more hours to fill as I waited for my boyfriend to return from his job in London.

On one of those days, I tried *The Innocent* again.

Not much happened in the first ten, twenty pages, but there was something about it. Brighton was not Berlin, but many aspects of my circumstances chimed with the innocent-abroad theme of the novel. By page forty, I removed the dust cover to preserve it and was then fairly sure I was going to go the distance. The book expended a lot of time and type on establishing character and setting, in which a Post Office engineer had been sent to Berlin in the 1950s to help the Americans tap into Russian communications. The protagonist then strikes up an affair with a Berliner. I didn't realise the extent to which I was being lured in by the prose at first, but there was a moment about halfway when I nearly dropped the book in horror. The Victorians would have called this sensation fiction: stories that pluck and twang at the nerves. Those Victorian forebears were sometimes cheap and formulaic, but the effect that McEwan creates in *The Innocent* is skilfully done by fashioning a sense of safety, intimacy and privacy, then disrupting all three in the worst way possible.

Then there's 'that' chapter. The novel's 'innocent', Leonard, finds himself in a situation in which he has to dispose of a body. The only means available to him is to dismember it and transport it in a suitcase. It takes a whole chapter.

In interview, McEwan has since said that no one ever reads the chapter.[15] There's certainly some truth in this but not for me. I was revolted by it. But then, it is supposed to be revolting. The squirming difficulty that people experience in reading the chapter is nothing compared to what the character is having to endure. It certainly does not glamorise violence; there's no sense of authorial revelry or tie-straightening.

I completed the chapter on the bus home from work and was relieved that I no longer had to check over my shoulder for passive readers.

I was a slow reader, so it wasn't until about a week later that I was approaching the end of the novel. I was at that point, familiar to almost any reader, where I couldn't put the book down. I was in the closing pages and – forgive me – needed the loo, so I took the book with me. While enthroned, I read the novel's denouement. The details of it sound facile without context but work perfectly in the story. The plot turns upon the presence of a real-life character in Berlin at the time, one who passed the secret of the comms-tap to the Russians. The protagonist's friend who lives down the hall, who we've encountered several times in the novel, is called 'George'. Only at the end of the book do we discover his surname: he is George Blake.

'Oh my God!' I said aloud on reading it. 'Oh my God!' as the book slipped through my fingers and tumbled to the floor. And open mouthed in wonder: 'Oh. My. God!' I felt the reaction in my body. It was shock, and I was trying to process it. It was as if the book had become suddenly sentient and had reached out, responding through its proximity to the only other book in our flat – Blake's autobiography.

At three points, the book had electrified me. At three points, the print and paper had risen from the page and become something in the air, in the world. This wasn't passing the time, it wasn't entertainment; this was feeling. It was actual. It was something. A real thing. I had no idea fiction could be like this. Quite accidentally, I had, at last, learned to read.

xviii

We often don't recognise the moments when our lives change. We fail to register the significance of events and sometimes claw for them in hindsight. We try to find meaning in them, searching for the hinge in our experience. This wasn't that. I knew. I knew straight away that my life had changed. I'd never known that books could do this, and now I did. I'd never felt sick to my stomach reading, and now I had. I'd never had prickles reading a book, and now I had. A book had never left the page and entered the world, creating sensations in me, pleasant or not, and now it had. It was rapturous; I felt like my life had begun.

xix

What does this mean that someone can suddenly acquire the ability to read at the age of twenty-one? The fact that it coincided with being out and not having to do the work of lying to those I loved, feeling that some semblance of a future awaited me, suggests that I was settling into myself. I was in a place where I could be myself, and I was being myself.

Since the age of twelve, I'd been trapped, held in place face-on to a cocked fist, flinching with my eyes closed, waiting for the punch to land. I waited for years. But it never came. Instead, when I opened my eyes, I found help, not harm.

It was as if so much bandwidth had been consumed in an effort to act and be someone else, there wasn't room for any of the good stuff. I may have learned to read – but not to *read*.

Children aged about four to six acquire the ability to recognise letters and can recognise words in the world when they encounter them (but not know what they mean). This is called emergent literacy. Alphabetic fluency (ages six to seven) includes basic word recognition and decoding strategies for unknown words (using illustrations or contexts to help). Ages seven to nine is a transitional phase in which fewer decoding strategies are necessary and basic word recognition becomes automatic. The intermediate stage (ages nine to eleven) is one in which students begin to read to learn about new things and start to write in different modes. Independent reading should be easier by now, which also means that longer materials can be tackled. Finally, there is advanced readership (eleven to fourteen), at which point the pupil becomes fluent and can read completely independently, using the skill to take up difficult or challenging information.

Literacy is, of course, much more complex than this. For one, reading is not natural. It isn't something that can be entrusted to just happen, like learning to walk or having the impulse to speak (thanks to the FOXP2 gene). There is no gene for reading. Neither is there a single part of the brain that is activated in reading. Reading is an acquired skill that forges links across the temporal lobe (responsible for awareness, processing and decoding of sounds), the frontal lobe (speech, reading fluency, grammar and comprehension) and the angular and supramarginal gyri. The latter two elements serve to conduct the orchestra of the brain, so that its user can recognise 't' and 'o' and then infer from the syntax and lexis whether those two letters express motion in the direction of approaching or reaching a particular location or whether they are identifying a person affected by or receiving something. These are the mechanics of reading.[16]

xx

For me, advanced readership means something else as well. It refers to precisely these moments when the device, the brick of paper, the codex, disappears and takes on a transparent form. Like when someone goes to a play and, for the first time, stops seeing actors talking their lines at an absurd volume and instead, in a moment of tension, thinks, 'Oh, don't do that. You'll be caught for sure.'

Advanced readership is when so little cognition is required in the act of doing it that the mode and means of delivery disappear. Instead, it's more like a fibre-optic cable is pulsing the stuff directly into you. It becomes impossible to look at a word without reading it. (Take a moment to think about just how amazing that is.)

With stories, their present becomes your present. Your body dissolves and your feelings of delight, disgust and desire are dictated by the ink on paper and not by the materiality of your surroundings. It was like I was no longer reading the black print – I was in the white spaces around it, and had found there a new universe.

More practically, I quickly learned that you didn't have to say the words in your head. It was like I'd installed an interpretive bypass and could go straight to understanding the word without having to subvocalise it. Next, I learned that it wasn't necessary to read each word individually. Instead, it was possible to process several words in a single fixation of the eye. If antidisestablishmentarianism can be captured in a glance, then it stands that a third of a line consisting of shorter words can also be received and processed in a single glance, rather than the dozen or so it takes when words are read singly. Why weren't we taught this at school? Reading there seemed only to be a punishment, a fine for some wrong. The idea that I might, on any given page, brush up against the very best that has been thought or said, that what I read might be a means for my exploring the recesses of the soul, might tell me about what it is to be a human, might show me beauty and mystery and awe – none of this was ever present when I read at school. There was never any question of being carried away by a chore.

Learning to read – really, to read – is the single most accessible means of living your life with greater intensity. Nothing has taught me so much about the world as fiction has.

xxi

I wanted more! I was like a computer with only a BIOS, sufficient to power up but not to actually do anything. I wanted software. I wanted data. I wanted lots and lots of data.

The next morning, I phoned the gift-giving friend and tried to explain to her that books were really good. I tried to tell her that this literary novel that was being advertised in railway stations and bus shelters was a good novel and lots of people should read it: 'That Ian McEwan, I think might be a very good writer. Have you read him? You should read him. He's really good. I think he might be famous one day'. She listened to it all patiently, even making it to the end of the loo story before she 'really had to get going'.

It was a few years later, after I'd read hundreds of novels, that I finally put together the planetary weight of my beginner's luck. That friend was PA to Tom Maschler – inventor of the Booker Prize and chairman of Jonathan Cape. Maschler was responsible for publishing people like Ernest Hemingway, Bruce Chatwin, Gabriel García Márquez, Martin Amis, Joseph Heller, Salman Rushdie and, of course, Ian McEwan.

The next day, a package arrived in the post addressed to me. It was a giant brown envelope stuffed full of book catalogues from publishers I'd never heard of: Jonathan Cape, Chatto & Windus, The Bodley Head and Virago. There was a note explaining that she could get me 50 per cent off.

xxii

But I didn't know what I wanted. I didn't know who J. G. Ballard was or Margaret Atwood or Angela Carter. It was a rare moment of self-awareness, because I knew that I'd captured something so precious, I couldn't risk wasting it on a misinformed impulse. I was trying to hold on to sand. If left alone, in time it would blow away on the breeze. But if I held it fast, the tighter my grip then the easier it would run through my fingers. This needed care. I needed expert help. There was a bookshop in Brighton, gay-friendly and less imposing than Waterstones, which seemed to be for people that knew what they were doing. The bookshop was called Read All About It. I explained my predicament and the husband-and-wife duo handled me as carefully as an injured bird.

'He's done a few novels, but he's more famous for his short stories.'

It was just my kind of commitment: stories, some of which were only a few pages in length. I paid my £3.99 and left the shop with the book wrapped in a paper bag, proudly announcing myself to the world as a reader.

McEwan's collection *First Love, Last Rites* (1975) caused a furore on publication, lauded and lambasted for its deft prose and lewd content. For me, the effect of reading the stories was not so much impressive as concussive. I entered a world of crazed narrators. The subject matter was both disgusting and compelling. Entering the psyche of a child abuser for twenty minutes is no pastime, but the effect was never prurient or exploitative. In those pages, action wasn't thrilling, violence was not glamorised and sex was not erotic. Every thought and idea seemed to have been distilled into the fewest possible words, creating a general impression that the writing of the stories had been easy. Decades on, without ever having returned to them, I can remember most of the stories.

xxiii

And I was off. Thanks to my friend the PA and the folks at Read All About It, I read Carrie Fisher, Jenny Diski, R. K. Narayan, John Fowles, Hanif Kureishi, Alan Hollinghurst, Don DeLillo, A. S. Byatt, Charles Palliser, Barbara Pym, Chinua Achebe, David Leavitt and more. I spent 10 per cent of my week's salary on a Barbara Vine – new out in hardback. By then, the seemingly imposing *Foucault's Pendulum* that had intimidated me in the Manchester bookshop display was out in paperback. I whizzed through it and found it not so challenging after all. The conclusion in which the protagonist is resigned to his fate made my spine shiver. And later, when my boyfriend's job took him to Paris on a business trip, I joined him and went to see the Foucault pendulum swing in space at the Musée des Arts et Métiers.

By about the twentieth novel, without fail I'd get through a hundred pages a day of whatever I was reading. Even if the Iris Murdoch was a bit boring, I'd knock it off in a few days and be on to something else before the end of the week. With so much space to fill, I sucked everything in like a collapsing star.

I quickly devised an amateur theory of novel length and worked out which, for me, was the best kind to devote my time to.

The 100-page ones were like Japanese miniatures, to be admired and inspected closely. These were titles like Penelope Fitzgerald's *The Bookshop*, Amit Chaudhuri's *Afternoon Raag*, Adolfo Bioy Casares's *The Invention of Morel*, Patrick Süskind's *The Story of Mr Sommer* or anything by Anita Brookner.

The 200-pagers generally dealt intelligently with a single issue – Jenny Diski's *Nothing Natural*, Abdulrazak Gurnah's *By the Sea* or, more recently, Paul Lynch's *Prophet Song*, which is a nice idea and perfectly executed but that's about the life of it.

The 300-hundred pagers tended to be the more traditional kind but mostly could have been 200 pages if the editor had stood up to the author (too many to mention here).

At 400 pages, the novels were into a weird hinterland between the traditional and the capacious, like Salman Rushdie's *Midnight's Children*, the second half of which I can never remember.

It was at 500 pages that I felt the magic started to happen. I still do. These weren't vignettes. Nothing about them was dainty. Entering them was like spinning down a hotel corridor, diverting into every room, colliding with the lives therein and making sense of it all by the end. Just like George Eliot put all Middlemarch life – from the land labourers through to the clergy and those dabbling in politics – into her book, Michel Faber crammed all of the detritus, grime and perversion of Victorian London, from the capitalists to the maids to the sex workers, into *The Crimson Petal and the White*. Likewise, Leo Tolstoy, not satisfied with just Moscow, wrestles all of Russia into *Anna Karenina*. More recently, there's Paul Murray's *The Bee Sting*, which is like *Middlemarch* crossed with *Derry Girls*. Or there's Richard Powers's capacious *The Overstory*, about those touched by trees, in which the story becomes a complex root network that reveals all manner of connections between plant and human life. By the time you crest page 600, it's not so much a novel about the forest but the entire planet.

By the time you've made it through books like Hilary Mantel's *A Place of Greater Safety*, Rohinton Mistry's *A Fine Balance* or Wilkie Collins's *The Moonstone*, it's not so much that you've put your head around the door of another life. It's not even like staying a weekend. Reading a two-pounder is more like a short-term tenancy. That's what I call them – 'two pounders'. Not their cost but their weight. I've learned that I'm not so interested in the kind of novel that if you flung it might startle a sparrow. I like the books with so much crammed into them they could smash a window.

xxiv

Meanwhile, I'd been working for a finance company and got made redundant after three months. They slung me what was to them some loose change; to me, it was more money than I'd ever seen in my life. The most valuable part of the package, though, was one-to-one career consultancy. I didn't know what this was but, out of a job, I had nothing better to do, so went along to meet my consultant, Mr Chamberlain.

Together, we did the sorts of things one might expect: CV spruce-ups, interview training, exploring different ways of finding meaning-ful work. He was kind and supportive, and I noted that except for Margery Kim, my college teacher, I'd never met another grown-up that took me seriously. We did lots of psychometric tests (all the rage at the time) coupled with an array of verbal and numerical reasoning tests. A week or so later, we met again. He had produced a thirty-page report about me, and when he handed it to me he said, 'You should have gone to university.' I'd got to know him at this point and he obviously liked me, so I dismissed the advice, writing it off because he was, like Margery, paid to be kind to people like me.

A fortnight later, interviewing for what would be the worst job of my life, I sat some tests, and as the sunbed-tanned branch man-ager breezed back into the room brandishing both my results and surprisingly white teeth, he said the exact same words: 'You should have gone to university.'

I was to be a recruitment consultant, selling salespeople to salespeople. My job was, it turned out, to shuffle liars around their chosen industries. I hated it. I hated the people. I was so unsuited to the job and the culture; I was like a zebra trying to make the move from black and white movies to colour. I couldn't sell anything. I couldn't have sold coal to a Victorian railway magnate. And al-though I'd had only a fleeting relationship with the truth in the past, much to everyone's dismay, I found it impossible to lie to clients. My Sunday-afternoon dreads were so acute they'd start on Thursday.

I used to drive the twenty or so miles to work and resented being there so much that rather than be two minutes early for work, I'd pull into a lay-by so I could read another page of *Brideshead Revisit-ed*. At work, I'd stuff the paperback down the back of my pants, put on my jacket and sneak the book to the loo to escape for just a few minutes into that prelapsarian world, that syrupy prose that emitted odours of spring lilacs and summer jasmine. It felt like I was living my real life around the interstices of this fake one, one in which I pretended to be both straight and capable of selling something.

Soon, to everyone's relief, I was sacked. No longer could I inflict my honesty on the company's clients. I hadn't failed to register that after two years in the fast-food job, I had spent nine months as a relief landlord. Six months in the cinema. Nearly three months at the finance firm and now only two as the world's worst recruitment consultant. At this rate, I would soon crest peak turnover and be exiting jobs before being invited for interview.

XXV

Mr Chamberlain was still eager and willing to provide advice and guidance off the books. He repeated that I should go to university, but I wasn't ready to hear it. So, he submitted and said I should start approaching places with no vacancies and say I'd really like to work for them: 'Then you're not in competition with a long list of other candidates.' I cascaded down my list, from the 'like tos' through the 'would considers' all the way down to the tenuous 'coulds'.

I got a call back from the local bus company. I would sit behind a counter and dish out weekly savers and bus passes to old dears and foreign language students. Occasionally, someone might threaten to throw you through a window because they wanted their coach ticket faster than you could write it, but when it wasn't busy, all you had to do was sit there. And I had 100 pages to get through every day. Kazuo Ishiguro, Henry James, Sue Townsend, Martin Amis and Vikram Seth were all snuggled away under my desk if a customer approached. I'd read at every available opportunity.

I served customers their tickets and this allowed me to buy a few books. It paid for cinema tickets. And working for the buses made it very cheap for me to do things like go book shopping for the day in Cambridge or nip up to town in the evenings to go and see a Sibelius or Britten at The Proms. I'd occasionally see a bus driver from the company that I was on nodding acquaintance with at these events. I liked the idea that they'd be driving a bus the next morning with threads of Mahlerian strings still ringing in their ears. Later, when I read Elizabeth Gaskell's tale of industrial life in Manchester, *Mary Barton*, it always made me think of this time, of using work, like soil, to sustain the life around it. Gaskell is writing about the city's factory workers:

There are botanists among them, equally familiar with either the Linnaean or the Natural system, who know the name and habitat of every plant within a day's walk from their dwellings; who steal the holiday of a day or two when any particular plant should be in flower, and tying up their simple food in their pocket-handkerchiefs, set off with single purpose to fetch home the humble-looking weed. There are entomologists, who may be seen with a rude-looking net, ready to catch any winged insect, or a kind of dredge, with which they rake the green and slimy pools; practical, shrewd, hard-working men, who pore over every new specimen with real scientific delight.

If you've not read Elizabeth Gaskell, may I urge you to. Every century there are only one or two figures that possess the storytelling gene and she has it. No one I've read can blend character, realism, psychological depth, empathy and compassion, all wrapped up in neat, nascently feminist narrative arcs, like her. Often the stories seem straightforward on a first read but develop prismatic qualities on a second or third. *Wives and Daughters* is as good as George Eliot's *Middlemarch*.

Throughout this time, I continued to think about university, but once you start earning a wage (and I think this applies more to people on lower wages), it is incredibly difficult to stop.

In the days before emails, memos used to be circulated and people would have to sign their names to prove information uptake. One day, my manager put in front of me a notice about staff development. Anyone interested in taking a course with the Open University would be able to get 75 per cent of their fees paid. The fees were only about a fortnight's pay, but that's still a fair sum when you're not earning much. The company would also gift a week's leave for a summer school and paid time off for the sitting of examinations.

I'd heard of the Open University, from both a full-of-herself colleague at the finance firm, who had often talked about her achievements in doing a course with them, and from the Willy Russell film *Educating Rita*.

I did a little checking and went back to the MD of the bus company to ask if they'd contribute to an arts course. I wanted to study literature and philosophy.

xxvi

Before I knew it, I was in correspondence with the MD and it was immediately clear that 'of course' they would help me. This is probably the most 1990s thing that happened to me. A bus company, willing to support someone interested in learning more, to invest actual money in them, give them extra time off, all so that they might feel a little more fulfilled and satisfied in their work by studying the arts.

The company will have got tax relief on the fees that they fronted up, but the time off, the encouragement, the assumption that this was a good thing to do – this was altruism.

With a peculiar mix of insecurity and arrogance, I'd believed I was 'settling' for this company when I deigned to work for them, but now I feel enlightened by the thought that they were never undeserving of me; it was I who was the lucky one.

The Open University is one of the most profound engines of social change in the UK. In terms of impact, it comes a close second to the Education Acts of the nineteenth century that diverted tens of thousands of children into schools by rule of law. By the beginning of the twentieth century, working-class literacy was transformed and there was a new, mass reading public.

Established in 1969, the Open University was founded by the Labour government under Prime Minister Harold Wilson. It was part of a commitment to radically modernise British society: to contribute to the economy while also promoting greater equality of opportunity. Planning commenced in 1965 and the university accepted its first enrolment of students six years later in 1971, with an intake of 24,000. It swept away fusty notions of what a university should be, with its multimedia delivery consisting of traditional primary texts, pre-prepared and printed course materials, lectures on cassette, lectures on radio, and TV broadcasts, covering everything from Umberto Eco on semiotics to advanced astrophysics.

Since it opened the gates to its ivory towers, well over two million people have studied with them. It has grown into the largest academic institution in the UK and even today, you can sign up for free courses in 'Babylonian mathematics', 'plate tectonics' or 'teaching secondary music'. Its estimated impact on the UK economy is nearly £3 billion. Aligning with its initial mission to widen participation to higher education, 28 per cent of the Open University's under-graduates are from the 25 per cent most deprived areas in the UK. More than 37,000 of its students have a declared disability.[17] The university offers open degrees, which means that students can take any blend of courses they wish from a wide variety of subjects and once they have reached the required credits, can take their degree. For that reason, they don't have traditional pathways. When I did it, for example, it wasn't possible to do an English degree, only an arts-themed one.

xxvii

Any number that suggested kind Mr Chamberlain might, in fact, be right, I would be thrilled with A mark in the fifties would be a huge win. Even something in the forties would be great. Anything. If I could pass, I might be able to believe that the world might be different.

The reading materials arrived, wrapped tight in cardboard, heavy as a hod. Printed on the casing was the instruction 'Urgent Educational Material'. It was as if the institution understood these materials were a matter of life and death. I unwrapped it to find five A4 books. They said they were introductions to history, litera-ture, music, philosophy, and art history, but they weren't. Not really. These were introductions to another mode of being.

There were a few set books. Geoffrey Best's history of the Age of Equipoise in Britain from 1851–75 and Charles Dickens's *Hard Times*. My heart sank when I first learned this. The only thing I knew about the Victorians was that they seemed a horrible bunch of prigs who sent children either down mines, up chimneys or kept them close at hand so they could whack them with a cane. The Victorians were who the Tories wheeled out to bolster any and all attempts to justify worker exploitation, to espouse 'self-help' and family values. The fact that Margaret Thatcher longed for a return to 'Victorian values' besmirched, in my young mind, an entire century's people.[18]

Although I'd read dozens of novels at this point, they had all been contemporary fiction. Within those worlds, I'd visited everything from New York's Park Avenue skyscrapers to the bodegas of Harlem with Tom Wolfe. I had spent time between the wars in Japan with Kazuo Ishiguro in *A Pale View of Hills*. I used the Booker Prize like it was a reading list. Every year I read all of the nominees, as well as the also-rans mentioned in the literary pages for being unfairly omitted from the list. So, I'd spent time on a slave ship in Barry Unsworth's *Sacred Hunger* (another two-pounder), I'd accompanied a spirit child in Nigeria in Ben Okri's *The Famished Road* (as epic, intimate and dazzling as a dream) – and then there was Martin Amis's *Time's Arrow*, a neck-spinning Holocaust novel told entirely in reverse. (I also possessed a freakish ability to correctly guess the Booker winner each year. Even in the year that everyone put their money on Michael Ondaatje's *The English Patient*, I was sure that the outsider, Barry Unsworth, was going to win. That year, they both won.) These were challenging books to read, but there was something about the language and setting of 'classics' that seemed unnavigable, and 'not for me'. In these, the language always seemed to be falling over itself to say more than it actually said.

The physicality of the Dickens novel was flimsy and insubstantial, porous. An old, well-to-do Victorian gentleman stared out at us from the cover – an arrogant-looking fuck, bald pate and mutton chops. The kind of expression that said, 'I'm so rich, I commission my own porn as oil paintings.' The book was the type of paperback that, at 400 or more pages, could rest, fully unfurled, with recto and verso flat on a table without so much as wrinkling the spine. Though new, the paper smelt old. It was the kind that would start to turn caramel in a matter of weeks. The font was large, indulgently serifed, bespeaking the fruity exuberance of Dickens's language.

Many of Dickens's novels purport to be about some wider subject (the law, capitalism, nepotism) but most of them invariably turn out to be concerned with education in one way or another. *Hard Times* (published in weekly parts in 1854) was inspired by Dickens's visit to Preston to observe a long-running industrial dispute. But instead of exploring the nuances and power dynamics between the masters and the hands – as, for example, Elizabeth Gaskell did in *Mary Barton* and *North and South* – it is education and utilitarianism, the hot philosophy of the day, that the novel careers into.

The novel opens with a school official's speech to his charges:

Now, what I want is, Facts. Teach these boys and girls nothing but Facts. Facts alone are wanted in life. Plant nothing else, and root out everything else. You can only form the minds of reasoning animals upon Facts: nothing else will ever be of any service to them. This is the principle on which I bring up my own children, and this is the principle on which I bring up these children. Stick to Facts, sir!

His emphatic annunciation is punctuated, beaten out by his 'square forefinger'. This is Thomas Gradgrind, a dedicated entrepreneur concerned only with numbers and truth: 'In this life, we want nothing but Facts, sir; nothing but Facts!' You get the point. Being at the wrong end of Dickens's characterisation can often feel a little like when you test a pair of binoculars indoors and everything is suddenly massive and unbelievably close.

The aptronyms continue with Gradgrind's best friend in Coketown, Mr Bounderby. He identifies as a self-made man who pulled himself up by his bootstraps after being deserted as a child (none of this turns out to be true). He employs many of the other characters in the novel.

There are two little Gradgrinds: Tom and Louisa. They are both stuffed to bursting with facts.

Tom, a sullen and resentful boy, takes a job in Bounderby's bank, which he eventually robs, framing one of the town's workers for the crime. Louisa's hand is gifted (some might say trafficked) to the rather paedo-y Bounderby, a husband more than three times her age. With an uneducated heart, she obediently accepts Bounderby's proposal because her father seems to approve of it but then falls into a soft-core affair with another man, which completely devastates her. With one child wishing an early death for herself and the other proving to be greedy and a psychopath, the outcomes of a fact-filled education are laid bare. At least they are in this fictional world.

Many of the other characters that populate the novel are visiting circus folk, passing through Coketown to entertain the ground-down workers. This cast of colourful characters are revealed as poor but empathetic, uneducated but intelligent, disparate and unrelated but loyal and familial. Among these, Mr Sleary, the circus master, is a dilettante, an armchair philosopher, a theoretician whose theme is education and people's need for entertainment. He is crippled by asthma and pants his words through empty lungs, his plosives fail to pop and there's a wheeze in his lisp, but Dickens puts more sensible words into his mouth than that of any other character.

He's given a monologue at the close of the novel, when he addresses a broken Mr Gradgrind: 'People mutht be amuthed. They can't be alwayth a learning, nor yet they can't be alwayth a working, they an't made for it. You mutht have uth, Thquire. Do the withe thing and the kind thing too, and make the betht of uth; not the wurtht.'

If you admire comic writing, *Hard Times* is not funny. If you admire drama, there is only melodrama. If you crave subtlety, there is only blunt heavy-handedness. It is this last that can be so grating to the unwary reader.

I couldn't bear the novel when I first read it, something exacerbated by its being compulsory. The book left behind little more than the impression of my never wanting to be trapped in a world with those people again, with their humourlessness, their ill-explored suffering – as overworked and laboured as Dickens's arguments – and the scum of coke smuts on everything. Even the print looked mucky on the page. 'The people must be amused!' I wanted to cry on finishing it.

xxviii

In later years, *Hard Times* became for me a much greater, more articulate novel, adept at foregrounding and pre-empting much of what is happening to reading, literature and the arts in education today.

The children in the novel are taught 'facts'. Of the two protagonists, educated in this way in the novel, one marries so badly she nearly dies. Tom, the psychopath, proves unable to understand or comprehend the feelings of others. By being denied a playful, arts education, Dickens says, Tom develops no theory of mind. But so what? This is just Dickens's notion of what a fact-filled education does. We should consider the source – and as a novelist, he would say that, wouldn't he?

But there's contemporary data that supports this. We know that the reading of fiction increases both empathy and one's empathic vocabulary for contemplating and understanding the feelings of others.[19] We also know that the reading of literary fiction specifically leads to improved performance on theory of mind tests.[20] Without access to any neuroscience, Dickens was proven to be right about what exposure to fiction can achieve.

Books and fiction change you in even bigger and more permanent ways. Books effect real changes in the brain; they can make you into a different person.

In 2013, a group of neuroscientists at Emory University sought to explore the short- and long-term effects of a novel on connectivity in the brain. They did this by measuring changes in resting-state connectivity of the brain and looking at how long these changes persist.[21] The trial subjects undertook an fMRI scan on nineteen consecutive days. For the first five days, the subjects went about their business as usual. For the next nine, they read a ninth of a novel each evening (Robert Harris's *Pompeii*, in case you're interested), with fMRIs taken each following morning. The final five days were another 'wash out' period.

The team discovered that the reading of fiction had created lots of new brain activity across different centres throughout the brain. In some cases, these changes were short-lived, decaying rapidly on completion of the novel. But there were also long-term changes in connectivity which persisted. The reading of fiction in particular created the impression that the brains of the subjects had undergone something resembling a workout.

Most surprising was the additional evidence the team discovered for 'embodied semantics'. This is like reading about some exciting incident in an Ian Fleming novel, but when our eyes scan the words 'kick' or 'run', those parts of our brain that operate our limbs are activated. It doesn't matter that it was James Bond performing these feats during an unlikely escape from a villain's lair. The same goes for words like 'lick', 'chew' or 'feel'. It even goes for abstract terms like 'pain' and 'anger'. This means that when we are reading, we are not passively learning what's going on in someone else's head, but – and this is a big difference – we are getting to experience a little of it as well. The brain scans present like the people reading are living some of these events too.

How can you look at the brain scan of a reader and decry 'But fiction isn't real'? As far as brain structure is concerned, those experiences have rewritten some pathways and junctions in the brain as clearly as if you'd had Ernst Stavro Blofeld fling his furry puss, all sharp claws and anger, right in your face

In *Hard Times*, the criminals and psychopaths, unable to imagine the existence of other minds and having never been exposed to them, can only look to themselves and the satisfaction of their desires. Their own happiness, they believe, makes the world a better place to be. No one else matters. Starved of fiction, stuffed with facts, fed only bran and no sugar, all meat and no vegetables, their imaginative diet is so low in nutritious fiction that their lives are a wreck. The novel is genius.

xxix

The novel's significance does not conclude there. Since the first time I read it, I've had to return to it numerous times, mainly to teach it. And as the drive towards STEM subjects in schools gets ever harder with every year, the novel seems to take on even greater importance. One of the striking things about it is just that: the fact that the STEM-first war on the humanities has been grinding away since at least the 1850s.

In the three years between 2019 and 2022, the number of students taking STEM A-levels rose by 3.5 per cent. This rise is reflected in an equivalent drop of 3.3 per cent in humanities subjects. As the popularity of English literature fell in this period (with nearly 20,000 fewer students taking it), the A-level dropped out of the top ten most popular for the first time. It was subjects like business or economics that shunted it on its way.[22] But there's a much bigger story here, not just about English.

There is currently an alarming decline in school attendance. In 2020–21, 12.1 per cent of pupils were persistently absent. A year later, the number was 22.5 per cent.[23] There are many drivers at fault here, among them the chronic underfunding of schools; the effects of Covid and lockdowns; anxiety and mental health issues (where in 2021, one in six children were identified as having a probable mental health issue, up from one in nine in 2017); poverty and housing (especially when families are moved into emergency accommodation many miles from school, for example); and finally there's special needs and disabilities (which can leave children unable to attend due to lack of support).[24]

But it is also about how pupils feel about school – and that matters too. If schools are inhospitable places to be, we need to change them.

Positive feeling towards school is strongly associated with student engagement and academic achievement.[25] This tells us that liking school matters. It gives you a distinct advantage. But in a world in which pupils are the conduit through which OFSTED assesses a school or where the success in an exam may matter more to the managerially inclined in a school than any notion of broader educational achievement, it is easy to see that the emotional state of the child can easily slip through the cracks. It's not that children shouldn't study STEM, more that you can't expect anyone to thrive at something that they are neither interested in nor particularly talented at. The Tory government's policy of favouring STEM at every stage of education is not only threatening the future of the creative industries in the UK, but as subjects like music, art, drama and English literature cede time and funding to them, government policies risk alienating those pupils interested in pursuing those subjects. 'People mutht be amuthed,' one might say. But it's not just about amusement and diversion – happier pupils attend school. Happier students do well academically. Happier students even do better in STEM subjects.

xxx

In early January 2023, Prime Minister Rishi Sunak set out plans to make maths compulsory for everyone to study up to the age of eighteen. When *Mission Impossible* and *Spaced* star Simon Pegg heard the news, he lost his shit. I saw the expletive-ridden stream on social media, delivered while sitting in his car, and nearly cheered as I watched it:

> So Rishi Sunak, our unmandated, unelected Prime Minister twice removed, has decided it should be compulsory for children to learn maths up until the age of eighteen. What a prick! What about arts and humanities and fostering this country's amazing reputation for creativity and self-expression? What about that? What about the kids that don't want to do maths? I hated maths. I dropped maths as soon as I could, and I've never needed it other

than the skillset I acquired at the age of twelve. But no, Rishi Sunak wants a fucking drone army of data-entering robots. What a tosser! Fuck the Tories.[26]

I'm guessing that's his name off the Sunak honours list.

The Prime Minister's policy, like so many others, began to disintegrate soon afterwards when it was discovered that the UK was already unable to recruit sufficient maths teachers to instruct the under sixteens, never mind beyond. The point was also quickly conceded that no students should be forced to study the subject at A-level.

A novel like *Hard Times*, for all its faults and lack of subtlety, could not be more prescient; its basic tenet being that you cannot educate people in only one way. Just like you can't teach someone to read by employing only one method. They need fact *and* fancy if they are to have any hope of growing into a rounded individual. They must be amused.

xxxi

The sharp-eyed among you will by now have noticed that *Hard Times* is not evidence for the role of fancy in children's education; it merely depicts it. While this is true, there is one recent story that makes the real case very persuasively. With the government pushing arts and other 'frivolous fun' subjects to the periphery of education, one Yorkshire school went in the opposite direction. Feversham Primary in Bradford took the decision to integrate music, drama and art into their daily timetable, meaning that pupils ended up doing as much as six hours of music a week. The effect was spectacular. The school went from being in special measures (OFSTED's lowest possible rating) to performing in the top 10 per cent of schools nationally for reading, writing and maths. It is currently rated as 'outstanding'.[27] Despite a challenging demographic, with 90 per cent of students having English as an additional language, the school emphasises inclusivity, fostering a positive environment where children of diverse backgrounds learn harmoniously.

Mr Gradgrind, I am sure, would not care for the school, but the results speak for themselves.

xxxii

There were very few in-person sessions with the Open University. In the first of them, we were asked to do some icebreakers. Our group of three exchanged names, at which point I was immediately asked, as I am every day of my life, 'That's an unusual name. Where's that from?' In most situations I just want to get through the conversation with as little friction as possible, so I lie and I say what I said then: 'Oh, it's Irish.'

The third member of the group leant in and, in an accusatory tone, said, 'Well, I'm Irish, and I've never heard of *that* name.'

Ladies and gentlemen, meet Sandra. I would later learn that Sandra does not suffer fools. She and I went on to become such good friends that I now call her my third sister. Her son, who is now thirty, still loves this story because it articulates so much of the no-nonsense nature of her character. She is also evidence of the kind of social change that the Open University makes possible for people like her and me. On the night, she wheedled a full and complete explanation from me (after completing her degree, she went on to qualify as a barrister). After which, she insisted I accept a lift from her partner, and by the time they dropped me off, we were friends.

We would call one another when we got to sticky points in our Urgent Educational Material, consulting about bits of theory or exercises we were tasked with completing. By the time the literature essay came around, we decided to work together on the skeleton of a plan for the assignment. I was on the chair and she was on the bed with her notebook. We sat in the warm, dim light of the bedroom in our little flat, and I revelled in leafing through the reading materials and constructing 'an essay'. I felt like a student. We were students. And here we were, studying.

In the days that followed, in the same chair in the same bedroom, I wrote up the essay, printed it, sealed it up and sent it off in the post to be marked. Another three Schrödingerian weeks, in which I was both a success and a failure.

Sandra's essay arrived back and, in her excitement, she phoned me to tell me that she had narrowly missed a first. I was happy for her. As inexperienced as I was, I knew to try to keep my expectations for my own attainment in check. There was going to be an exam, long in the future, and I was sure I would perform terribly at it, so I wanted to build a bit of a buffer with the marks from the coursework components. But there was no getting around the fact that we had worked from the same plan; the signs were positive.

The next morning, mixed in with the birthday cards congratulating me on turning twenty-five, my assignment arrived. I hadn't narrowly missed a first; I had been given one mark above a fail. It was obvious I'd been given a sympathy pass. It was too early in the course to tell someone that they were completely out of their depth. This was the mark that accompanied a simpering smile and a feeble 'keep going'. This was the kind of mark you were awarded for effort but not for achievement. Forty. I read the comments and they turned my stomach.

How much easier things were when one didn't care, I thought. I believed I had tempered my expectations sufficiently and was now without a coping strategy for something so devastating. I felt like I'd failed kind Mr Chamberlain. I was now glad I hadn't got round to letting him know that I was dipping my toe into higher education. I thought about Margery Kim and was now sure that I was right and she had pandered to me all along. It made me feel sick at the thought that despite all their skills and experience, my ability to fuck everything up was so acute, I was still able to prove them both wrong. I'd failed myself. I felt like I'd failed everyone. It was the same story, so familiar to me but this time so painful because it mattered. The literature section of the course was the one I was supposed to excel at because it was the one I wanted to pursue. In my hands was evidence to the contrary. Although the comments were encouraging, this was what you said to failures.

That night, we gathered in one of Brighton's pubs to see in another year on earth. Everyone who had met me in the last few years had seen me with a book about my person, in my hands, protruding from a jacket pocket or wedged down the back of my jeans, and no matter the frequency with which I saw them, it was always a different book. They had watched the bookshelf in our flat fill up and seen the new ones brought in to house more, the shelves of which soon began to bow under the weight of even more books. Everyone that knew me knew the direction my life had taken. Everyone wanted to know only one thing: how I'd got on. The cheeks on my face soon began to ache with the smile I wore, not minding.

4 The greatest benefit we owe to the artist, whether painter, poet, or novelist, is the extension of our sympathies ... Art is **the nearest thing to life**; it is a mode of amplifying experience and extending our contact with our fellow-men beyond the bounds of our personal lot.
– George Eliot, 'The Natural History of German Life', 1856

If a young man has trained his muscles and physical endurance by gymnastics and walking, he will later be fitted for every physical work. This is also analogous to the training of the mind and the exercising of the mental and manual skill. Thus, the wit was not wrong who defined education in this way: 'Education is that which remains, if one has forgotten everything he learned in school.'

Albert Einstein, 'On Education'

Education is like ice: harmless in small quantities, but a sufficient amount is glacial. You won't notice its advance, but when it comes, it crashes through your life, lifts you up and takes you on with it, leaving the remnants of your past in its wake.

The fact that I was not derailed by my poor result was a bit of careful planning on the university's part and a little luck on mine.

By the time the results were returned, we were already well into the next section of our introductions. It could have been, for example, philosophy or history but instead, it was musicology. We were given bits of Handel and Schubert and, using the pieces, were tasked with learning the basics of musical analysis. Since the age of maybe three or four I could read record labels and sleeves, so fascinated was I by music. So, when it came to an 'introduction', written for someone that had never thought, studied or written about music before, I had a head start. The basics I had. I could distinguish phrasing; I knew my bass clefs from my trebles, my semi- from my demiquavers, my minims from my crotchets and my Bs from my C-flats. I wasn't a talented musician, but none of it was new to me.

One night before the assignments arrived, on the bed in my flat, Sandra and I were working our way through Schubert's 'The Trout' (set to the poem 'Die Forelle' by Christian Friedrich Daniel Schubart).

'The phrases are like sentences. You can hear where they end,' I explained.

'I can't hear it.'

I whistled the tune of the first five bars of the song.

'Can you hear it ends on the same note that it started on? It resolves.'

'How can you do that?'

'What?'

'Just whistle a tune like that?'

'I don't know. I just can. Then the third line, that one finishes on a different note to the one it starts on,' I whistled the line. 'It doesn't resolve, see. It signals the change in tone that's about to happen.'

We had a similar conversation about discriminating between time signatures without seeing the sheet music or the differences between major and minor scales. Being able to whistle a tune and hear phrasing isn't an advanced skill. What it meant, though, was that I wasn't having to learn that stuff and could just do the course materials. By the time my awful English result arrived, I was already thinking that I might find the next assignment a little easier.

Looking back, it presents as tenacity, the fact that I was able to keep going. Friends would say how determined or disciplined I was. I used to say I was neither; I just really wanted change (which I suppose is the same thing).

It was also luck. Luck shuffled the pack and the card that rose to the top of the deck was musicology, otherwise I would likely have dropped out.

i

Students drop out of their studies for all sorts of reasons. Some struggle with self-motivation and are unable to cope without teacher or parent supervision. Others find the workload overwhelming. Many are used to being the big fish in the smaller pond of school or college, then cannot cope when placed with their intellectual peers. There are any number of family or social issues. Illness is a common one. But an increasingly important reason is stress and mental health. Wouldn't you be stressed if you'd borrowed £50,000 and placed it all on black?

One of the persistent difficulties in trying to address university drop-out rates is the lack of information. There are statistics, and we will get to some of those in a minute, but an enduring characteristic of the non-returning student is that many of them have had enough. They stop attending and don't respond to any form of communication. In many cases, we, the university, never get to find out why a given student arrested their studies and disappeared. Even if a student did tell the university, there's the possibility that they might not be prepared to give the real reason or even that they might not entirely comprehend it themselves.

A student dropping out is the worst possible outcome for everyone. The student today has taken on significant debt in terms of fees and living expenses, the government has handed over the fee income to the university, and nobody in the system benefits from dropping out as an outcome. The student is in debt and all the worse off because they have no degree that might accelerate their future income to help them with the repayments. The government is in the hole for the fees it handed over to the university. And the university, that you may think is the winner in this scenario, has to explain to all concerned how they have failed the student. It's terrible press for the university, the faculty, the school, the lecturers and the tutors.

In July 2023, the Department for Education announced in a press release that there was to be a 'crackdown on rip-off university degrees'.

> Students and taxpayers will be better protected against rip-off degree courses that have high drop-out rates, don't lead to good jobs and leave young people with poor pay and high debts, the Prime Minister and Education Secretary have announced.
>
> Prime Minister, Rishi Sunak, said: 'The UK is home to some of the best universities in the world and studying for a degree can be immensely rewarding. But too many young people are being sold a false dream and end up doing a poor-quality course at the taxpayers' expense that doesn't offer the prospect of a decent job at the end of it. That is why we are taking action to crack down on rip-off university courses, while boosting skills training and apprenticeships provision.'[1]

What are 'rip-off' university courses? No one is entirely clear, but it seems to be those that don't lead to a high-paying job. I suppose it's degrees like music or fine art that they are taking a pop at (both departments are, as I write, being closed at an institution I used to work at). But what about courses like nursing, in which the student is never likely to achieve what the government might consider a 'good' salary? What about teachers? What good is a nation of law-yers and bankers when there's no one to teach their children?

No. 10 refused to clarify what 'rip-off' meant. It would be the job of the Office for Students to decide which courses offered poor value for money. No one would be drawn on how this would be decided. Was this another announcement that was going nowhere, like so many before them? Unlikely, as there were some specific policy an-nouncements: 'The government will also reduce the maximum fee that universities can charge for classroom-based foundation year courses to £5,760 – down from £9,250 currently.'

Tory governments have, since the election of the Cameron–Clegg coalition in 2010 – the one where Nick Clegg promised in his man-ifesto not to raise university tuition fees then oversaw an increase of 300 per cent – only made the environment for the arts and humani-ties more hostile. Funds (for both research and teaching) have been siphoned off into STEM subjects.

Cutting the fees that universities can charge for foundation level qualifications by 38 per cent is obscene. It will have a deleterious impact on widening participation because most of the institutions offering them will simply withdraw them. It is working-class people that will be hardest hit by this decision. Working-class people that might otherwise go to university, earn multiples of their pre-university salaries and end up paying a great deal more tax. If I seem biased, it's because the courses that squeaked the gates to university open to me were these same foundational ones.

Universities are no longer in the business of running loss-making courses. Up and down the country, those degrees are being closed and will continue to be for the coming years. The kinds of students that attend foundation courses are not cheaper to teach. While the content might be aimed at a lower level, those students need more help, support, feedback and encouragement, not 38 per cent less.

The worst-value courses for everyone involved are not those in which the graduates of one degree earn £2,000 a year less than the others; they are the ones that have high drop-out rates. In these situations, everyone is a loser.

The subject with the highest drop-out rate in the UK isn't drama, fine art, music or English literature; it is computer science, where nearly one in ten first years don't make it to year two. In second place is business studies, third is communications and fourth is engineering.[2]

There is an obvious conclusion here: too many students are being driven to study subjects in which they are not fully invested and that they never really wanted to do.

The statistical story is the opposite one when we look at the other end of the scale – universities with the best retention rates. Oxbridge take the top two places, but after that, it's the arts that win out. The rest of the top five for students that complete their studies comprises the Royal College of Music, the Royal Academy of Music and the Courtauld Institute of Art (which specialises in art history, curating and conservation).

I wonder what the earning potential is of these students? And do they much care whether their university education is going to lead to a 'good' (which is Tory for 'high-paying') job or not?

What is also hidden by these statistics is that the universities at the bottom of these tables all serve the most precarious communities. And among non-completing students you will find higher proportions of minority ethnic, disabled and low-income students. These groups more commonly have lower incomes and competing responsibilities (like caring or paid work) alongside their studies.

Even the ones that complete with a great degree are less likely to have parental or their own networks on which to draw to find high-paying work. These are the universities which are trying to, forgive me, 'level up' their communities, while the number crunchers are singling them out for providing poor value for money, for 'ripping off' their students.

Universities are measured and pressured to provide access for students with multiple indices of deprivation, but when universities meet or exceed these targets, they will likely find themselves dropping through the rankings. This is because that group of students have slightly lower completion, continuation or progression rates. None of it is because a university is bad at taking care of those groups of students – more that a lecturer or professor does not have capacity to intervene in the lives of those students. We can't give them money, can't do their childcare, can't look after ailing parents, can't work their full-time jobs for them.

Meanwhile, the universities that don't meet these access requirements and don't take their share of these kinds of students from lower-income neighbourhoods look amazing in the rankings because they are underperforming in a metric that is not counted.

Basically, the game is rigged against institutions that are trying to help. And it makes me angry because the game is rigged precisely against the institutions that have historically tried to help people like me.

'Value for money' is a stick made by politicians to ensure the ongoing perpetuation of privilege across the system, and it creates an absurd situation in which the same people that implement the policy then seek the right to bemoan the impact of the policy.

'Value for money' forms the basis of many of our relations in consumer-capitalist culture. But we don't ask if the sun represents good value for money. We don't ask if our friendships represent good value for money, our sex lives (at least, I hope not!), our birthdays, our sleep. These things are, more or less, free.

The question can only be asked in England because students are charged so much. What about elsewhere? In Italy, a student can expect to pay £700–£3,000. Spain, about £600–£1,800. In Russia, the figure is around £1,000–£3,500. Switzerland is around £700–£1,100. But in countries like Austria, Denmark, Finland, France, Germany, Scotland, Ireland, Sweden and Norway, tuition is either free or a nominal amount to both home and EU students.[3] There's a very easy way to make all this go away for students in England, a simple solution in which no one ever need feel ripped off ever again. No fees, no problem.

ii

Sandra and I whizzed through the rest of the module, becoming better and better friends, even revising for our first exam together. I got through the year almost unscathed. When the marks came through, I'd performed acceptably in the exam, putting me well clear of my hoped-for pass. I took a moment to mentally thank Mr Chamberlain, without whom I wouldn't have taken the odds. Before I knew it, I was into my second year.

The bus company was again supporting me. This time, they were contributing 75 per cent of the fees to a course devoted to the cultural milieu of the European Enlightenment.

Now, as well as whatever I was reading, when the boss was away I'd take out my books on the Enlightenment and drape those across my knees under the counter. One moment I'd be scratching off a weekly saver for someone too nervous to do it themselves, the next

I'd be in Salzburg with Mozart; a coach ticket to Colchester, then I'd be in Paris with Diderot planning the *Encyclopédie*.

As the months went by, I spun down a colonnade of books, lectures, essays and more books.

Mixing two parts tenacity, one part ability and three parts hunger to learn makes for a kind of alchemy. Now, I wanted to see how far I could get the glacier to go.

iii

I was growing tired of all my time off being consumed by studying part-time. I'd already done two years and there was another four to go. I wanted to find out if I might be any good at this, and I wasn't going to be able to do that while stamping bus passes for forty hours a week.

The boyfriend had got us a deal on a nice hotel on Lake Derwentwater. With my second-year exam done, off we went to tour the lakes in the lush mossiness of late autumn. One day, we visited the village of Grasmere. I'd had it in my head that I wanted to see Wordsworth's grave. Understandably, boyfriend was less interested in such an outing and instead went for a wander in the town.

One of our set texts that year had been Thomas Gray's 'Elegy in a Country Churchyard'. I'd taken to carrying a £1 Penguin copy of *Palgrave's Golden Treasury* around with me, and once I was in the churchyard, thought I'd try a little site-specific reading – inspired as it was by the death of a poet. I leant by the wall near Wordsworth's grave and read. Buried deep in the poem is the line that Thomas Hardy later dipped into for the title to one of his novels. Hardy's working title for the book was 'A Winning Tongue Had He', but at the last moment he switched it to the first part of line seventy-three of Gray's poem: 'Far from the madding crowd's ignoble strife'.[4]

I was somewhere around this section of the poem when two tourists, laden with heavy camera equipment and clunking accents, lumbered into the graveyard. They talked loudly to one another, and I watched as they photographed a grave from every possible angle. The wrong grave, one of a different 'William Wordsworth' from the end of the nineteenth century. My little pilgrimage was over. I slipped my book into my jeans pocket. I had thirty minutes until we said we'd meet up in town. What could I do?

Suddenly, I knew. On an impulse, I walked into the village to find a phone box, yanked open the half-ton weight of its door and stepped inside. The stench hit me. Years of grief and drama had all combusted in this confined space. Now it was my turn.

I dialled directory enquiries. After all the Forster, and an odd phase of being obsessed with Wittgenstein (the phase has never fully passed, if I'm honest), there was nowhere else for me to go. When the woman answered, I asked for Cambridge admissions. I took down the number.

How on earth was I going to go to university? I didn't earn much and we needed all of it. The grants system that had been in place for my sister a few years previously was long gone, chipped away at until nothing was left.

In 1990, Thatcher's government introduced student loans via the Student Loans Company, aiding those in areas of reduced state aid. Initially, 28 per cent accepted, with an average loan of £390, but by 1995, uptake doubled to 59 per cent, averaging £1,250, with, from memory, 3.5 per cent interest.[5] (Today, students face £45,000 debt at levels that rose at one point to 13.5 per cent interest but now settle around 6–7 per cent.)

And what I mean about the glacial power of education is that none of this actually mattered to me. Whatever the reality was, I would have made it work. If we stayed together that would be great, but nothing was going to stop me. Alone would be fine too. I'd manage. I didn't really care how big a home might be, just that there were lots of books in it. How can you expect anything to change if you're not willing to change anything?

Except, Cambridge admissions quickly answered their phone and put me right.

'You need to apply through UCAS and applications for this year are already closed,' I was politely informed. My iron will seemed to be rusting rather quickly. But didn't they understand? I was Urgent Educational Material! What they were telling me was that it was a year before applications opened again and that those applications would be for places starting in the September of the year after. We'd all have our own jet packs by then. Two more years! I'd already wasted twenty-six of them.

I hung up and redialled to get the number for admissions at the University of Sussex. I shoved another hot and moist ten-pence piece into the slot and asked Sussex if they accepted applications for mature students. I took down the details and ten minutes later, when I met up with my boyfriend at Wordsworth House on the other side of town, I recounted my tale of woe with the tourists in the graveyard but omitted my adventures in the telephone box and the few minutes in which I thought I was moving to another city.

A few months later, I was sat in the School of English common room waiting my turn to be called. Boys, overdressed in ill-fitting suits, sat lankily on the edges of chairs with their parents. The boys were being nudged to sit up straight, do up their top button and were being coached on rehearsed answers. The women, by comparison, seemed much more self-possessed.

I'd call myself an anxious person but I wasn't worried about the interview. I was looking forward to talking with someone that really understood books.

iv

We don't interview prospective students any more. But we do read a lot of personal statements that are a part of the student's application process. Their variety is surprising. Some come straight from the heart. Without any noticeable structure, the applicant just goes for it, explaining why they must access Urgent Educational Material. They tell us about their passion for books, for reading and for understanding the world. They tell us about their favourite authors and why they like them, that they can't wait to learn about new authors that they are sure they will like just as much. These are the applicants that will do really well. Their engine is already revving.

There are a few other types of statements. The worst are those that have had lots of help and guidance from people that are much better educated or more mature than they. They coolly espouse their interest in Zadie Smith or Jane Austen but avoid going into any detail or exploring any of their feelings around these works. They have also followed the strict formula that is laid down on the UCAS website – which is fine, just not so great when you have to read dozens of them. Many forget to convey any sense of passion. It's the passion that will motivate them to keep going. It will keep them interested in their degree, even if they're not so interested in Marxist semiotics, for example. It's really only the passion that matters – everything else can be taught.

v

When my Sussex interviewer asked me what I'd been reading recently, I told him, 'Tom Wolfe's *The Bonfire of the Vanities*, *Middlemarch* and, before that, Graham Swift's *Waterland*'. We then had a conversation about Swift's indebtedness to the nineteenth-century novel, then Wolfe's, then in turn to George Eliot's *Middlemarch* and her other novel *Romola*, featuring Savonarola and his bonfire of the vanities. My head spun with all the connections I'd missed. Through all of which I nodded my best 'interested' face. He then gave me a poem to read – W. H. Auden's 'Musée des Beaux Arts', the one about Bruegel's *Fall of Icarus* – and asked me what I thought of it. Before I'd left the room, I had a place to study English full-time.

vi

In my first class, four of us out of about ten were mature students. We had been assigned a fearsome lecturer, Dr Mary Dove (the namesake of the Agatha Christie villain from one of the Miss Marples, *A Pocket Full of Rye*). Dr Dove: the name implies a feathery softness, lightness, buoyancy. She wasn't like that. She was exactly what one would expect of a university lecturer, as dishevelled as she was opinionated. It was her job to steer us through a first term of Shakespeare.

Dr Dove was the most direct person I think I'd ever met. The comments on our written work were sparse and when she disliked something, she told you. You would be left under no illusion about what you'd done wrong. The shape of armour, though, always bespeaks the human beneath. There was something in her manner in the classroom, a kind of bedrock assumption that everyone, young, older or old, deserved to be there.

Students' needs are different, and for me, what Mary was offering was what I needed. I had distrusted the kindness of the Margery Kims and Mr Chamberlains. Instantly, I knew that Dr Dove wasn't going to lie to me or pat me on the head. If I could get her to write 'good', I knew I would have earned it.

I was still working part-time on the bus tickets, but I was determined to do as well as I could, so I threw myself into university work. At the end of the term, the lecturers had to write reports on three-ply carbon paper: white, pink and the bottom, smudgy yellow copy was given to us. It smelt of the dentists. Mine said something about being the best-read student she'd ever taught. There might have been a little hyperbole in this because I later learned that Dr Dove had taught Martin Amis. But who knows, maybe he had been a bit of a layabout, and I had never, before or since, caught Mary on a lie.

vii

The next term's teaching groups were announced and, in class, Mary apologised to several of us who were going to have her again. She set us big, difficult books to read like Samuel Richardson's *Clarissa* or challenging essays by Hélène Çixous. Some complained at having to read so much – a remonstrance I didn't really understand, but nonetheless a common one.

And that was it. I was completely in love with Dr Mary Dove.

I did modules just because she taught them. By my second year, we were drop-in friends. If her door was open, I'd put my head round it. We'd go for a cup of tea and I'd tell her about what I was studying and reading. Her passion was medieval interpretations of the Bible – that and TV's *Blind Date*. For those that don't remember it, this was the *Love Island* of the 1990s. In all my years of knowing her, she never missed an episode. We shared a very similar interest in books

– contemporary fiction, including a little crime. In my youthful glee, I tried to get her interested in *The Matrix*, which she watched patiently and concluded with a cryptic, 'Well, I can see why *you* like it.'

The next year began. The evenings darkened. I was always called away from the university to do my new job of helping kids with their GCSEs. I had left the bus company and had set up on my own as a tutor – teaching English at first but most kids also needed help with their maths. There was some irony in me helping others through their GCSEs.

Leaving the campus on these evenings, I'd walk past the library, which I always saw as an Atkinson Grimshaw painting. His work always depicted houses from the exterior in a dull, crepuscular and grimy setting. Punctuating the darkness would be warm glowing windows, where the viewer was invited to covet the snug of those sheltered by such a home. As I watched those in the library, I longed for the freedom to study into the evenings. They no doubt felt imprisoned by their work, but from the outside, it looked like freedom. The thought never quite surfaced, but what would it be like to just do that? I never told anyone that I was thinking of staying on to study at a more advanced level; I assumed they would laugh.

Throughout that second year, I would drop in on Mary and I'd tell her about what we were reading in the philosophy or Victorian literature classes I was taking. We talked about William James, Martin Heidegger, Elizabeth Gaskell and – of course – Thomas Hardy.

viii

The social realism of Gaskell's industrial novels appealed to me on a surface level. I was reluctant to read the Hardy we were set, and I hastily wrote him off as a pedlar of misery porn, a disinterested god toying with his playthings, driving his protagonists into the tightest and very nastiest of corners. There seemed at the time to be something cruel, prurient, even pornographic in this. An author, sat at his desk, concocting the very worst outcomes for his characters.

We were set *Jude the Obscure*, which was *so* tragic that the dial succeeded in rotating from drama through to tragedy, eventually overclocking its way back into comedy. Hardy makes clear the obstacles that intelligent men of the labouring class encountered in trying to go to university (it is Hardy's story, after all – he had been desperate to go). Given my circumstances, I ought to have loved it, but the school-age taint on Hardy remained strong.

Elsewhere, we were asked to read *Tess of the D'Urbervilles*, and again it felt like an elaborate, slow-motion mouse trap that took 370 pages to close.

The novel expertly lays bare the double moral standards that existed between the sexes in the nineteenth century (a husband admits a previous sexual history to his wife and is forgiven, but when she discloses hers, she is cast from the house).

Perhaps it was the pace at which I was reading most things as an undergraduate, but at the time, I couldn't see anything in the novels beyond a thicket of misery. Hardy was more of a realist than Dickens, for example, but no one reading those stories could believe the world is, or was, really as bad as all that. The book confirmed my feeling that I never wanted to return to Hardy.

ix

Meanwhile, higher education was about to be hit with the biggest changes it had seen in a generation. It was the year of the Dearing Report.[6]

There is no one moment, no key decision, no policy announcement that is responsible for the current crisis we see in the humanities and for English in particular. The Dearing Report, however, is pretty close to the smoking gun.

After what felt like 150 years of Tory rule in the UK, in which monetarism and market forces were driven like tanks across lawns and through corridors and lecture halls, the university system that the Labour government inherited in 1997 was chronically underfunded. Institutions were competing for increasingly scant resources. Class sizes had ballooned, staff numbers had shrunk, efficiencies had been harvested until the yield consisted only of chaff.

The Dearing Report was the first large-scale review of tertiary education since its massive expansion after the Robbins Report in the '60s. A lengthy 466 pages, it was commissioned in 1996, under John Major's Tory government, and reported to the New Labour government a year later.

Its message was a well-meaning one that saw universities as engines of social mobility and change but also sought to address 'an immediate short-term problem with the funding of higher education'.[7] The funding shortfall it was trying to address was in the billions.

A basic tenet of the report was the belief that 'tuition contributions will enable students to be more demanding of institutions if they are making a direct contribution to the costs of their tuition'.[8]

The introduction of a service model to education was supposed to enhance customer satisfaction. Such an idea has only gained traction in the decades that followed. But for me, the basis of this idea is incorrect. Universities are not like shops where you enter, place your money on the counter and walk out with a terrific handbag. Instead, the student is paying for access to expertise and to facilities, and if they engage with the programme, they will emerge changed. If they pay their fees and don't work, they will get nothing. Universities are less like shops and more like a gym. I've been a member of any number of gyms over the decades and I'm still the same weight. Is that their fault? If the lockers are being broken into, the machines are poorly maintained or there are too many people in the pool, this is all on the gym. If the gym advertises itself as 'world class' but it turns out not to be, that is on them, too. But what if the gym is run very well, but I don't attend and so fail to become Chris Hemsworth? Is this on them, too? The consumer model doesn't fit in this way, and there are more examples.

If the person in the handbag shop is rude or no good at selling handbags, you could go to another shop. But students, once in place, are extremely unlikely to move. They live there. Their friends are there. They've invested time in studying in that particular place. If something goes wrong, how are they supposed to take their business elsewhere? If you decide after a couple of weeks that you don't like your handbag, it may have depreciated a little but you can sell it on. A degree is not such a mobile commodity.

The consumer model breaks down at so many points in the comparison that it is hard to see why it is believed to be of any use by anyone involved. The model damages both parties and serves neither.

Empowering students as consumers of their education meant that they would have more choice. But what even is student 'choice' when most degrees have rigid entry criteria? A student with three 'D's at A-level cannot choose Oxbridge, no matter what rhetoric is deployed at the ballot box. Choice and tough selection criteria are not conceptually compatible.

X

In the run-up to the general election of 1997, Tony Blair and Robin Cook, the future Foreign Secretary – in what would turn out to be a pedal note of all parties in opposition, be they Conservative, Labour or Liberal Democrat – explained Labour's stance on tuition fees. Blair had repeatedly said his party had 'no plans to introduce tuition fees for higher education'.[9] Robin Cook was equally clear that 'tuition costs must be met by the state'.[10] But after just two months in office, Blair went ahead and introduced tuition fees.

It was in the November of 1997 that Labour's Education Secretary David Blunkett proposed what would become the Teaching and Higher Education Act 1998. This introduced tuition fees for the upcoming academic year (which were, at least, means-tested for lower-income families). The long-dwindling maintenance grant was also put out of its misery, to be replaced instead with a student loans system – though the maintenance grant returned soon after to support those from the lowest-income families. In 1997, the fear was not so much the cost but the fact of an eroded principle. Once a 'fee' was chargeable for education, the worry was that it would become the norm and future governments would find it easy to raise them.

The Overton window on tuition fees had just shifted significantly to the right.

Labour MP Ken Livingstone accused his party of, according to BBC News, 'whipping away a ladder of opportunity which they themselves had climbed'.[11]

Had the Tory Party won the 1997 election, they would almost certainly have introduced fees, but would they have killed the maintenance grant too? We will never know. Instead, David Blunkett went down in history as the individual who ended free higher education.

xi

In the summer before my final year, I was readying myself to study with Mary again. I read all of Chaucer and Margery Kempe and did my best to get through *Piers Plowman*. I saw that Cardiff University was advertising a one-day conference on medieval literature, so I signed up and Mary invited herself along too.

We left Brighton at the crack of dawn, drove across the country and arrived for the 10 a.m. start. The conference finished around 4 p.m. and it was time to drive back. I was tired. Then it started to rain, the kind that makes the roads glass. The windscreen sloshed with water the instant the wipers completed their stroke. It beat on the roof. I opened the window to defog the screen but had to close it because it was letting too much rain in. I'd switched the radio off because we couldn't hear it over the rain. The only thing to do was to slow down to about twenty miles an hour. That and talk.

xii

Mary told me that she'd applied for promotion but that it was a slow process and she wouldn't know for a while.

'What have you applied for?'

'Senior lecturer. It's the most important one. It's also the hardest.'

'And you're a lecturer now?'

A long 'Yeah' came in response.

I knew she'd returned to England from Australia, where she'd also had time out to have a family, so presumably would have been further up the academic scale if she'd stayed.

'What's so hard about senior lecturer?' I asked her.

'It's the first one where you are really judged by your peers. With a PhD, you have someone to help you through and most people aren't doing anything else, so there are fewer things to contend with. But you can only get senior lecturer off the back of a book, and you have to have been working while you're writing it and no one's supervising you. Senior is all I want. Senior means they think I'm a serious researcher.'

We weathercocked from that subject to the – to me – astonishing fact that Mary didn't own an alarm clock. This is why I loved these conversations – trapped in a car, gallons of rain and lots of traffic meant there was nothing to do but reveal interesting things about yourself.

'I like to wake up when I'm ready to wake up.'

I was aghast. That was it. I wanted that life.

Were there really employers that left you alone to get on with your work and didn't mind how you did it, as long as you did it? I thought of the bosses I'd had over the years and how far such an idea was from anything those micromanagers might comprehend.

Mary broke the silence, cutting across my thoughts: 'Hey, you know what you should do. You should do a PhD.'

I nearly drove us off the road.

xiii

I'd thought I was making friends but what I'd accidentally done was find a mentor. For people that come into education – or indeed any industry – from an unusual background, mentorship is absolutely key. If, for example, more than one generation of your family has completed higher education, there is a bedrock assumption within you that things will probably turn out OK. There are people around you that have been in and through similar experiences. The lack of such a support network is why under-represented groups find themselves disproportionately negatively represented in the kinds of statistics in which they'd rather not figure: rates of access to higher education, drop-out rates, earnings potential, the likelihood of attending a top university, and the likelihood of getting a first-class degree.[12]

Mentorship goes a long way to help students from under-represented groups. Counted among its effects are enhanced confidence, self-awareness, learning ability (from others' experiences), capacities for self-reflection, abilities for more nuanced and realistic goal setting, as well as exposure to other perspectives. There's also the obvious benefit, whereby you now have someone to whom you can go to with 'stupid' questions like 'what's a senior lecturer'. The mentor can also share their own experiences. Without realising, the mentee has established a network. Being mentored puts you in the game – especially important when you weren't aware one had commenced.

Mary would balk at such an idea, but I desperately needed someone to give me permission to want something different and, absent-mindedly, she handed it to me.

xiv

My final year passed quickly. I'd worked hard throughout, navigating my way from Chaucer to Derrida with a bit of Homer for good measure. My application to stay on had been submitted, and my dissertation had been handed in. I ordered a copy of *How to Get a*

PhD from a shop in the city, so as to avoid the gossipy staff at the university bookshop. The schools were beginning to slow down and parents wanted to give their kids a break over the summer, so there was less tuition for me to do. I was going to be thirty, and I was waiting for my results like they were my GCSEs. The days dragged.

One evening, I was walking into Brighton to meet a fellow graduand when my phone rang. The number was withheld.

'Hello?'

'Do you know who this is?' Of course I did. It was Mary, speaking as if she was in a John le Carré and the feds had tapped her phone.

'That thing you wanted is a yes.'

'What? What do you mean.' I thought I knew what she meant but I wanted her to say it because until she did, I knew it wouldn't seem real.

'I can't say. But that thing you wanted is a yes.' A pause. 'You mustn't tell anyone.'

'Tell anyone what?'

'I'm the chair of the exam board. I could lose my job if I tell you what was discussed, but it's a yes. I thought you'd want to know.'

'A yes?'

'Yes, a yes.'

XV

I stumbled across financial support from one of the research councils to continue my studies and after a summer of walking on air, I was back in the classroom studying for an MA. As the nights drew in and the leaves in the trees began to sound a little more brittle on the breeze, I was, thanks to a little grant, able to stay at the university through those crepuscular hours.

Those starting as undergraduates were now paying fees.

There were protests on campus. Posters went up with the daubed face of David Blunkett as the villain who had ended free higher education.

But did he really? The answer is both 'yes' and 'not so much'.

xvi

For people over the age of forty, there is an assumption that up until the end of the 1990s, university tuition was free: a civic right. But for the vast majority of the history of higher education, fees have been a regular part of the university funding model. There was only a short window between 1962 and 1998 in which university provision was completely free to the student. For the rest of their history, with the exception of prestigious scholarships, university fees have been the norm for nearly 1,000 years. But this is not to say that the fee burdens that students are currently labouring under is in any way normal. It's a complicated picture. Let's start in the nineteenth century.

At this point, the Oxbridge colleges had been opening their doors to students in one form or another since the eleventh century. For England, that's the story for hundreds of years, though universities spring up elsewhere. In Scotland there was St Andrews (1413), Glasgow (1451), Aberdeen (1495) and Edinburgh (1582). The University of Dublin dates from 1592. There wasn't much change until the nineteenth century, when there was a sudden upsurge: Durham University in 1832, King's College London by royal charter in 1829, London University in 1826 (latterly UCL), Queen's College Belfast, Queen's College Cork (latterly University College Cork), Queen's College Galway (latterly University of Galway) in 1845 to name a few.

Most universities at this time charged fees, some had state grants, most had local grants and engaged in regional fundraising activities; many also benefitted from endowments. There was variety from one institution to another but the fees that students paid accounted for roughly a third of the cost of delivery.

Throughout the nineteenth century, Britain was at the centre of a global economic boom. But while it had made headway early on, innovation and experimentation are costly and rival nations like Germany had plenty of natural resources and were catching up in terms of productivity. Not for the last time, there was a sense at home that more needed to be invested in technical scientific education. It was an Edwardian push for STEM. If local talent was to be attracted, fees must be kept down.

Even though the state was now supporting universities, fees still only represented between 25 and 40 per cent of their income. This means that the universities were now dependent upon public financial support.

In 1919, the University Grants Committee (UGC) was formed to advise the government on the distribution of its funding to higher education institutions. The committee was formalising a process that had been in operation for three decades at that point. It met until it was disbanded by the Thatcher government in 1989. Throughout its history, the committee was run and chaired by academics (most famously by Sir John Wolfenden from 1963 to 1968, now remembered for his 1957 report recommending the legalisation of private homosexual acts between men). The UGC played an important role in cushioning universities from the whims of any given government, while helping to maintain institutions' relative independence from political interference.

Published in 1960, the Anderson Report on higher education

recommended that grants should be offered to students. There were marches in Bristol, and at Senate House in London students staged an eleven-day sit-in in favour of the report's recommendations. Fees still existed, but like a benevolent uncle at dinner, the state insisted on picking up the bill.

Over the next few decades, the university system continued to grow, with the student population tripling between 1962 and 1980 (a shift from about 4–15 per cent of young people). The rising cost of free higher education was something that any political party was now taking notice of.

Although fees had always been there in the centuries-long history of universities, it was only a matter of years before free higher education was seen by many as a civic right. This idea is known as the Robbins principle, from the 1963 Robbins Report in which the authors 'assumed as an axiom that courses of higher education should be available for all those who are qualified by ability and attainment to pursue them and who wish to do so'.[13]

With the formation of a national Universities and Colleges Admissions Service (formed in 1961 and still going), all applicants were granted access to the university admissions processes.

The freedom with which universities were able to operate for those few decades, while still using funds sourced from taxation, seems tied up with that post-war wave of public-service generosity. Higher education was seen as a worthwhile long-term investment in society. With the majority of their income sourced from public funds, universities became less adept at raising money locally, focused as they were on research and teaching.

The two had for centuries gone hand in hand – one informing the other and vice versa. But it was the 1980s, and everything was about competition, marketisation and reducing the tax burden – that and enormous shoulder pads. In 1985, for the first time, the teaching and research components of university funding were separated. Historically, the money was a 'block grant', but now research monies flowed towards those institutions that were seen as research intensive. The UGC required institutions to submit research statements across thirty-seven subject areas, then graded the quality of the research outputs from each institution. The grade received dictated how much the institution would be granted from the pot. In the decades that followed, the process would undergo numerous name changes. There would also be numerous changes to the process, with each iteration making it disproportionately more difficult for the humanities to score highly – further reducing their share of an already-shrinking pot of money.

In the mid-1980s, the idea of top-up fees was proposed by the Conservative government, but a backbench rebellion parked the matter until the Dearing Report in the '90s.

This brings us up to 1998 and the fees that were introduced by the Labour government and David Blunkett. In the longer history of university funding, the upfront £1,000 contribution to teaching seems paltry by comparison. While the introduction of fees wrought so much damage, except for the brief window between 1962 and 1998, these were probably the lowest fees ever charged for university tuition in the history of their existence.

xvii

My 'yes' now a reality, it was all change at Sussex. A couple of people stayed on from our degree but the majority came in from elsewhere. A few came from Cambridge, one of whom amusingly possessed anti-imposter syndrome. Shortly after introducing herself, she proclaimed that although she had got a 2:1, because it was from Cambridge it was equivalent to a first from anywhere else!

The year passed in a snap, with the last part of it reserved to work on a long dissertation. I chose Forster. As a university teacher now, I find it funny that I worried then about submitting a 'satisfactory' piece of work, while oblivious to the impression an MA student would create by travelling cross-country and staying at archives for a week, ploughing their way through mounds of Edwardian cursive in commonplace books, letters and diaries. I was there when they opened the doors to the archive in the morning and stayed until dark. In the evenings, I bought a sandwich from the supermarket because it was all I could afford and monastically returned to my rooms. I couldn't meet the expense of any of it, but I wanted to do the work as best I could. With reams of notes spilling from my bag, I went to return my key at the end of the week and I nearly wept when, with a swoosh of his hand, one of the porters waived the accommodation bill. I decided Oxbridge wasn't so bad.

All done and on to a PhD. I attacked it with such vigour that I would lay out all the materials I'd need by our bed at night. Then, on waking and before making coffee, I'd grab the laptop, lever it open, unfurl any of the books I was working on, spread them across the bed and get to work. I did this every morning.

Progressing through the different phases of university study, it becomes obvious that as you specialise, the groups get smaller. They diminish in such a determined manner that at the beginning of your PhD, only you and your supervisor know as much about your work. And after about two to three months, it's just you. The first year is consumed with making plans and constructing bibliographies of materials to consult.

The second year is when it gets hard – all the work is still before you, and you still don't know your subject that well. Mary was always helpful. But I couldn't even talk to her about the books I was getting out of the library, ones in print since the nineteenth century with their folded pages still uncut. If no one had bothered to make it past page eleven in 150 years, what did I think I was doing?

xviii

In my final year, I sat for so long typing at my computer that I began seeing stars, like a cartoon cat who'd been bashed on the head with a frying pan. The thesis was printed, bound and submitted and I began the long wait for my viva. In the empty space between submission and examination, I struggled to fill the time. I'd been offered a little teaching alongside Mary, as her duckling.

I read and reread reams of novels like A. S. Byatt's *Possession* and David Lodge's *Changing Places*, *Small World* and *Nice Work*. It took only a modicum of awareness to recognise these were wish-fulfilment reads.

They had a darker side, though. They signalled just how impossible it was to get into academia. With all the universe of the imagination available to draw upon, with all the possibilities for characters to reach a point of happiness and stasis and to be rewarded, what strategy did these novels choose? The characters didn't become rich, famous, marry the prince or princess, become President – no. Instead of the hero slaying an ogre, saving the world or preventing detonation of a nuclear bomb, the protagonist does something much more difficult and challenging: they secure university employment.

xix

By 2003, the debates and complaints about the £1,000 fees had begun to dissipate. After ministers had cracked their knuckles with those fees, they were already considering something more substantial.

May 2003 saw another turning point in the war on the humanities: a loud proclamation by a public figure, questioning the economic value of one of the fustier corners of history. To my knowledge, it was the first time that an Education Secretary had so publicly attempted to draw a strong link between education, its utility and that its function should be to contribute to the economy.

Charles Clarke took up office as Secretary of State for Education and Skills on 24 October 2002 and stayed in office until December 2004. It was several months into this post when he gave a speech at University College, Worcester – one whose content quickly travelled beyond the walls of the lecture hall in which he delivered it. He was reported as having said, 'I don't mind there being some medievalists around for ornamental purposes, but there is no reason for the state to pay for them.'[14] Clarke only wished the state to support degree courses of 'clear usefulness'.

What does 'clear usefulness' mean? Was he proposing degrees in plumbing, hedge trimming, lollipop-ladying? What about students who want to go on to teach English or history? Is that useful? Is sports science useful? What about business studies? That seems useful, yet it's one of the worst-performing degrees in terms of outcomes.

What Clarke actually said was even worse: 'The medieval concept of a community of scholars seeking truth is not in itself a justification for the state to put money into that. We might do it at say a level of a hundredth of what we do now.'[15]

Presumably, when Clarke said those words in the lecture hall in Worcester, he must have heard the click of the massive bear trap into which he'd galumphed. Was he really proposing a 99 per cent cut to funding for the humanities? Was he really so ignorant of the activities of humanities scholars as the unquenchable thirst for truth? Didn't he have advisers?

Taking a pot-shot at medievalists like that was a risky move. If my friendship with Mary had taught me anything, it was that you don't mess with medievalists. Both they and others were decidedly upset. A Cambridge medievalist called him 'a philistine thug', and the president of the Association of University Teachers was astounded that 'a secretary of state for education can … have such a terribly narrow view of what education is'.[16]

Clarke, a Cambridge maths graduate, was fixated on the role of universities as principally contributing to the economy and presumably did not stop to reflect on the fact that many of his Cabinet colleagues at the time were history graduates – among them, future Prime Minister Gordon Brown.

The Cabinet at the time was, as it usually has been, dominated by individuals with a range of educational backgrounds, from metallurgy to economics:

- Prime Minister: Tony Blair, Oxford University, law
- Deputy Prime Minister: John Prescott, University of Hull, economics
- Chancellor: Gordon Brown, University of Edinburgh, history
- Lord Chancellor: Lord Irvine, University of Glasgow, law
- Foreign Secretary: Jack Straw, University of Leeds, law
- Home Secretary: David Blunkett, University of Sheffield, politics
- Environment Secretary: Margaret Beckett, Manchester College of Science and Technology, metallurgy
- International Development Secretary: Clare Short, University of Leeds, politics
- Transport Secretary: Alistair Darling, University of Aberdeen, law

- Health Secretary: Alan Milburn, Lancaster University, history
- Northern Ireland Secretary: Paul Murphy, Oxford University, history
- Defence Secretary: Geoff Hoon, Cambridge University, law
- Work and Pensions Secretary: Andrew Smith, Oxford University, PPE
- Trade Secretary: Patricia Hewitt, Cambridge University, English literature
- Culture Secretary: Tessa Jowell, University of Aberdeen, arts, psychology and sociology
- Education Secretary: Charles Clarke, Cambridge University, maths and economics

Were they useful? Conversely, did he believe that Margaret Beckett's degree in metallurgy was useful to her given her political career?

For me, the whole thing was based on a simple misunderstanding as to what tertiary education is supposed to do. The fundamental error is the assumption that all subjects are content-based. That a university lecturer has knowledge, and all they need do is stand up and say educational things in front of some students, that the students then write down and that knowledge is now converted, delivered. Is that what learning is?

Higher education is a process through which people learn and acquire skills. It doesn't much matter what you study at degree level, only that you study. In one of the many responses to Clarke's bumbling, Tam Dalyell, who was at the time the Father of the House of Commons, having been an MP for four decades, explained that after he had switched from maths to history at Cambridge he found 'it was a very tough degree actually, in those days. I think any degree is valuable. It's not so much the subject as what it does to create methods of thought.'[17]

Clarke was merely the first minister to say aloud what many have since thought or put into policy. Years later, in a Q&A with the public, Clarke sidestepped the chance to double down on his ideas. He was asked if he thought there was too much funding of pointless research and he replied, 'Classic "blue skies" research has the point of extending human knowledge which is immensely important even if it doesn't have an immediate application.'[18]

Too late. The damage was already done. The humanities had been teed up ready for the incoming coalition government to whack them down the fairway.

For me, the essence of a functioning society is one that has a healthy, well-informed relationship with its past – principally because any notion of the present is founded upon it. Fascists seem to love a populace that are ill-educated and ill-informed; perhaps it makes them easier to manipulate, uncritical in their thinking and open to half-truths about the past. In fact, whenever a political question arises, a good starting question is: what would Hitler want in this situation? If the fascists want rid of something, that's sufficient reason to cling to it until we fully understand what it is that's being surrendered.

xx

Near the end of my PhD in 2004, I was standing in the corridor outside Mary's office, but I wasn't waiting for her. Instead, she'd lent the use of her office so that I might have a familiar environment for my viva voce examination.

There is nothing like a viva. Everyone has a viva story as vivid as their coming-out one. I'd worked for over three years on mine but some battle on for five or ten years. Then it all comes down to whether or not an examiner had their boiled egg that morning done just the way they like it. I heard gruelling tales of hours-long exams in which the PhD student would be trying their best to answer their questions but also trying to interpret the tenor of those same questions as to whether or not they indicated failure.

In a viva, there is no mark. You pass and dance off into the sunset. Or you might be sent away to do a small or large sum of corrections for up to a year. Worst, you fail and are offered a lower class of degree. Anything can go wrong. Anything can be asked of you.

Outside in the corridor, I couldn't hear any talk coming from Mary's room. Could I normally tell if Mary was in there with someone when I called? I couldn't remember. Some laughter would be a good sign. People walked by, oblivious to the fact that my life was in the balance.

I heard the movement of furniture, then I saw the door handle tilt. My stomach turned. As the door opened, doing my best to look ready, I grabbed the handle on my bag, hearing the rattle of its metal hinges as I lifted the heft of the thesis therein.

xxi

The room was like a scene from a novel. The walls were lined with books and it was a beautiful summer's day outside. It must have been postgraduates and staff out on the lawns because the undergraduates were away on summer break. I could hear their excited talk punctuated by short bursts of laughter.

I was hoping for some news about the thesis, eagerly awaiting what they thought. But instead of the usual 'How do you pronounce your name?' I got, 'Oh! That's a Texier, isn't it?' It was the external examiner eyeing my bag.

'It's a…?'

'Texier. The brand.'

I didn't know but it seemed polite to confirm that it was. The bag had been bought in a shop in Paris over a decade ago (on the Foucault's pendulum trip).

I listened eagerly to what she said, hunting for clues as to what any of this might mean for the outcome of my PhD.

'When I was a child, my mother was put in charge of opening their first shop in London. You don't often see them nowadays, but I can't not notice them.'

'What do I say?' I thought. Talk more about my bag? Ask about the mum? Instead, I clicked open the bag and pulled from its guts my thesis.

'Yes, we should begin.' A gesture to the other examiner, who took the cue and began: 'Well, Dr Cregan-Reid…' He continued but I'd stopped listening.

xxii

I'd achieved what I had been working towards for years; surely that should mean I'd feel some modicum of success? I'd phoned my bank to get 'Dr' put on my bank card, but after that, there didn't seem much to do.

I had a brief foray into non-fiction writing in which I accidentally secured a high-powered literary agent who I was sure was going to catapult me to fame. We worked together for months on a book idea about an amazing young Victorian, George Smith, who had discovered the *Epic of Gilgamesh* in the nineteenth century. The book went out on a strict ten-publisher, ten-day auction. I thought all my problems were about to be solved, but when bidding closed nobody wanted it. I hit the ground like a safe.

I was also in a staggering amount of debt. It was so bad, some of my possessions made me feel sick. I discovered there is nothing more exciting than getting indebted for something you want and nothing worse than possessing that thing afterwards.

I was, at the time, employed on casual lecturing contracts with three universities. In any given month, one or two of the institutions would simply forget to pay me. Payday always felt like a really shit form of gambling in which you never won, only waited to see if you'd lost. If I didn't get paid, I was unable to pay my bills. At any moment, it felt like the whole thing might collapse. Debt inveigles its way into so many parts of your life that it becomes a malignant weight you carry everywhere.

When I finished my first degree, I was put off reading for a few weeks afterwards, but this didn't happen with the PhD. There was some crossover between what I wanted to read for pleasure and what I might need in the future for teaching.

I'd read George Eliot's *Middlemarch* when I was about twenty-four. I was too young for it. It didn't leave in me any strong desire to return to it. I thought it without humour – correct. I thought there were no villains in it – incorrect. Unsensational – again, incorrect. Without mystery – absolutely incorrect. I remember rolling my eyes in contempt when in the novel's opening two sisters are talking about jewellery, bickering over who they may or may not marry. I remember feeling the sheer weight of the unread pages in my right hand and reflected that I couldn't take another 900 pages of this.

I had to reread it for teaching and when I did, I discovered something quite different. Some sentences made me shiver in recognition (the protagonist marries an older man). The hair on my arms stood up as I read of couples speaking and struggling to interpret one another on the most basic level. I was awestruck at Eliot's ability to polyempathise – to feel her way into every corner of everyone in the novel.

There are any number of comparable novels from the period: Harriet Martineau's *Deerbrook*, Margaret Oliphant's *Hester*, Dinah Craik's *Olive* or Olive Schreiner's *The Story of an African Farm*, in which intelligent, capable and ambitious women are put into conflict with their society. However, none writes with the empathy or scope that Eliot does.

Much earlier in her writing career, in an 1856 essay for the *Westminster Review*, she explained:

> The greatest benefit we owe to the artist, whether painter, poet, or novelist, is the extension of our sympathies. Appeals founded on generalisations and statistics require a sympathy ready-made, a moral sentiment already in activity; but a picture of human life such as a great artist can give, surprises even the trivial and the selfish into that attention to what is apart from themselves, which may be called the raw material of moral sentiment ... Art is the nearest thing to life; it is a mode of amplifying experience and extending our contact with our fellow-men beyond the bounds of our personal lot.[19]

That last sentence is one of the most powerful defences of fiction I've seen in my reading career. And most critics never get, or take, the opportunity to articulate their ideas and put them into practice so fully and completely as Eliot does. As a novelist, she has that outstanding ability to control and mould the chaos of life, yet still convince you that she is presenting it in its entirety.

xxiii

Middlemarch is about so many things: families, a town, medicine, politics, reform, debt, public faces and private lives. The list goes on. But what is really incredible about what Eliot achieves in the book is that the novel seems to be about the very nature of reading itself. Not so much the activity of reading but what it materially does to readers. As Eliot recounts what happens in the heads of her characters, as she shifts with acuity from the frosty, old, impotent Casaubon to the young and idealistic Dorothea, as readers we obediently follow her. What is amazing about reading fiction like Eliot's, fiction specifically about empathy, is that the very act of us readers empathising with the characters also rewires our brains to become more adept at empathising.

As our eyes scan the lines and circles of text before us, the symbols before our eyes are changing what is behind them. This happens in a number of ways.

First, in a randomised trial in 2013, researchers set out to measure one of the impacts of reading literary fiction. They were interested in 'Theory of Mind', the idea that someone can understand the motivations or feelings of others: empathy and sympathy to you and me. These two faculties are what enables us to form complex societies, social relationships, intimacy, all of what makes us human. But we don't really know much about how to teach this skill or foster it in others.

In the trial the researchers undertook five experiments, which led them to conclude that the reading of literary fiction led to better performance on tests of affective and cognitive Theory of Mind, specifically compared against the attainment of subjects reading non-fiction, popular fiction or nothing at all.[20] They were able to prove that the reading of literary fiction improves our faculty for empathy and understanding others. What's great about Eliot is she doubled down on this faculty by recounting the actual thought processes her characters undergo while attempting – or more dramatically, failing – to empathise: to do the very thing that you are subconsciously learning how to do while you're reading her.

Second, the neural pathway for basic interpretation is very well laid down in neurotypical humans. Light bounces into the eye and hits the retina, causing an electrical jiggle down the optic nerve to the back of the brain, where the information is processed in the visual cortex. From there, it is rerouted back towards the front where it lands in Wernicke's area, which deals with the comprehension of speech. It's then shunted along to Broca's area in the frontal lobe, which is specific to speech production, and finally to the sensorimotor cortex, where the photons of light and the concept finally come together in unison as, for example, 'cat'.[21] As brain activity goes, it's pretty straightforward. You can draw a 2D diagram of this sequence quite easily.

But try to track the brain activity involved in reading the opening of chapter 29 of *Middlemarch*:

> One morning, some weeks after her arrival at Lowick, Dorothea – but why always Dorothea? Was her point of view the only possible one with regard to this marriage? I protest against all our interest, all our effort at understanding being given to the young skins that look blooming in spite of trouble; for these too will

get faded, and will know the older and more eating griefs which we are helping to neglect. In spite of the blinking eyes and white moles objectionable to Celia, and the want of muscular curve which was morally painful to Sir James, Mr Casaubon had an intense consciousness within him, and was spiritually a-hungered like the rest of us.

To draw a diagram of your brain activity while you were reading that, you'd need something 3D and sculptural. Upturning 1,000 giant pans of recently boiled spaghetti might give you something like enough material to draw that diagram. The reason it's so complex is that not only are you having to do a great deal of extra interpretive work by looking at the lines and shapes and recognising them as letters, then words, then phrases, punctuation and sentences, but there's an additional layer of interpretation beyond that as the meaning seeps into your consciousness that is causing areas all over your brain to flutter and buzz in association with these words and their meanings. Put simply, reading, and reading fiction particularly, is a workout for the brain. Reading literary fiction, the kind that challenges your limits of understanding and your world view, really does make you more experienced. And more experienced equals smarter.

xxiv

The best fiction does not make clear its argument. Instead, it fires up a collection of shared ideas and feelings about which there is no absolute conclusion. It presents them on the page and asks us what we think. And what we think is conditional on our experience.

When I reached the conclusion of *Middlemarch* post-PhD, I was struck by just how different a book it was. There was one story in particular that leapt off the page. It was young Fred Vincy's.

The novel has seven central characters and Fred is certainly one of the least significant among them. At the beginning of the novel, he's blunt, plain-thinking and – as the son of the town's mayor – entitled. He is expecting to inherit a fortune from his uncle and lives accordingly. Meanwhile, his ailing benefactor dangles the legacy before Fred like he's teasing a cat with a toy mouse. Fred is in love with Mary Garth and hopes to marry her one day, but his financial ineptitude is a barrier to them. He involves himself with get-rich-quick schemes that inevitably fail, leaving him worse off. Fred's uncle later dies and, to everyone's surprise, Fred is left practically nothing. He is deeply in debt and even worse, he had convinced Mary's father to be a guarantor for one of the loans that Fred defaults on. Fred goes down and takes all of Mary's family down with him.

Fred's shock at the damage he has caused drives him to reassess his life, curtailing his ambitions and instead committing himself to something much more grounded: estate management alongside Mary's father. It's work that Fred commits to fully. And in time, he finds he has a talent for it.

His story unfolds over hundreds of pages and concludes with him being given sole responsibility for looking after the very estate he ought to have inherited. This places him in a position sufficient to marry Mary.

As I read the penultimate chapter, the idea that someone in such terrible debt could be forgiven, could have a future, could be redeemed, was worth loving, proved overwhelming. As I learned what became of him, the tears in my eyes made the letters blur, skitter and dance about the page. It was an embodied response to the simple fact that our future penetrates and begins to change us long before we see its presence in our lives. *Middlemarch* made it possible for me to imagine a different life.

XXV

A few weeks later, a letter plopped onto the doormat from a research council I'd applied to for a fellowship. The envelope was decidedly thin. I stood in the porch of our house and tore it open. On a single page, they told me that they wanted me to get in touch with them for further information because my application for a two-year fellowship had been successful. I was going to be paid to read books and write about them.

I planned a book. I wrote the kinds of articles that insecure early academics write: complicated ones with some very long words in them ('entelechy', anyone?). The years passed quickly, though the hope of securing a permanent job was never far away.

At my first proper job interview, conducted by one of the most senior professors in my field, I was ill-prepared, even stumbling at the first question. I performed so badly that I've never been able to look her in the eye since. With a few more failures learned from, I kept on applying.

At the next interview, instead of being asked about my name, folk just wanted to know where I'd got my bag from, just like at my viva. In the afternoon, when I went to attend the panel interview, I walked into the building and there before me was a Foucault pendulum. I stood for a moment, watching it swing back and forth. I thought about looking at those copies of Umberto Eco's novel piled up in the Waterstones window back in Manchester, when the book had seemed out of reach. I watched it for a short while, smiled to myself and walked on.

I stood and waited in yet another corridor. I was called in. As I was taking my seat in front of the five-person panel and before anyone could say anything about my bag, I said, 'You've got a Foucault pendulum.'

'A what, sorry?'

'A Foucault pendulum. It's a nineteenth-century invention to prove the rotation of the earth. [Pause, blank faces.] The pendulum swings, but throughout the day it turns on its axis as the earth turns. I think it's called the Coriolis effect. At the end of a swing of the pendulum, it pauses and by the time it swings back across the plane, the earth beneath it has spun a little to the... [visibly performs a compass-point ritual taught in childhood] east. It happens over and over until the pendulum goes full circle to the right. [Has he finished? No, not finished.] Well, in the northern hemisphere that is. It would be to the left in the southern.'

An hour later, I was only halfway home when I got a phone call from the head of the panel. I'd slain the ogre, scaled the castle walls, charmed the prince. I'd got a job.

xxvi

By the time I started lecturing at my first job in 2006, I'd already done a lot of teaching, so I noticed that the introduction of fees and their increases had changed the student demographic as well as their attitudes.

The 2001 Labour manifesto promised, 'We will not introduce "top-up" fees and have legislated to prevent them.'[22] Instead, under

Charles Clarke's aegis, fees tripled. On 1 July 2004, the Higher Education Act 2004 became law, allowing universities to charge between £0 and 3,000. The idea was that a new 'fees market' would be created. This backfired when not a single institution opted for anything other than the maximum £3,000. Suddenly, there were relatively few students who could afford to study without having to take on additional paid work. Students juggling paid and university work became the norm.

Student loans to cover fees were also introduced. For the six years 2006–12, university fees returned to the same level that they had been at for most of the preceding two centuries: representing something in the region of a 30 per cent contribution towards the cost of delivering a university degree. Labour's reasoning was that the expansion of the university system – that had been driven by Prime Minister Tony Blair's much-repeated pronouncement of 'Education. Education. Education.' – had outrun the taxpayer's abilities to fund it. (It would be quickly forgotten that one of the Tories' pledges in the 2005 election was to abolish fees.)

All of a sudden, there was a catastrophic drop in the number of mature students. Instead of constituting around, in my experience, 30–40 per cent of the student population, when I'd speak to 300 students in a lecture hall, I'd find there would be two or three sat together at the back. There were other, more subtle changes too.

There was understandably an increase in consumer behaviour. It's not that all students began behaving like this, more that none had previously and now one or two did. You'd sometimes hear students dividing up their fees into the cost to them per hour of tuition. None of these calculations ever included the extensive costs of examining, maintaining the buildings, the books in the library, the staff in the library and, in all the subject offices, the fact that we were discussing fees in a clean, tidy, heated and furnished room. Essay marks were more frequently queried on the grounds of the effort that had gone into them, rather than their actual quality. There is little that is unreasonable in any of these queries, only that they were significant by their absence before the rise.

In the years that followed, these changes in student behaviour and the varied approaches to their studies normalised. They didn't spread but instead became a normal part of the justifiable discussions that we have with students and their parents. The reason for this settling of attitudes may have a historical precedent. It also made what happened in 2010 so radical, shocking, even outrageous.

As 2009 drew to a close, it was obvious to all that this was the end of the fourth Labour government and would likely be the last for a while. A deepening crisis in higher education funding meant another review was commissioned. It was to be headed up by Lord Browne of Madingley. He was a former chief of BP, and this would be his first high-profile role since he'd resigned from that company after it was discovered he'd lied in court. There was some cynicism in Labour commissioning a review that wouldn't report until after the general election, essentially kicking the can down the road to be dealt with by, almost certainly, another government.

xxvii

Middlemarch would not be the last time reading affected my life.

We'd been in a relationship for nearly seventeen years. I had been struggling for the past few and I fixated on the precarity of being on the receiving end of funding that was only ever temporary.

Historically, our relationship had also felt equally precarious, without any legal standing. I often felt depressed and anxious and saw these two causes as the root of my problems.

In January of 2006, we undertook a civil partnership and in hindsight, it was weird. There were no photos. There was no party. I'm not even sure we told that many people.

The relief that I expected the imminent arrival of never came. I felt no more secure.

In the following weeks, I shifted the blame to the fact that I still didn't have a job. But when I got that, I still felt off and thought I was waiting for the contract to arrive. Then it did. Start dates, hours of work, my job title, all of it articulated that I had not wasted my time in working for it for nearly half my life. So why did I feel so bad?

It would be easy to imagine that a group of PhDs all competing for academic jobs would be like *The Hunger Games*, but it wasn't like that in the least. We were only ever happy for one another's successes. Every time someone got a job, it made it more real, more likely for the rest of us. So, when I told one of my friends and she asked 'When's the party?', she meant it. But it hadn't occurred to me that this was something to celebrate.

Around the same time, in the corridor at Sussex, I bumped into Laura Marcus (later the first female Regius Professor of Rhetoric and English Literature at Edinburgh).

'I heard you've got some good news,' she said.

'I've got a job.'

She raised her hands in a muted 'hurrah'.

'And is it full-time?' I nodded that it was, and she 'hurrahed' with a little more dynamism.

'And is it somewhere,' she hesitated, sifting for a better word, 'good?'

I said it was and told her where. She gulped and put a splayed hand to her chest, then told me that she had done all her postgraduate work there.

Treading more carefully, she continued: 'And is it permanent?' By the time I'd confirmed that it was, with students walking by either side of us in that bustling corridor, tears were already running down her face.

I was touched that she cared so much but equally struck that I didn't seem to.

Why didn't I want a party? These were the things that were supposed to make me feel better, but they were making me feel worse. Much, much worse.

Instead, I slipped into the ravine of a depression so deep and well camouflaged that no one even knew I was gone.

A few days later, I was chatting on the phone to a friend and we were, for some reason, talking about Woody Allen's 'Bergman' period – the series of films that took on big subjects and had few, if any, jokes in them. I was talking about one called *Another Woman* and explained, 'It's the one where an academic rents an office in New York because she wants to focus on finishing her book. But it doesn't break her writer's block because through an air-vent she can hear the therapist's office next door and becomes obsessed with one of the young female patients.'

I was supposed to be working on my book but I was too unsettled, so rewatched the film instead. It turned out that what I'd recalled was only a minor subplot of the story. It was really about the dissolution of a long-term relationship. And then someone recited some Rainer Maria Rilke.

I couldn't believe what I'd heard. I went to my study, found my copy of the 'selected' and there it was.

'Archaic Torso of Apollo' is a simple four-stanza poem, a piece of ekphrasis in which the speaker describes their response to a sculpture. The statue of Apollo is only a fragment, so the speaker remarks on what is lost and what may be implied from what's left and how the power of the artefact is likely greater than its whole would have been. Imagination is greater than evidence. The sculpture's power seems untamed by its incompleteness. It possesses such potency that it seems to address the speaker of the poem directly. Power emanates from it like the corona of a sun. The poem concludes 'denn da ist keine Stelle / die dich nicht sieht' (for there is no part / which doesn't see you). Then the last five words, clenched like a fist: 'Du mußt dein Leben ändern.'

'You must change your life.'

The wind knocked out of me, I packed a bag and left. I'd intended to stay with a friend for a couple of days, but felt so much relief on departing, I never went back.

xxviii

My first few years as a lecturer were exciting. On the surface I was energetic, eager to get involved and make a home for myself in my new job. Beneath the veneer, I was struggling with the same book that I'd started after my PhD several years before.

I was also experiencing the indignity of one of the country's first gay divorces. Nobody knew what the legislation was, so the whole thing proceeded at the pace of Dickens's Jarndyce and Jarndyce, a probate case that people are born into and later die out of without the case ever concluding. I was trying to work out how to pay back a massive debt on my junior lecturer's salary while living alone in a rented London flat.

I couldn't keep going. The burden of it all seemed too much as I strained under the weight of expectations fast becoming unmet, of not becoming all the person I wasn't yet and might never become – all very Hardy.

My inability to push through anything, to see anything to a conclusion, worked its way beneath my skin and into my DNA. The road into academia had taken so much out of me. I had cashed in every single one of my achievements to date when I started the job, and to make it through my probation the university would inevitably want more. I could see where I wanted to go but had no idea how to get there. The stress of it made me ill. I developed a skin complaint, coming to the surface as if to show the chaos of what was beneath. At first, the epidermis peeled away like tissue paper, revealing angry and reddened skin below, before finally it cracked open like the bark of an oak tree. I was put on round after round of antibiotics, and I swirled downwards into lethargy, self-disgust and depression. I went to see doctors, then specialists, then consultants, but none could tell me what infection or autoimmune disease I had. As the days began to shorten, and the rustling leaves became a touch more sibilant, term began and my then manager wanted to know why I hadn't been more productive over the summer.

I watched my new colleagues breeze through their days like a gliding bevy of swans as I thrashed to stay afloat, as eager to succeed as I was to avoid attracting attention.

I flung myself into relationships like one leaping into a river with a stone about one's neck. I dumped and got dumped. As my skin worsened, I didn't want to go out, refused to see friends, and couldn't focus on the work that I needed to be doing to make any headway. The only thing I had that could lift my spirits a little was running outdoors, ideally in nature. As my enthusiasm for it continued to grow, I became more and more fascinated by our body's relationship with its environment. And because by now nineteenth-century literature was my job, and I knew that Hardy was one of the most important writers of the period, I dutifully went back to reread *Tess* (in the same way as an architect might read up on architraves or load-bearing walls: without necessarily expecting to enjoy it). And when I did, I found I was reading a different book.

Hardy's Geppetto-like manipulation of his characters was still there, but he was doing so much more.

This time, the pages were luminously alert to life. I was more forgiving to the tragic elements of the book precisely because if you want to show a world with no beneficent, all-powerful being at its centre, then tragedy is really the only genre fit for this. But what I had never seen before was that he was obviously, to my eyes, the first post-Darwinian novelist.

Darwin's *On the Origin of Species* had been published decades before Hardy's *Tess*. In *Origin*, Darwin presented his theory of natural selection: species evolve through random variation and the resulting organisms most suited to their environment are those most likely to survive and reproduce. As such, the future members of the species are increasingly made in their image. Beautifully simple, yet the implications of that theory are ones the Victorians struggled to understand. It's little wonder they did; 160 years later, we are still grappling with that theory's implications as it fights for elbow room on curricula throughout the world – ironically, in environments hostile to its reproduction.

Hardy didn't struggle with the theory of evolution by natural selection in the least. He's a post-Darwinian novelist not because his plots and characters mechanically act out Darwin's ideas or align themselves with his thought. While some of his characters are more suited to the modern world than others (and as a result survive and thrive), what Hardy does in his fiction is present an entirely Darwinian worldview.

This is how he describes the simple act of a field being harvested in *Tess*:

The narrow lane of stubble encompassing the field grew wider with each circuit, and the standing corn was reduced to smaller area as the morning wore on. Rabbits, hares, snakes, rats, mice, retreated inwards as into a fastness, unaware of the ephemeral nature of their refuge, and of the doom that awaited them later in the day when, their covert shrinking to a more and more horrible narrowness, they were huddled together, friends and foes, till the last few yards of upright wheat fell also under the teeth of the unerring reaper, and they were every one put to death by the sticks and stones of the harvesters.

From the same novel:

The outskirt of the garden … was now damp and rank with juicy grass … and with tall blooming weeds emitting offensive smells … She went stealthily as a cat through this profusion of growth, gathering cuckoo-spittle on her skirts, cracking snails that were underfoot, staining her hands with thistle-milk and slug-slime, and rubbing off upon her naked arms sticky blights which, though snow-white on the apple-tree trunks, made blood-red stains on her skin; thus she drew quite near to Clare, still unobserved of him.

There are numerous passages like these in the novel that show Hardy's environmental empathy – a vision of the world that focuses on human stories but does so by placing them in the proscenium of all the other life with which they interact.

When the book was first published at the end of the nineteenth century, it caused great offence because of its sexual frankness, pessimism and its unwavering depiction of women's oppression. But there's also the novel's *juiciness*.

It's a book so utterly alive to life that it trails and slithers, creeps and crawls on every page. It's suffused with slime, spittle, milk and blood. Stare at the pages long enough and you'll see lacewings, moths and damselflies fluttering at the peripheries of your vision. Life is huddled in every corner of every paragraph – it's there close up, in the distance, in the skies, beneath the winnowing grass. Everywhere, it is at all times trapped in the struggle for survival.

This world of lush succulence, of juiciness, in which sex is seemingly ubiquitous, had Victorian readers as enthralled as they were appalled.

It's easily forgotten that Hardy was not at the time the grand old man of letters that he became. Before he was the stately, stale, pale male of nineteenth-century literature, long before his books were thrust into the hands of unwilling and bemused school kids, before his work was adapted for Sunday evening TV, people were enraged, shocked and/or disgusted by his work. He was not writing from the centre but from the fringes. He was anti-establishment, fiercely so. He wasn't polite; he was punk. In all the talk of Hardy as the champion of the underdog and the downtrodden, it is too easily forgotten that Hardy, for at least the first half of his life, was the underdog and the downtrodden.

And when *Tess* hit the shelves, the outraged were as disgusted by the suggestion of sexual assault as they were by the goading subtitle of the novel, *A Pure Woman*. There was also outrage because Hardy refused to make easy moral judgements about the sex lives of his characters but presented a world in which society and nature are utterly at odds. (Indeed, it is the friction between the two that is so commonly the source of tragedy in his later work.)

After reading *Tess* for the second time, I got it. Not only could Hardy easily shift his and our focus from an insect to a human, from lichen to lapwings, from horses to hyacinths, but in doing so he was making the Darwinian point that all life is sympathetically, dependently, connected.

I wanted more!

I read his fiction. I read the poetry. I read biographies. I read his letters. I'd have read his shopping lists if I could.

xxix

I don't think I'm overstating things to say that Hardy fixed me. My life was nothing without books like this. My life would be nothing without books like this. The book began to repair neural circuitry, and as my skin grew back, this time it held in place. As my fascination took root, I found new purpose.

A few months later and I had spent so much time with Hardy that it would have been remiss of me not to put a course together, but when the day arrived to deliver the first lecture, *Far from the Madding Crowd* was notably absent from the reading list.

I'd been a lecturer for a few years at this point. If I were to count my wins, it would be that I didn't own an alarm clock. I was taking on more responsibility at work. The book I was working on now had a great many words in it.

In 2008, the housing market crashed so hard that I was just able to reach up to the bottom rung of the property ladder. I bought a flat that had holes in the roof, a kitchen where if you leant on one side of the surface the other end would rear violently upwards. Nicotine and tar ran down the walls in brown tears as I cleaned them. But it was mine.

Since leaving Sussex University and Brighton itself, I'd seen very little of Mary Dove. We stayed in email contact, where she would occasionally send me bits of gossip or book recommendations. One day, a copy of Suzanne Berne's *A Crime in the Neighbourhood* arrived in the post. She'd recently read it and knew we had a similar taste in books (the non-medieval at least). She then got in touch when she was made professor. She heard in April 2008 and took up post that September, with the idea that she would give an inaugural lecture at some point in the future.

The following year, I turned forty. A trauma for some but I was beginning to feel that I'd found my place in the world, so I wasn't riven by the usual concerns. I invited Mary along to a party and she explained that unfortunately she already had plans and signed off 'Wishing you a manageable hangover and much happiness in the years to come'. It was the last I heard from her.

Six weeks later, her son wrote requesting I ring him. Mary had died a couple of days before. She had gone into her garden in Lewes on a warm Friday evening to enjoy a glass of wine and had died there, in her chair. She hadn't even reached retirement.

I've got the Suzanne Berne in front of me now, on my desk as I write. It's still pristine because for fifteen years, it has remained unread. In the interim, it has taken on necromantic properties. I feel, while the book is unread, there is something about our friendship that is still ongoing. The process of gift-giving remains in a transient phase, where I can hold the book in my imagination, delaying its arrival like I'm still holding the idea of her mid-air. Maybe

I'll read it one day – but it still feels like an act that would disregard the memory of her. Because she held back the briars to help me slide through to so many open fields, I feel like she's the only one that really understood it all, what it cost. She gave me so much in the time that I knew her and some of that remains in that unread book. The things she gave me, without cost, proved invaluable.

Financial debts used to haunt me, but they can always be repaid. Now, though, it is the reckonings of friendship that trouble me. They are the ones most difficult to settle.

5 Much of the writing is strong and fresh. But there crops up in parts a certain rawness of absurdity that is very displeasing, and makes it read like **some clever lad's dream** ... There is real feeling in the writing ... There is stuff and promise in him: but he must study form and composition, in such writers as Balzac and Thackeray, who would I think come as natural masters to him.
– Anon. reader's report rejecting Hardy's first novel

Mr. Wopsle's great-aunt kept an evening school in the village; that is to say, she was a ridiculous old woman of limited means and unlimited infirmity, who used to go to sleep from six to seven every evening, in the society of youth who paid twopence per week each, for the improving opportunity of seeing her do it.

Charles Dickens, *Great Expectations*

Sometimes, you do so little of what you're supposed to it feels like real life is happening in the displacement activities around it. It was 2007, and I was still working on a book I'd begun four years previously. I was stuck. Recently divorced and in a job not going well. One of my bosses would pass me in the corridor and practically roll his eyes in wonder at how someone like me ever got hired. Another would point at my clothes and laugh, 'Ha! You look like a builder, or something.'

Every day, I struggled to muster the motivation to open the document I'd jokingly named 'Doom.doc' on my desktop. It was one of those jokes that wasn't funny any more because it was true. I was working on the deep history of literature, examining shifts in narrative endings in the nineteenth century, which had been interesting once. Most of my time, though, I spent not working on the book. I spent years prioritising trivial tasks or convincing myself I was reading around my subject. From the desire to find some detail in a book, I could spend half an hour looking for it, open its pages, and I would be away. In the preceding days, I'd found a copy of Anthony Trollope's *Cousin Henry* under the bed and read the whole thing. It's a neat little tale about a will and the consequences of failure to act. Underneath it was Henry James's *The Spoils of Poynton*, also about a bequest but this time the characters argue so long over who gets what from the inheritance that the whole place burns down and no one gets anything – it sounds terrible but it's brilliant.

Days before, the book I had been looking at because I needed to check something was *Great Expectations*. I was ready to do some work, at last. Back at my desk, I read the first three-line paragraph of the novel, which led to the next. By the time I'd got to Pip encountering the convict who grabs him by the ankles, turns him upside down and violently shakes any valuables from his person, like an omelette from a pan, I slid from my desk back to my bed and over the next few days, read the whole thing for the fourth or fifth time.

i

It had been a few years since I'd followed Pip into adulthood. Since I'd seen how that pip, thumbed into the ground, might grow into something strong enough to withstand a storm.

Rereading a novel takes you back to a place you think you know to revisit friends you've made along the way. I was forty and I'd last read *Great Expectations* something less than a decade ago. And, as is the case with rereading novels, I didn't expect it to be all that different from the last time. I was wrong.

Classics, real, true ones, are like rainbows. They are things of magnitude and beauty. But they don't exist on their own. It's our perspective that makes them.

Is this what makes classics 'classic'? Their capacity to produce new insights, reveal new layers, points of view, coigns of vantage, with each encounter? It seems that at key moments in our development, something about us *and* the books that got us there changes too. Quite by accident, my procrastination succeeded in revealing an important truth about the nature of stories.

I'd taught *Great Expectations* any number of times in the past but hadn't always reread it because there simply wasn't time. The book had already succeeded in attaching itself to me like it was a field of burrs I had careered through. What had always surprised me in the teaching of it was that the students never responded to it in the same way. Everyone knows the feeling of talking to friends about a film or book you loved only to discover they hated it. This is no revelation. People are different. What's not so straightforward is the fact that books like *Great Expectations*, or any of its ilk, have not been out of print for 150 years or more. That should at least make them interesting. It's the life experience, the values of the reader that change, and that has a lot more to do with age than we often care to acknowledge.

Reading isn't just a means of learning how to navigate the world, it's also about finding one's place in it. There's a name for this kind of novel, devoted to its protagonist finding their place in the world: *bildungsroman*. The form reached its peak in the nineteenth century with novels like Stendhal's *The Red and the Black* (1830), *Jane Eyre* (1847), *David Copperfield* (1850) or Flaubert's *Sentimental Education* (1869) – and, of course, *Great Expectations*.

These coming-into-being novels are often a key part in readers' journeys to and through adulthood. And if you take a poll among your reading friends, you'll likely find that for some it's the teeth-gnashing passion of *Wuthering Heights* (1847) or Holden Caulfield's acuity for spying all things 'phony' in *The Catcher in the Rye* (1951) that haunts them. Albert Camus's *The Stranger* (1942) is another that tends to generate adolescent apostles, and Truman Capote's evisceration of Jack Kerouac's *On the Road* (1957) – 'That's not writing, that's typing' – needs to be understood in the context that Capote was, at the time, twice the age of the majority of that novel's devoted readership.*[1]

These books are like parties: you have to be the right age if you're going to belong in them. I remember going clubbing in my early forties and I looked so out of place, people would come to me asking what drugs I had to sell. I was too old to be at a club on a Thursday; I should have been at home watching *Spaced* or at a more age-appropriate dinner party. The point is, sometimes you have to be the right age to read something and *get* it. If you're the wrong age, or don't have the correct assortment of struggles, insecurities and experiences, that lifelong friendship between you and a book may for ever be denied. As we progress through life, it's as if our emotions present a moving target, a twitchy bullseye that Katniss Everdeen would struggle to hit. When some stories let fly their sentiments from the page, the target has all too frequently moved on. It's like turning up at a theme park and finding yourself too tall to ride the teacups.

Like many, when I first read *Great Expectations*, I was swept up in Pip's perilous journey into the happy ever after of his adulthood. In my late twenties, I reread it, this time noticing the tone of regret that dripped from each paragraph, thick as syrup. Another rereading

---

* Capote is much reported as having said this but in fact said different versions of it multiple times, referring to different writers. The first time he used the phrase, he was name-calling several writers: 'But yes, there is such an animal as a nonstylist. Only they're not writers. They're typists. Sweaty typists blacking up pounds of Bond with formless, eyeless, earless messages.'

in my thirties, this time I knew things were badly wrong at home and the ending was revealed to me to be not in the least happy. Instead, the way the novel closes merely restates Pip's own pathology of having too-great expectations of himself, of those around him and, most perilously, of his future. His fatal flaw is laid bare in those closing moments: Pip possesses a persistent failure to foresee that things will not turn out well.

It seemed a more existential novel that time around too. My jaw dropped when I read:

A man would die tonight of lying out on the marshes, I thought. And then I looked at the stars, and considered how awful it would be for a man to turn his face up to them as he froze to death, and see no help or pity in all the glittering multitude.

Now, with the burden of a messy divorce, a couple more bad relationships under my belt, a static career and a friend's recent, sudden and untimely death, I found the novel to be different once again.

Towards the end of the novel, Pip has a chance to look back and reassess his close friendship with the perennially loyal Herbert. It was a friendship that Pip had tested to the extreme. When I got to that part and read:

We owed so much to Herbert's ever cheerful industry and readiness, that I often wondered how I had conceived that old idea of his inaptitude, until I was one day enlightened by the reflection, that perhaps the inaptitude had never been in him at all, but had been in me.

It was like one of my secrets had been read aloud on the national news, and I blushed in shame at all the times I'd blamed others for my own defects and limitations.

Dickens is not given enough credit for these insights. I suppose it's because they are not sustained in a way like they are in the much more serious Eliot. He wants to be done with emotion as quickly as he can because he's got a joke up his sleeve and he can feel it working its way free.

There are any number of rereading experiences. Some books are like a guest house that you return to, only to find everything just as you left it. You're different, but nothing in the room has changed. There's nothing new to discover about the place. And sometimes, this is just the holiday you need.

Then there are stories that we don't so much carry around but instead grow with us. For me, these might include *Middlemarch*, *Hamlet*, *The Tempest*, *Tom's Midnight Garden*, late Jane Austen (the sharpness of her pen and that confidential tone!), about half of Hardy and at least a quarter of Dickens.

The worst kind of rereading is when you go back and find the room has aged badly. Really badly. The unhospitable books I've revisited would be stories by someone like Ian McEwan. On first reading, decades earlier, the quality of the prose amazed me, but going back, I found the worlds that he writes about to be rather claustrophobic ones, riven by class prejudice and homophobia.

When I reread *The Comfort of Strangers* (his second novel), I re-encountered the couple who are into S&M, where we know something must be off with the husband because he frequents gay bars that play stupid and inane pop music and he is familiar with the gay clientele. The denouement is that he's actually a bit gay and a psychopath and a murderer.

In 1997's *Enduring Love*, the queer villain, Jed, is killed by the heterosexual hero protagonist and seems to reclaim his masculinity in doing so. (This was an A-level set text, by the way.) In McEwan's world, homosexuality is so extreme that it is placed on a continuum with psychopathy. Once I'd made this connection, it made it challenging to read his later work without tarnishing those precious early reading memories.

Great Expectations is decidedly not like this. The space of the book only grows with rereading; it becomes a better friend. There are only a handful of novels and stories like this, where something floats from the page to make your blood fizz and tingle. The best books draw you in, so that the feelings being relayed become yours. The two of you mix and a third space is opened up into which you temporarily step. Three lives begin happening simultaneously.

The novels that can cast this kind of magic are not locked in a frame: they do not look the same from every angle, they are *prismatic*. No, they are *fractal*, becoming more complex the closer you look, every pause revealing more and more depth. But that's not right either because it makes them static. Instead, real classics are *sculptural*. Their texts may be set in stone, but as we move around them, as our place in the world changes, so does their aspect. Light hits them differently and reaches our eyes, creating new shapes. New patterns, dynamics, symmetries and shapes emerge – always there, just that you weren't correctly positioned to see them before.

What really cooks my onions, though, is the revelation that hidden somewhere in the pages of *Great Expectations*, pages that my eyes have scanned numerous times at various stages of my life, there are hidden sentiments that a future version of me will see and instantly comprehend in a way that I could not and cannot today. There are ways of seeing the world not yet revealed and sympathies yet to be apprehended.

Those sentences are already there. When I get to them, the bones in my arms will be a little thinner, but the hairs will still stand up. Lines of print are waiting to pinch tears from eyes a little more wrinkled than they are today. Patiently, magically, those words await my arrival.

ii

For years I floundered with writing. The world of whackydemia is a brutal one: publish or perish! Vend or vanish! At least the reading was fun. Another six years went by before the book was finished.

Meanwhile, there were revolutionary changes in higher education that would create difficulties for the existence of the humanities. While there was a chance that a newly elected government might actually reduce the fees that the Labour government had introduced and address the climbing debt burden of young people, there was about as much chance of enquiring of a man's height and being told he was 5ft 11in.

Those panicking in 1998 that Blunkett's introduction of fees was not a sticking plaster but the thin end of the wedge were proven right. The Browne review had been commissioned by the outgoing Labour government and was not set to report until after the general election.

In the Tories' 2010 manifesto, they kept their cards close to their chest on fees by saying they would 'consider carefully the results of Lord Browne's review into the future of higher education funding, so that we can unlock the potential of universities to transform our economy, to enrich students' lives through teaching of the highest quality, and to advance scholarship'.[2] In the Liberal Democrat manifesto, they were so confident of their position that they put in bold typeface, 'We will scrap unfair university tuition fees so everyone has the chance to get a degree, regardless of their parents' income.'[3] (The Tories had said something similar in their 2005 manifesto.)

The 2010 election resulted in a hung parliament. Whomever the Liberal Democrats wanted to form a coalition with would control Parliament. Anybody that knew anything about leader Nick Clegg's background could foresee which way he was going to go. Clegg, while a student, was said to have been a member of the Cambridge University Conservative Association but later commented that he had 'no recollection of that whatsoever'. Not 'that's incorrect' or 'untrue', just that he had 'no recollection' – this is despite his name appearing in their register.[4]

The Lib–Con coalition was formed.

The Browne Report, commissioned in 2009, appeared late in 2010 as *Securing a Sustainable Future for Higher Education: An Independent Review of Higher Education Funding & Student Finance*. It rejected the idea of a 'graduate tax' because it would require an 'additional £3bn a year until 2015–16 at least; additional spending continues until ca. 2041–42', meaning that it could take thirty to forty years for the government to recoup the costs of the student's education. Furthermore, that such a tax would provide 'no incentives [for universities] to focus on quality, access or student experience.'[5] From my perspective, it's hard to countenance the notion that after having world-leading institutions for about a thousand years, English universities could not be trusted to focus on 'quality', and instead had to be financially incentivised to do so. There was also the inherent belief that an increase in fees would improve standards among institutions as they competed with one another for students.

The contribution model, whereby students put up a fraction of the cost of teaching them, was completely abandoned. They would now be charged £9,000 a year to fund the entire delivery of their degrees. The idea of higher education as a civic right was gone in an instant. Students would now be consumers and their choices would dictate and reshape the universities of the future. While for-profit educational institutions had been the greedy monster of tertiary education in the US since the 1940s, turning generations of young adults into debt-serfs, the UK system would be for ever changed by these fee hikes.

iii

In the following January, it was discovered that the research undertaken for the Browne Report looked decidedly thin. It had spent only half its research budget and conducted only one opinion survey of students and parents in order to gather information about fees and what people were willing to pay. This was supposed to be research that was paradigm-shifting, that would change the landscape of higher education, that would rank in significance next to the Robbins or Dearing Reports. How could it be that the total cost of research was a meagre £68,000? How could the majority of that be spent on a single opinion survey comprising 178 people, where the questions posed assumed an upper limit on fees of £6,000?[6] I understand that research cannot be exhaustive, but 178 seems pitifully small given the review has resulted in, to date, £206 billion of personal debt in outstanding student loans.[7] That figure is forecast to be around £460 billion, or half a trillion, by the 2040s. They spent half the research allowance.

The new arrangements effectively privatised government higher education spending via the new loans system. Tax subsidies were transformed into individual debt.

The amounts of debt that our youth live with is so extreme as to seem a kind of psychological warfare on the young. It also has no precedent.

In the entire history of universities, no students, to my knowledge, had been asked to contribute such a high proportion towards their tuition. There was little doubt that the Lib–Con government looked to the US university system, one in which the role of the state seemed to be smaller and less complex. But only the most cursory of glances could sustain such a view. In little more than a decade, the English university system went from being the super-efficient rival of US universities to out-pricing the vast majority of them. The average cost of attending a public university in the US in 2021 was $10,388, which in that same year was equivalent to around £7,600.[8] By 2021, fees in English universities had increased to £9,250.

iv

In 2005, the monitoring culture of universities took a big step forward with the introduction of the National Student Survey (NSS). League tables arrived soon after, in which institutions would trade punches year on year for a better place in the rankings. The key outcome of the NSS is whether or not the student is 'satisfied' with their degree. They are asked this as they are gathering exit velocity in the final term of the final year. (Any lecturer will tell you that this is when students are at their most strung out.) Over the years, one of the interesting outcomes of the survey is that evidence shows that overall satisfaction levels are, depending where you look, either the same – with one study concluding 'there is no statistically significant difference on student satisfaction rating between Russell

Group and Non-Russell Group universities' – or worse in Russell Group universities.[9]

It's not just about how students 'feel' about their degree. Evidence also shows that 85 per cent of students go on to pursue further study or meaningful work and this number is fairly static across the entire sector.[10] The Russell Group seems to be producing less-satisfied students, while their student outcomes are similar to that of any other institution.

With higher education in England now among the most expensive in the world, a couple of things happened. One was that I never taught a Scottish student ever again. Scottish students contribute nothing to study for their degrees as long as they stay in Scotland – where they are spoilt for choice for world-leading universities.* The other change was that parents and students quite understandably began to enquire more frequently, 'But what job can you get?' For people studying economics, law or medicine, dollar signs spun in their eyes as they were regaled with stories of prosperous careers in high finance or some kind of private practice. The fee burden was a worthwhile risk to offset against that kind of future income, one that would extinguish debt with alacrity.

What about young people that were interested in being teachers or nurses? It makes some sense to ask students to contribute towards the tuition that will enable them to secure a high-paying job in the private sector (i.e. not public service). But the idea that the sole beneficiary of an education in pedagogy is the individual that undertakes it is wrong. No teachers are in it for the money and where would we be without them? Don't they, throughout their careers, foster thousands of young people into adulthood, equipping

---

*   Welsh students studying in Wales pay a discounted rate of £9,000 (instead of the £9,250 they'd pay if they studied elsewhere in the UK).

them to become citizens? By that, I mean people who participate in society, are socially engaged, vote, feel like they belong, understand how the media works, how our political system works, are responsible, contribute, possess values, and value things like cultural heritage (in all its forms). I could go on.

Teachers contribute more to society than they get from it. I don't want to set up a banker as a straw man in this argument. Bankers do contribute to society and what they produce contributes to the economy, to progress and most aspects of our society in myriad ways. And they are richly rewarded for it. Teachers aren't.

From 2010 onwards, fees were a barrier to any humanities students.

The loan terms changed regularly but to provide a snapshot, repayments started once the debtor crested £15,000 in earnings. The interest charged was linked to that charged by high street banks (money was cheap then). Once you earned over £15,000, you had to pay back 9 per cent of your earnings beyond the threshold. The payments were deducted before tax, so the repayments would feel closer to 5–7 per cent. Loans unpaid at the age of sixty-five were written off. In 2023, the threshold has understandably risen for students in England to £25,000 and the repayments remain at 9 per cent. Loans are written off forty years from the point at which repayments were due to commence (as opposed to 2022's thirty years). Interest on the loan is charged at Retail Price Index (RPI) rates. In October 2022, the RPI rate was 14.2 per cent. RPI is volatile at the moment, and that means that no one knows what they are going to pay because no one can predict what next year's interest rate is going to be.

Sadly, the way that fee repayment arrangements have matured over the years has made things worse for poorer students or those on lower pay but great for richer ones. In other words, great for those students who move into high-paying industries, less so for those that don't. Unlike, say, a credit card, the amount you owe does not dictate how much you pay each year but how long it will take to settle the debt. And because interest accrues annually, those on lower or middle incomes will end up paying considerably more for their tuition than higher-income graduates. The difference between what a low- and high-earning graduate will end up paying for their tuition can be as much as £30,000.[11] According to forecasts by London Economics, for men in nursing the average total repayments increased from £24,400 to £42,000; for women, the increase was £10,700 to £26,000.[12] At the time of writing, there is a recruitment crisis in nursing. In June 2023, more than 900 schools were advertising English-teaching vacancies for immediate start; there are currently over 3,000 vacancies being advertised on LinkedIn for maths teachers.[13]

Does much of this sound like a 'loan' to you? Can't you shop around for loans? Who's heard of loans deducted by your employer and done so before tax. That doesn't sound like a loan at all. It sounds like a tax, a hypothecated tax (i.e. a tax for a particular form of expenditure, like National Insurance used to be).

The young are in an impossible bind. In 2000/01, the average rent of an unfurnished property was £345 pcm.[14] Adjusted for inflation, that should be £623. Instead, it's £1,221.[15] House prices are out of reach and on top of this, over a third of young people are having to pay an additional tax that almost no one over the age of thirty-five is subject to.

This environment is one that is hostile to any but those seeking to enter the highest-earning professions. But the Lib–Con government had more plans for disrupting the arts and humanities, this time poisoning at the roots and making sure that there were fewer young people even interested in a subject like English.

V

It takes a lot for an Education Secretary to secure such sustained public opposition that 110,000 signatories petition for your resignation. That's how many people wanted Michael Gove out of office before his new curriculum launched in September 2014.[16]

It started, as it so often does, with a man with a plan to modernise. Michael Gove, an MP since 2005, was considered by some party members as a future leader of the Tories. To everyone else, he was an ultracrepidarian with the look of a startled frog. Michael Gove, a Cabinet minister who distinguished himself by being even more reviled than both George Osborne and Jeremy Hunt, who described economist John Maynard Keynes as a 'homosexualist', who said 'many of us are familiar with the fact that homosexuals thrive primarily on short-term relations', this redoubtable intellect, whose levels of confidence were inversely related to his competence, was disastrously put in charge of the English curriculum for the UK.[17]

At the Tory Party conference in 2010, Gove's speech made it clear that he was going to drag English literature into the twenty-first century. He was going to save children from 'the shadow of ignorance and the chains of dependency'.[18] Gove told the conference, 'I can't rest when more than 800 primary schools can't even get half their children reading, writing and adding up properly.'[19]

In Gove's attempt to modernise education, his so-called radical plan emphasised the study of predominantly male, exclusively white and all-dead writers. This is a bit like modernising a car by removing the engine and making a hole so that the driver's feet can propel the vehicle by flitting across the asphalt.

Gove's special adviser at the time was Dominic Cummings, the now-infamous architect of much of the political chaos of the last decade. There is a famous motto, coined by Mark Zuckerberg, which characterises the behaviour of disruptors: 'move fast and break things'. It typifies the nature and speed at which these changes across our education system were rolled out.

Over the next couple of years, plans were shared. There were consultations but everything moved very quickly, which doesn't sound very conservative. It soon became clear English literature would be ceding space to STEM in the new curriculum. Worse, the GCSE wasn't even going to be compulsory any more. The post-Gove version of the English GCSE was like the previous one but with a bit of English literature thrown in. The standalone English literature GCSE after Gove became optional.

Plans were announced in 2013. Gove was going to drive up standards and he promised to make the Conservative Party 'the party of the teacher.'[20] He should have asked them first. With a couple of exceptions, they didn't see it the same way. At their next conference in 2013, the Association of Teachers and Lecturers passed a motion of no confidence in Gove.[21] The following month, the National Union of Teachers (NUT) unanimously passed a vote of no confidence in Gove and also called for his resignation.[22] Kevin Courtney of the NUT said in a TV interview that the curriculum looked more like 'a personal, ideological crusade' and that the 'timetable for change was dangerously and recklessly short'. Moreover, Courtney added that it was 'massively under resourced' and 'massively rushed'.[23]

Some teachers liked it, or at least those that they found to front the Department for Education's publicity.[24] And there were some advantages to the new curriculum. It was, on the whole, simpler than the preceding one. Some teachers felt there was less scrutiny. The outgoing curriculum had stratified student performance into levels and the new curriculum abolished them.

Gove claimed in 2013 that the National Curriculum his government had inherited was 'insufficiently supportive of those who wanted to ensure that people acquired that stock of knowledge'. He went on to state that his plans encouraged creativity.

> Creativity depends ... on making sure that you master certain skills, that you acquire a body of knowledge before then being able to give expression to what's in you. If you're musically gifted or want to pursue creativity in the way in which you write, you need, first of all, to learn your skills. You need to able to secure a foundation from which your creativity can flourish ... If you're going to write, if you're going to move, if you're going to persuade, if you're going to inspire, then you need to be able to know how the English Language, which is a wonderful instrument, can be used and tuned in order to move hearts, in order to persuade people. And you cannot be creative unless you understand how sentences are constructed, what words mean, how to use grammar. ... Unless there's that solid foundation, creativity can't flourish.[25]

If you read it quickly, it sounds sensible. If you're going to race F1, you need to learn how to drive a car. If you're going to play first violin for the Berlin Philharmonic, you need to know your scales. Where I think Gove's analogy fails is in his interpretation of what counts as core knowledge, especially in English.

vi

The contentious issue of excessive grammar instruction in primary schools was a hallmark of Gove's curriculum reforms. Children as young as six were introduced to complex grammatical concepts, a move that many argued was detrimental to total engagement with all a language has to offer. A learner driver doesn't need a detailed understanding of engine mechanics. They need to learn how not to crash into things. A novice cellist doesn't need to know that in order to sound an 'A', the string must vibrate exactly 440 times per second. It's not that this information is worthless, but you don't need all that extra knowledge to handle a car or a horsehair bow. And that's the point – one 'plays' a cello. Language use, like music, is a form of creative play, and excessive focus on grammar detracts from this essence.

The best writers, the ones that you really admire at the level of the sentence, play with their sentences. They write and rewrite (either on the page or in their head) until they have something that works, that's musical, has the right rhythm. No writer ever thought, 'Now, what I need here is a subordinating conjunction.' Grammar just does not have the same kind of application that a content subject like maths does and the tragedy is that our current curriculum pre-tends that it does.

Forgive the brag, but I've got a first-class degree; I've got a dis-tinction at MA; I've got a DPhil; I'm a professor, which means I can't get any higher up the academic ladder; I've published four books and countless articles; and I've made series for the BBC that have been broadcast in 200 countries. Yet if you asked me what the sub-junctive was, I'd have to look it up (see what I did there). That's how inessential it is to both the studying and teaching of advanced Eng-lish. My all-time favourite meme from social media is one depicting an aged and wizened Scrooge: "'I am the Ghost of Christmas Future Imperfect Conditional," said the spirit. "I bring news of what would have been going to happen, if you were not to have been going to change your ways.'"

English is not maths. You can't teach it like algebra, then construct sentences in the hope that x + y will equal z.

Since the Gove curriculum began, teachers, parents and academics have all worried that English was being turned into a content-based subject, something to be learned like the recitation of the times tables. (While we're on the topic, in the new curriculum, times tables were back, too. Were they useful? I'm fifty-four and I still can't remember what 6 multiplied by 9 is.)

Forcing kids to learn unnecessary grammar and times tables – it's like when teachers in the 1980s used to say, 'You won't have a calculator with you everywhere you go.' We showed them, didn't we! With a phone and a smartwatch, my answer would be, 'No, Miss, I'll have two, and that's not counting my laptop, two iPads and fifteen smart speakers.'

vii

The new curriculum heavily emphasised the importance of grammar, focusing on the kind of content that might be assessed by computer.

Digraphs were taught to Year 1 students, where two letters combine to form one sound, facilitating the learning of common words like 'rain' and 'look'. Split digraphs, altering vowel sounds, were taught across Years 1 and 2, providing access to numerous words in the language. While the terminology is complex, it's all quite basic stuff and learning them provides access to hundreds of common words in the language.

There was also an increased emphasis on synthetic phonics, a controversial method of learning to read by sounding out words letter by letter. While synthetic phonics had long been a staple in

primary education, they were part of a larger approach that included reading along with a (relaxed) adult, contextual decoding where
the pupil works out from clues in the text and paratexts what the
word might be, and reading or writing without books using clay,
sand or paint. Nothing beats practice when it comes to learning to
read.

A way not to convince a child that reading is fun is to have them
sit a compulsory phonics exam in Year 1, then again in Year 2 if they
don't perform well enough, and have the school or teacher in the
frame for your result.[26] Don't get me wrong, I'm not denigrating
the work of teachers. Primary and secondary education is running
on fumes – some schools can't even afford to stay open for the full
week because of the heating bill. There's practically no funding for
special educational needs, for example. Teachers are left to cope as
best they can. The system is held up by a great deal of goodwill. If
any teacher submits to the pressure and works into the evenings or
at weekends – as many do – the government will have that too and
recalibrate it as the new normal. Are there any other professions
where a fifth of people, having worked for years to get through the
door, leave within the first two? Post-Covid, even ambulance services and the police have better retention rates than the teaching
profession does.[27] And if teachers do manage to stay in the role,
there's clipboard-wielding OFSTED inspectors poised to ruin their
career with a single word: 'Inadequate'.

I think the idea is that government want to spot slow readers, but
teachers say that even their sharpest students fail the phonics test.
Moreover, a child might learn to pass a phonics test but does it mean
they are likely to become a reader? A 2016 study undertaken by researchers at University College London concluded that the way that
reading is being taught is 'uninformed and failing children'.[28] Part of

the research undertaken was a survey of 2,200 teachers, where out of 936 comments from the survey, all but one responded negatively to the screening test.

From our children's first engagements with the written word, reading is turned into a boring chore.

The 2023 National Literacy Trust survey explains that just two in five children enjoy reading (43.4 per cent) and this is the lowest figure since 2005 (when the question was first asked on the survey).[29] Only one in three children (34.6 per cent) enjoy writing in their free time, a number at its lowest since 2010.[30] The evidence around synthetic phonics all points to the fact that the phonics test is most effective at teaching children… to pass synthetic phonics tests.

Further down the line, between the ages of six and ten, pupils find that English has persisted in being boring. Weird grammatical terms await them, like fronted adverbials. When the teaching of these was introduced, parents were red-cheeked in their failed attempts to help kids with their homework.

The test at this level is called the 'SPaG', and it checks spelling, punctuation and grammar at the ages of ten or eleven. I had a look at one of the papers and there is plenty that is good about it.[31] But there's also questions like:

- Circle the subordinating conjunction in the sentence below.
- Which option makes the sentence start with an adverbial?
- Circle the two determiners in the sentence below.

I don't think my students need to know any of these to achieve a first-class degree in English literature. They could probably achieve top marks at university while still maintaining only a glancing acquaintance with, for example, the dash.

viii

It's at secondary level that school kids start to do all the good stuff, and it's also where the strangling of English fully begins.

Between the ages of eleven to fourteen, the new curriculum lays down that students should be taught to 'develop an appreciation and love of reading, and read increasingly challenging material'.[32] But the selection must include both pre-1914 and contemporary literature, including prose, poetry and drama; Shakespeare (two plays); and some 'seminal world literature'.[33]

Looking across the exam boards of selected texts, the range currently on offer is: *Macbeth, Romeo and Juliet, The Merchant of Venice, Much Ado About Nothing, Julius Caesar, Macbeth, Twelfth Night, Henry V* and, my favourite, *The Tempest*. It could be worse, I suppose. They might be doing *Cymbeline*.

While one teacher I spoke to told of a school that boasted of teaching *King Lear* to Year 7s (aged eleven to twelve), the common consensus is that teachers tend to choose the first two. *Macbeth* because it's the 'Napoleon' play – short and violent – and *Romeo and Juliet* because there's a good film of it.

When I spoke to English teachers, I was expecting them to hate the fact that they had to teach such difficult and advanced stuff to teenagers. I was wrong.

Without exception, they all said that Shakespeare matters because he's endured in a way that no other writer has. They also said that he's good to teach because he deals with the big stuff that all humans deal with at some point: love, loss, jealousy, ambition, belonging, displacement, anguish, depression and so on. They also said that unlocking the language is, for some kids, revelatory.

The teachers are happy but the kids aren't. 'I don't think

Shakespeare was writing for fifteen-year-olds,' one said. 'Trying to explain some of the jokes in *Much Ado About Nothing* to mixed-ability kids and trying to convince them it's hilarious. Explain things like "civil as an orange" and they'll just stare at you.' A child once asked this teacher, straight-faced, 'Did Shakespeare write anything in English, Miss?'

I was asked to read *Romeo and Juliet* long before Baz Luhrmann filmed it. I found it incomprehensible. The nuances of aristocratic romance, where members of the church were kind and supportive, did not connect with me at all. The dick jokes in the opening scene may have, but our teacher shrunk from mentioning those. If I was interested in anything at the time, it might have been things like social justice, class and being gay in a straight world. I might not have been able to articulate it but those themes would have engaged me. It's for this reason that when I heard of pupils doing Shakespeare at an even younger age, I balked.

Yet again, though, I am wrong. So wrong. There are definable and demonstrable benefits to the study of Shakespeare.

Time to Act was a major research study, the results of which were published in 2024.[34] The randomised trial ran across forty-five state schools in lower-income areas. In the randomly allocated intervention group, schools 'delivered 20 hours of Shakespeare teaching' using Royal Shakespeare Company approaches, while the control group schools delivered the National Curriculum. The team tested the two groups of pupils at the end of the intervention. Comparing language use with control group, this is what they discovered the intervention group had achieved:

- use of 13.8 per cent more 'sophisticated' words (outside the 2,000 most commonly used words);

- 24.3 per cent higher use of rarer verbs;
- use of 20 per cent more clauses within sentences and clauses at greater length;
- 8.9 per cent greater use of complex sentences;
- use of 27.4 per cent more words relating to emotion.
- use of 6.7 per cent more abstract vocabulary (words relating to emotion, cognition and concepts outside of the physical world).

These were nine- to ten-year-olds. And it doesn't stop there. The trial also assessed the children's levels of confidence in their ability to learn more generally:

- 17.3 per cent were more confident in their ability to work out what to do next when stuck;
- 13.8 per cent were more confident with language;
- 12.6 per cent were more confident in taking a considered approach to tackling work;
- 11.3 per cent were more confident in their own ability as a good learner;
- 9.9 per cent were more confident in wider problem solving.

Twenty hours' study of Shakespeare works more like a spell than an educational intervention.

If my feelings about my first Shakespeare are on a continuum with other kids', then giving them The Bard seems a bit like feeding them broccoli: just because they don't like it, doesn't mean it's not really good for them.

ix

Feelings are such an important part of our literary experiences and they are a complex ecosystem. On days at work when I'm feeling a bit impatient, I sometimes struggle when a student's first comment about a book is whether they 'liked' it or whether they liked this or that character. But feeling really does matter in English. And it matters probably most at secondary-school level. An error of text choice at this stage can be like pouring bleach on the soil of a seedling.

This from a secondary teacher.

> You've got to get them to enjoy the text first and engage with it, then you can start doing the difficult stuff ... I tried Browning's 'My Last Duchess'. It's quite challenging for them, but they loved it. When they got to the last lines and suddenly realised what he'd done [the narrator of the poem strangles his wife], in one of my classes, one of the kids read it, paused and said, 'What a bastard!' It was kind of okay in the context of the class because they suddenly realised that the speaker of the poem was manipulating everyone.

It's in moments like those that readers are made. Emotions matter.

A 2015 scholarly article examined the psychology of reading, of tracing the potential of fiction to 'transform emotions, both directly through the events and characters depicted and through the cueing of emotionally valenced memories'. They concluded that 'emotions experienced during reading may have consequences after closing the covers of a book'.[35]

The effect is now pretty well established. Fictional stories are so potent they make us feel more than 'true' ones do.[36] Recent research by the National Literacy Trust reported that nearly half of children and young people 'agreed that reading made them feel better'.[37] Borne out by my own conversations with teachers, this literacy research makes the strongest possible case for putting feeling and emotion at the centre of the classroom in the teaching of English.[38] And just how wrong I've been in the past to disregard those student responses.

X

All of this is assuming that the children even 'do' English literature. Just as English had been made more boring to study at primary school, so too had the curriculum been tweaked here and there to make life for people interested in pursuing it more difficult.

In September 2015, the three existing English courses were replaced. Where previously, students either took *only* English or *both* English language and English literature, English language became compulsory for all and English literature was relegated to optional.

While pupils would still get to read a little literature on their language GCSE, it would mostly consist of excerpts and passages among a morass of 'vocabulary, grammar, form, and structural and organisational features ... using Standard English where appropriate'.[39] Ask a teacher what they think about the English language curriculum, and they will tell you.

A recent survey on recruitment to A-level English subjects highlighted some typical responses: 'Students hate the GCSE and seem to be being taught "English by numbers". It is definitely putting them off', 'The new GCSE specifications have really killed the joy of English', 'GCSE syllabuses just aren't sufficiently stimulating and engaging – students are switched off.'[40]

At the end of it all is the exam. As outmoded and irrelevant a mode of assessment as might be imagined. No one in your professional life is ever going to lock you in a room with 300 strangers to write in silence for three hours recalling all the quotations you memorised. I once did just this at university. It was a Victorian literature exam and for it I learned a ton of quotations. I went as far as learning two long paragraphs from the 900 pages of William Thackeray's *Vanity Fair* – a great, wild, intelligent and rambunctious novel that poked fun at Victorian propriety. I was sure I'd be able to use the material somewhere. Actors might find this easy but I didn't. It took me a week before I had it all in my head. When the day came round, I turned over the exam paper and in question one there were the Thackeray passages, used as a prompt for some angle I'd not revised. I had wasted my time. I couldn't even use them in a different question because it would look like I'd copied them from the exam paper. All I got out of the experience was this dumb story.

Finally, Gove's curriculum also got rid of the coursework components of both English language and English literature, which contributed significantly to the GCSE scandals of the pandemic. Now there are fewer pupils coming through the English literature GCSE, it is no surprise to learn that the A-level version, under the Gove curriculum, has also tanked.

The numbers are in rapid decline: between 2012 and 2019 there has been a 31 per cent drop in students across all English subject specialisms.[41] English language is so despised at GCSE, the numbers of students taking it at advanced level have dropped 42 per cent. For the literature-only option, numbers have dropped by 25 per cent and they're still falling. There is no equivalent decline in Scotland, where they enjoy a different set-up and examination system.

In a survey of teachers on the decline of English A-levels, teachers felt that the move away from reading for pleasure was one of the key factors in their decline. 'Students not enjoying GCSE English' was the top-ranked reason teachers gave as to why students were not pursuing the subjects further. Moreover, 'STEM being seen as the best option in HE and for employment' was the top-ranked reason identified for a decline in A-level English literature recruitment.[42]

The range of set texts varies from exam board to exam board, but in the one that I looked at (AQA), out of a dozen prose writers, all were white and one (to my knowledge) was gay.[43] There is clearly work to be done if A-level English literature is going to attract young people.

The stream of students leaving school with an English literature A-level is now at a drip.

xi

English is a subject that gives you a skill set. Skills are mobile, they are agile, they work across any number of disciplines and jobs. This is what stresses out kids that are good at those other content-based subjects. Equally, it stresses out government.

We should acknowledge that pupils respond better when they see their own interests, identities and cultures. Assessment also needs to be urgently addressed. Oracy is a key skill in all aspects of a pupil's later life, not just their employment. It is currently assessed but is not part of the pupil's grade. And without a coursework component, no one is really learning the importance of drafting and redrafting work, making selections in their edits, choosing, refining – these are essential skills not just for 'a writer' but for anyone literate.

We need to stop pretending that English is a content-based subject. Its remit is complex, its disciplinary boundaries are permeable. More faith needs to be put in teachers' abilities to deliver the subject. Instead, what we have is a rigid OFSTED regime, which has imposed an ideology across subjects that is examinable but not does not test proficiency, efficient but not holistic, transparent but unresponsive to the changing nature of the discipline. English language and English literature are not at war with other subjects in the curriculum. In fact, they complement them. They exist sympathetically with them. One might even say that they are foundational to those other subjects. The most historically significant scientists are great writers: Albert Einstein, Charles Lyell, Charles Darwin, Sigmund Freud. English should not be losing to STEM's gains. Such a dynamic should be setting off alarm bells.

The UK excels in arts and humanities, regularly dominating at the Oscars, for example. Our universities are among the best in the world. Why not capitalise on some of that success rather than managerialise them out of existence?

In one of the biggest and healthiest economies in the world, our children are being taught by rote and any attempt to inculcate critical thought in the curriculum is distrusted or stomped on by politicians.

As a result, our creative industries are increasingly dominated by those who have inherited their own safety nets through lucky parentage, the attendance of public schools, or a mix of the two. To break through from the working class, you have to be unbelievably talented, a one in a billion. There is no midlist of working-class people in the arts. Basically, you have to be Adele.

Arts provision and education in the humanities all seem part of the same continuum in which schoolchildren are reduced, in a Gradgrindian way, to what their financial worth might be to an employer. The driving ideology behind much of our compulsory education system is that it exists to make people that employers can monetise. I don't think I want to contribute to that sort of education. I like to read Dickens novels; I don't want to be in them.

xii

Soon after my first book came out, after working on it for many years, I was gifted one of the most powerfully instructive lessons of my life. I received a telephone call in my office from someone at the publisher, who revealed with some excitement that the book had sold 187 copies. Nearly ten years' work. Never again would I expend so much energy for so little outcome. I was determined, instead, to do something I loved and was passionate about. I wasn't going to write for the university to please the eye-rolling boss. I was going to do something fun.

Blogs were already passé in 2011 when I started one. It wasn't for an audience: I just wanted to play, to work on something that was, to me at least, fascinating. I had taken up running when I had been ill, and I now found that when I went out on those long runs, I'd return laden with ideas, like I was trailing dozens of clattering tin cans in my wake. I'd come in through the door, sit straight down at my computer and write something. Before I knew what was happening, I was writing a very different kind of book, a fun one. In the afternoons, I'd read to stock up on some material that would be jiggled about in my head when I ran the next day.

I was happy. I got happier when suddenly, after years of grind, I was promoted at work, won some awards for my teaching, received some funding to undertake research and learned that the book had been auctioned. I can remember at the time wishing these things could have been spaced out, even just a little bit. Even one of them, every couple of years, would have been good tidings aplenty to sustain me for a decade.

xiii

Meanwhile, government was at it again. In 2017, tuition fees were frozen. This meant that as inflation sky-rocketed, institutions were year on year having to make do with a great deal less, all the while paying more for estates, maintenance etc. Most institutions looked to boost the numbers of foreign students, to whom they could charge higher fees. This became a lucrative solution.

Next, the fallout from Brexit. The tenor of talk about immigration and the flurry of policy announcements made the UK appear a less inviting host to students from abroad. The number had dropped by 33 per cent in February 2024 compared with that time the previous year.[44] Both factors meant that there were large gaps in university finances – even in some of the more established institutions.

Then there was the lifting of the cap, too. In most countries, if the state is contributing directly to university funds, they want to make sure that when the bill comes in, they can pay it. For this reason, for decades there had been a cap on student numbers on university courses. Any university that was too free with its offers was fined.

In 2013, David Willetts, then Minister for Universities, announced that the cap would be lifted. Because the government was now contributing so little, it no longer mattered how many students any university recruited. Let there be a 'free market' for places in universities!

The UK was not the first country in which this had happened. Australian universities had lifted their cap on student numbers several years earlier. The plan was the same there: to drive up stand-ards as universities competed with one another. Some of the unex-pected results were that the amount government was required to invest in universities suddenly jumped, from around AU$12 billion to AU$17 billion. University funding had to be cut fast and hard while student numbers grew. There was concern about the inevita-ble fall in standards.[45]

When the cap was lifted in England, what happened was that sud-denly everyone wanted to go to the places with the best branding. Across the country, millions were spent on new staff in marketing departments so that everyone could compete for students. Anyone that works in the sector could tell you what happened. Some of the greedier institutions at the upper end of the scale basically swept the table. Instead of recruiting 180 students for a course, they took 400. No extra staff were hired to teach them. Neither did they care that they couldn't all fit into a lecture theatre; they just stuck TVs up in the hallways outside. It also didn't matter that they weren't able to house them. Instead, cheaper accommodation could be found in neighbouring cities (that the students did not want to live in) and they could be brought in by bus. Some universities even offered students four-figure discounts on their fees if they would defer for a year, just to make sure no one else recruited them.

As early as 2014, universities like Exeter, UCL and Bristol had, in only three years, grown their undergraduate numbers by more than a third. The likes of London Metropolitan, Bedfordshire, Bolton, East London and Liverpool Hope, in the same time period, watched their numbers drop by 20 per cent.[46]

The idea of a market in fees never actually happened. There might be a university that charges less than the current maximum of £9,250, but if there is, I couldn't find it. The best I found was

London Met, which charges £2,310 per thirty-credit module. You have to take four of these a year for a degree, which brings the total to £9,240.

xiv

After the first book took nearly a decade to complete, the second came much easier. I'd go out for those long-ish runs and at the end would take my phone out and start adding to the book in the street. About a third of it was written standing up in Greenwich Park. A couple of years is all it took. It was called *Footnotes* and bemused some runners, who discovered it wasn't really about running at all but alienation and the disembodiedness of modernity. At the launch party, my editor, knowing my history with the book, teasingly gifted me a clothbound copy of *Far from the Madding Crowd*.

The third book, *Primate Change*, took even less time.

Both books meant I was able to do things I'd never been able to do before. I exchanged conferences for festivals, academic journal articles for journalism. I juggled teaching with TED Talks and interviews. I popped up on TV. I had a blast.

It had been a long-held ambition to make a radio programme for the BBC and the third book enabled me to make quite a few. One series took me to Singapore, Boston, Groningen, Nairobi, Sardinia and Belgium – and to tiny, inaccessible villages in the Rift Valley in Kenya.

As the final episode was airing in 2019, an email dropped in from a senior colleague at another institution. She told me she had been approached as a referee for a possible professorship.

Later that year, surfing the exam season, I was worn out and stressed. My neck was sore – as it always is at the end of an academic year, but this time it seemed worse. I was basically a walking ironing board.

I was away at another institution doing something called external examining, in which you oversee and sign off to approve the standards of said institution. I'd given my end-of-year report to a room that did its best to look interested. During the formalities that followed, I idly opened my email on my phone and the academic next to me thought I'd taken ill. 'What is it?' they whispered. 'Are you alright?'

I showed her my phone and murmured, 'I've made professor.'

She interrupted the chair of the board and called the meeting to a halt so they could applaud me. I noticed that my neck and back had stopped aching.

A few months later, the title was made official just as news of a novel virus was emerging from Wuhan.

XV

It didn't take long for the virus to arrive. Like many, I was terrified. After decades of asthma, I had the lungs of a canary. While we Muggles were in lockdown, my (now) husband worked for the London Ambulance Service. He wasn't behind a wheel but he was going into the central London offices every day.

Meanwhile, the choking of the humanities at those earlier levels really began to show. With fewer students taking English literature A-levels and GCSEs, and a demographic dip – in which the number of people of a particular age suddenly drops – the numbers were down. With the cap lifted, more established institutions began cannibalising their subjects by cleaning the table of students, leaving fewer for other universities.

Worst of all, like many universities, the services of a data-analysis company had been employed to assess the future of our discipline at mine. Dire trouble was forecast, none of which turned out to be true, but I'm sure the university paid handsomely for it.

The only way forward was that most of us would have to be made redundant. The humanities, they argued, were now trapped in a raging Helm's Deep of a battle, fighting off throngs of neo-liberal orcs all thrusting their unfeasibly long ladders at our ivory towers.

It had been a long stretch to get my neck over the line and as soon as I'd arrived, it looked like I was going to lose my job.

Friends would ask, 'Why don't you get another job?' The academic job pages were like the deserts of Tatooine. I dredged the internet. The nearest vacancy at my level was 6,000 miles away in Shenzhen.

They'd ask why I didn't just go down a level? Another reasonable suggestion. But the universities that were advertising vacancies knew it was a buyer's market. At one point, there was a single English vacancy. They wanted someone with my qualifications but written in bold typeface at the end of the advert was 'there is no guarantee of any hours'.

Most people have negotiated crises like this. I had been made redundant before; most people have been. (If I hadn't been made redundant, I would never have met nice Mr Chamberlain, for example.)

Like many others throughout the pandemic, I was readying myself to be set adrift. I was absurdly, comically over-qualified in a quirky and discrete job market, one only really interested in hiring very specialised labour that was cheap or temporary – but ideally both.

xvi

By the end of 2021, the UK housing market was experiencing unprecedented growth, with house prices rising in practically all regions except in London, where many people were departing. We were one such couple. My husband and I went for a short break in Yorkshire and discovered houses selling for half the value of our London micro-flat. It ruined the holiday because the remainder of it was spent in intense planning, leading us to quickly list our flat and sell it within days, despite numerous barriers and uncertainties ahead. We chose York, and given I was unlikely to keep my job, I knew not to base our decision of where to live on proximity to an employer. It was much better to be somewhere we loved – and a bit of me liked being 275 miles out of arm's reach of my employer. We were not alone in all this. It's estimated that about 200,000 people left the capital for similar reasons, in search of greener pastures. It was probably also for a similar reason that I encountered a sudden upturn in the number of those wanting to study the fiction and poetry of Thomas Hardy.

xvii

The size of my Hardy course doubled. Some of the pull must have been what I'd experienced in my completion of *Far from the Madding Crowd* – namely that during yet another lockdown they were craving to be in another time and another place, looking at open landscapes and sunny skies.

Few of them knew much about Hardy's background, but his background is one of the reasons I admire him as a writer and also one of the reasons I think he's perfect to teach to the young.

He was born in humble circumstances in rural Dorset, the son of a bricklayer. Despite having little opportunity, Hardy flourished academically and was sent to a local school where he excelled. He was apprenticed to a local architect but found little satisfaction or success in the profession. He was ill-suited to it.

Later in life, Hardy penned a poem, 'The Self-Unseeing', about a simple childhood full of music. Like his best, there's harmony in the verse and it's all imbued with memory and the regret of time passing.

> Here is the ancient floor,
> Footworn and hollowed and thin,
> Here was the former door
> Where the dead feet walked in.
>
> She sat here in her chair,
> Smiling into the fire;
> He who played stood there,
> Bowing it higher and higher.
>
> Childlike, I danced in a dream;
> Blessings emblazoned that day;
> Everything glowed with a gleam;
> Yet we were looking away!

As a child, Hardy had taken to music, just like his father. From his mother, he inherited a love of reading.

Hardy's first attempt at fiction failed. Despite its ambitious portrayal of class relations in the capital, *The Poor Man and the Lady* faced repeated rejections from prestigious publishers like Macmillan. So began a long and torturous tale in which no one seemed capable of simply saying 'no'.

Hardy thought it was the beginning of his writing career. He wanted a commitment, when all he kept getting was feedback. The publisher's reader's report sent to Hardy from Macmillan explained:

Much of the writing is strong and fresh. But there crops up in parts a certain rawness of absurdity that is very displeasing, and makes it read like some clever lad's dream … There is real feeling in the writing … If the man is young, there is stuff and promise in him: but he must study form and composition, in such writers as Balzac and Thackeray, who would I think come as natural masters to him.[47]

Frustrated by the response, by being sent away to do homework, Hardy instead busied himself redrafting the novel, rushing a process that he ought to have prepared better for. 'I almost feel that I don't care what happens to the book, so long as something happens,' he wrote.[48]

The whole thing failed and the manuscript was eventually burned. Hardy instead decided to work on something the publishers could sell. *Desperate Remedies* was published a couple of years later in 1871 and received harsh criticism. *The Spectator* called the novel a desperate remedy 'for ennui' and thought it so cheap and trashy in its construction that the author's only motivation for writing it must have been 'an emaciated purse'.[49] It was a wounding review that Hardy could quote at length even in old age. But importantly, he learned from it. Focusing on the modicum of praise about the depiction of rural scenes, he set his next novel in the world that he knew, among the woods and furze land of his native Dorset.

His third book, *Under the Greenwood Tree* – widely regarded as his 'first' because of its recognisable subject matter – opens with one of the best first sentences in nineteenth-century literature: 'To dwellers in a wood almost every species of tree has its voice as well as its feature.' All of Hardy as we now know him is there. This is the writer who is going to explain and translate the rural experience to an increasingly urban world. This is the writer entrusted with noticing and understanding what it means to dwell in the natural world, to see and hear and feel its sounds and rhythms.

While he would experiment with themes and settings throughout his career and it took a long time for him to become an 'established' writer, Hardy had found a voice all his own. He'd found a fictional territory. By this third book, Hardy had become a writer but he never stopped learning and never stopped working. He believed creativity was found through habit, rather than a given. In his ghost-written autobiography Hardy's second wife's name is on the spine of the book, but it is obviously written by Hardy himself in the third person – he is said to have said, 'I never let a day go without using a pen. Just holding it sets me off; in fact I can't think without it. It's important not to wait for the right mood. If you do it will come less and less.'

Success is less about talent in Hardy's case than about perseverance. For him, creativity was borne of habit not inspiration. It's a great lesson for the young. We may know him today as that grand old man of letters, a facade that Hardy worked much of his life to create, but that writer was not born; he was made.

xviii

In the past, students had rightly asked why *Far from the Madding Crowd* was missing from the module. I'd explain about not having read it, but only as a footnote to things like, 'He spent half his life as a poet. To get a rounded sense of him as a writer, we need to read the first- as well as the second-rate.' (At least we were not doing the third-rate. I'm looking at you, *A Laodicean* and *The Hand of Ethelberta*.) But something deep inside me had put the novel in a tin, wrapped it in hay and stored it away for an unnamed future.

But now, as we swung into the second lockdown, I felt that the novel's time had arrived. I had a sense that I'd drifted into the end-game, that I might never get a chance to teach it.

Reading the novel now, as a professor, seemed as neat as a sonata, ending as it had begun – with the same theme but in a different key. And so, beset by a kind of 'last-chance saloon' feeling, I set it on the course, not really considering what the impact of it might be.

I'd never lived any of my reading life when I wasn't technically *still* reading *Far from the Madding Crowd*, so was I really ready to read it? Was I ready to have read it?

It was the epitome of a first-world problem: people were dying alone in care homes, livelihoods were being lost, people were being made homeless. I was about to lose everything I'd ever really worked for.

Even though the reading of it was rushed because of the pressures of teaching and lecturing, I marvelled as I read.

On one hand, I was steeling myself for an 'experience', porten-tously closing a loop that had been open for nearly four decades. On the other hand, I was reading it 'with a pencil in my hand' (a friend's term for compulsory rather than pleasurable reading). I was reading it so I could teach it: for the detail, with an eye on signifi-cant passages that related to the rest of Hardy's career or the politics of the 1870s, looking out for what the novel told us about the rural and urban experience. I was watching out for all the things that the students really enjoy discussing, issues of class, gender, power and so on. I was marking up sections that warranted especially close reading, where the cadence and imagery was as fine as in any of his poetry.

And on every page, as I read, I was trying to recall what my fifteen-year-old self had made of any of this.

The sheep this time around seemed positively captivating. How had my fifteen-year-old self not registered the dramatic tragedy of an entire flock being harried over a precipice by an inexperienced sheep dog? Not only does the whole flock perish, but they must be the only animals in all of Hardy's work not given any identity or individuality whatsoever. Singular or plural, they are just generic 'sheep'. One of his later novels, *The Woodlanders*, opens dramatically with a long shot of a horse-drawn carriage looming over a hill. We then zoom in, but instead of our narrator accompanying us into the carriage to tell us about its passengers, this is what we are given:

> The old horse, whose hair was of the roughness and colour of heather, whose leg-joints, shoulders, and hoofs were distorted by harness and drudgery from colthood—though if all had their rights, he ought, symmetrical in outline, to have been picking the herbage of some Eastern plain instead of tugging here—had trodden this road almost daily for twenty years.[50]

The old horse gets a description, a present, a past, a future, even a self. We are acquainted with what it's like to drag a carriage while we humans (readers and wagoneers alike) recline in easy ignorance. And this is not the only place he does it. There's a luminous account of what a town looks like from a bird's perspective in *The*

Mayor of Casterbridge, where even the language used is avian in tone. Humans weren't the world for Hardy; everything was. In his fiction, everything's connected – a sobering message during a zoonotic pandemic.

xix

The students loved it. You'd think the fact they chose the course would predetermine such an outcome, but this is rarely the case.

Any reading is tainted by the need of doing it. Some of this is procrastination. But it is also the fact that, as soon as someone within an institution sets a book, a reader knows that this is an 'approved' text. No matter the themes it might explore, somebody somewhere thought this book was 'OK' and it is from that point damned with obeisance and propriety. It is the equivalent of a vapid biopic that has been made with the approval of the family. When the subtext is 'our institution has approved this message', the truth value of any book diminishes.

This is one of the key things about books. If a teenager wants to find out about sex, they can, in the space of a few seconds, access some porn on whatever device is at hand. They might think they are learning about sex and intimacy but they are not. They are learning about porn – which is, for almost everyone, a closed semiotic system, referring only to itself.

Instead, a teen might turn to Flaubert's *Madame Bovary* or Patricia Highsmith's *The Price of Salt*, Caleb Azumah Nelson's *Open Water*, Ian McEwan's *On Chesil Beach* or Ali Smith's *How to Be Both*. They will learn more about intimacy and eroticism from these books than they will from any amount of dredging the internet. I don't mean that these books are necessarily 'right' about these subjects, but they are a part of the truth, a part of it that cannot be found elsewhere.

Books, novels, fiction, poetry, they articulate things about the world that no one will tell us. And when we read them, they make us weird, they make us outcasts. Readers are weird. In a good way. For example, if you walk down the street staring at your phone, no one will say anything. But if you read *An Instance of the Fingerpost*, or some such book, while you're walking, then you get the complete gamut, from 'Oh, what are you reading?' to 'You fucking nobhead!'

On the margins is where we live. We, regualr book buyers, make up only 4 per cent of the UK's population. We speak to one another in tongues via shared metaphors and experiences. The truth is what the best books have to offer you, yet validation by an exam board signals the opposite: that this book contains things that a bunch of squares feel comfortable with you knowing... at your age. Even the finest books struggle to endure this process of literary mummification. Few recover.

The best books are obscene, irreverent, graphic, offensive. They pull your heart out and leave you changed. All the classics that everyone's heard of: Shakespeare, the Brontës, Joyce, Hardy, even Dickens were considered obscene in their time. Likewise, the list of the most-banned books of all time are all household names: *1984* by George Orwell, *The Adventures of Huckleberry Finn* by Mark Twain, *The Catcher in the Rye* by J. D. Salinger, *The Color Purple* by Alice Walker, *I Know Why the Caged Bird Sings* by Maya Angelou, *Lord of the Flies* by William Golding, *To Kill a Mockingbird* by Harper Lee.

PEN America reports that there have been more than 4,000 books banned in the US since the autumn of 2021.[51] Today, it's predominantly issues of race, gender or paganism that puts books on the naughty step in the US; whereas actually harmful things like depictions of war or gun violence are fine. Gun violence in the US was, in 2023, responsible for over 40,000 deaths.[52]

In the US, it's conservative school governors, politicians and parents that are driving the piety binge. In Hardy's time, it was the lending libraries. Books used to be prohibitively expensive – as much as a week's wage for some. Many nineteenth-century novels were borrowed from lending libraries that functioned a little bit like Netflix used to do when they loaned physical copies of films on DVD. Mudie's Lending Library, the largest of these Victorian streaming services, would simply refuse to distribute a book they considered sexually explicit.

It was this kind of censorship that made Hardy's relationship with his fiction throughout his life not what one might expect. He wasn't precious about any of it. On the whole, he worked quickly and few of the novels made it into print without him having, in some way, to compromise his message. A number of his novels have different endings depending on which version you read. Many of them have sequences that have been cut or changed. The dramatic course of some of the storylines was morally corrected to achieve censor approval. His poetry, though – he wouldn't let an editor so much as move a comma. What is on the page is what was intended. Because Hardy knew he couldn't tell the truth in his fiction, he distanced himself from it.

Far from the Madding Crowd, though, is one of the few novels that appeared unchanged. It contained no sexual assaults, no sibling murders, nothing scandalous. I think it's the book's completeness that is part of the appeal and the reason that it is still a household favourite.

xx

With the novel finally read and the class taught, I was ready for my jaunt in higher education to be over.

It was such a strange experiment to have conducted. I never thought that I would come at last to the novel only in a moment of crisis. I always imagined a sunny someday when I'd sit down to read, when I would be both the same and a different person. The novel's ending is, for Hardy at least, a happy one. But it doesn't end well for everyone. There are corpses in graves and Sergeant Troy is left to play with his sword alone on the heath.

Closing the book, I felt not so much a sense of satisfaction but one of finality and of loss. I suppose it's a bit like completing your bucket list – the process is tremendous fun but getting to the end not so much, because, well, it's the end, isn't it?

I thought about the years I'd enjoyed in academia, when, like Hardy's unseeing self, 'everything glowed with a gleam'. But clouds had gathered while I was looking away.

6 And in time there will come a generation that has got **beyond facts**, beyond impressions, a generation absolutely colourless, a generation seraphically free from taint of personality, which will see the French Revolution not as it happened, nor as they would like it to have happened, but as it would have happened, had it taken place in the days of the Machine. – E. M. Forster, 'The Machine Stops'

Dad's favourite part of a fish was the eyes. He would spear them with the tines of his fork so they burst, then one by one pop them in his mouth. We could see his masseter muscles engage, the stubble on his face glinting in the light as he crushed the eyes between his tongue and the roof of his mouth. Then he would make a show of gulping them down. As kids, we would squeal with disgusted glee, but I now wonder about the source of this habit of his. Did it go back to when he was a child? Was it a means of claiming attention in the competitive environment of a large family? Or was it that in times of leanness (he was born in 1925) delicacies were hard to come by and he had learned to make do with the performance of enjoying these leftovers?

I don't know. I'm now the age he was when he became debilitatingly ill, and I'm still no closer to understanding the mess of conflicts that he was.

He was always into his schemes. If bailiffs weren't at the door in the 1970s, come to take away the latest Jaguar, Merc or Daimler he'd convinced some poor sod of selling him on hire-purchase, then we'd have ducks strung up on our kitchen door, blood draining from their beaks, because he'd swapped them for a driving lesson or some such thing.

When I catch myself in these kinds of behaviours, on a depressed spending spree or working some complex scheme, I dwell on this inheritance. I think, *I hope*, that my distinguishing characteristic is laughter. But when I feel my blood boil at some minor slight, it's my father that I think about.

He would want his distinguishing feature to be his intelligence and aptitude, but it was his temper. The second most distinguishing: jealousy. Together, they are like mixing a binary explosive.

I have one photo of him as a child, sat on the lap of some uncle. Legs astride and scowling at something off-camera. What is striking for me about this photo is the lack of warmth. It's not the serious faces – even though photos in which the subjects smile were increasingly common in this period – but the pose and manner. Presumably, the clan have all dressed up for this portrait, yet there isn't an ounce of familial tenderness to be seen. My great grandmother, presumably born in the 1860s, looks worldly wise, stern and forbidding at the far right. My father's mother is broad-shouldered and strong as a wing forward in rugby. She looks like she has no time for any of this as her eyes look inquisitively down the lens at us, looking back at her from the future. His cousins look like ones you'd very much regret beating at dice down the pub. From that day, down through to a century later, these are the connections and impressions that group sought to preserve.

I wonder what his childhood was like? I look at him in this

picture and hope to see some trace of the life he'd go on to live and the damage it wrought. He looks impatient here. Wilful, like the back of his shirt had to be gathered into his uncle's fist before being dragged onto his lap. His younger siblings seem docile and obedient by comparison.

Taken around 1931

He stands out in the picture. He's not dressed like anyone else and his facial expression is different too. He doesn't look like he belongs, and perhaps that is what he always sought, trying so many things, travelling so far and living in so many places. In the scored lines of that scowl is the future decorated police sergeant, the local hero that saved drowning children and disarmed dangerous drunks. While recuperating from injury in the line of service, he took up chess to pass the time and went on to play for his country in the Olympiads, becoming Irish Chess Champion in 1961 and '62. Meanwhile, he penned several hundred poems of varying quality, but some were good. And yet, and yet... He created chaos wherever he went. He went to prison at least twice and nearly ruined our lives.

I look at this picture and wonder what would he have made of his son, the gay English professor?

i

During the summer, his mum blanks out one day a week in her diary to do something with the kids. She is readying them and herself on one of these days when the phone rings. It is a prospective pupil for driving lessons. He's asking her if she can give him his driving licence. She explains that she cannot; it doesn't work that way. But she can help him fill in the forms. He lives nearby so she invites him round. If he is quick, he might catch them before they head off to Lytham St Annes for a day by the seaside.

She is herding the children down the path to manoeuvre them into the car when around the corner, a vision appears.

A tall man emerges in a kaftan and towering white head gear, robes billowing in the breeze as he walks. He wears long, pointed shoes that curl up at the toe and at the heel. She sees him in an instant and decides to distract the boy, steering him behind the short garden wall she will later clamber over, fleeing for her life.

There is no deterring the boy's curiosity, though. His interest is piqued from the moment he hears the man's voice. They start talking business. Within seconds, his articulate voice is loud enough to be heard the other side of the street.

'Mummy.'

If she ignores him, she might be able to make it through this transaction without friction and get on her way.

'Mummmmeeeeee.'

She knows from the timbre in his voice she's going to lose this one. Now it's only a matter of how long she can get him to hold out.

'Mummmmmmeeeeeeeeee.' More music in it this time.

She surrenders, but hits the ball back over the net with a 'I wonder where your sisters have got to?'

But he's not having any of it. And louder again, he cries. 'Mummy, is that—'

She implores the man to come again: 'Perhaps next week when the children are back at school.'

Then loudest of all: 'Mummy, is that man a queen?'

ii

He is the youngest, this ragged bundle of misunderstanding, broken ideas and fragmentary sense impressions. He is so distant from me, the 'he' before reading made its mark, it's like he's another person. He is spoilt but not a brat; shy but occasionally enjoying the spotlight, especially if he's dancing in it. He has a mop of brown hair so dark it looks black, skin so tanned the last thing he looks is Irish. His mother calls him 'Little Jai', Tarzan's diminutive sidekick from the TV show.

He nearly left the country when the family went on holiday to Jersey. The six of them piled into a car and drove for what felt like a week. Then a boat. Then a hotel.

At the hotel reception, he's plonked down on the treacle-varnished counter as his mum checks in.

'That's two rooms.'

He's not listening. Instead he is eyeing the bell, trying to resist chiming it like they do on telly.

The receptionist continues, 'Two adults and three children.'

The error brings him to his senses. 'No', he pipes up. 'No, it's four. Four children.'

The receptionist explains with a smile, 'Yes, there are four of you, but we are only counting children five or over. Children up to four are free.'

'But I'm five,' he lies.

His mother interjects, 'No, he's really four. He really is four.'

'No, I'm five. And my name's David.'

'He's not,' his mum says to the receptionist. 'He's really four. His name's not David. He just wants a normal name.'

Her interest piqued: 'Oh, what is his name?'

'That is an interesting name.' She turns to the boy. 'Where's that from?'

But he's lost interest and is now watching the people across the lobby walk into a metal coffin then disappear, like in a magic trick.

iii

Later in the holiday, some of them go on a tour of an old hospital. The rooms are drab and grey. The bedframes in the wards are vacated and rusty. There are bullet holes in the walls. Were the patients shot? Why would they be shot? Why would you need to shoot sick people? Real bullets. The war was real then, not just something from comics like cowboys. Whoever invented cowboys must be very rich, he thinks.

The hotel has everything. After dinner, in the basement of the hotel, there is a disco. Coloured lights flash on the empty dance floor. It's 6.30 p.m. and the children have an hour before it becomes adults only.

His mum and siblings goad him to dance for them. He doesn't want to. On and on they go. Why don't they dance?

'We'll have to go to bed soon,' they say. 'We've only got half an hour.'

He watches the DJ cueing up records. He has dozens of them. How can owning and playing records be a job?

'Dance. Go on.'

His mum says, 'If you dance, I'll give you anything you want.'

'Anything?'

'Anything!'

The boy considers the offer a little too swiftly. 'If he plays "Changes" by David Bowie, I'll dance.'

The two sisters jet across the dance floor, their arms straight, hands as rigid as fins, so as to move as swiftly as possible. They whisper into the DJ's ear. They scuttle back across the empty space like they are running across lava.

'He's going to do it. He's going to play it. You've got to dance now.'

The song fades. Through the diminuendo, the major-seventh chord that he knows so well sounds. The chord is perfect; its failure to resolve is the very essence of the idea of the song.

By the time the second chord sounds, he's on his little feet. By the time the backbeat drops, he's already on the empty dance floor. He shakes his hips, points, performs arabesques, a few spins. The beat often drops out but this is of no concern to him. It's then he can hear them clap and roar. He dips, swizzles, glides and curves through all of it. By the time of the stuttering chorus, everyone in the disco is watching and nothing can stop him.

Perhaps wanting to curtail the little boy's embarrassment, a few stragglers get up to join him on the dance floor. This is the wrong thing to do. Instead of being lost in his reverie, he throws up his hands, clearing them off the space. It belongs to him now. Only when he gets to the end of the song is anyone else allowed to join him, like it's a wedding and he's marrying the music.

iv

'Isn't that a girls' school?' they'd say – like that was a bad thing. Every time he told someone, anyone, that they went to The Hollies, he'd always get the same line. It was co-ed but only up to the age of seven. Once there was any chance of a boy getting within a pube's distance of adolescence, they were siphoned off to an all-boys' Catholic school across town, where they could sweat and stink and not brush their teeth through puberty. The boys at The Hollies were only ever walk-on parts. They were permitted to join in at skipping but on sufferance. It was the girls that had all the ceremony and tradition. They had indoor and outdoor shoes, like characters in Jane Austen. They had summer and winter uniforms. They had elocution lessons from which they'd emerge at playtime, index fingers in their mouths like they were about to blow their brains out. Then, popping the digit from their mouth on the plosive, they'd sound out the elongated vowels of 'sP-ooooooooon'.

v

He dances with his sisters at their school disco. He's so small, they are the ones that do the lifting when they jive. They have the strength to throw him up, down, across and around their bodies. The nuns watch from the sidelines, big smiles on their faces.

He loves the darkness and the noise of the discos. He likes discos so much, he pens acrostic lyrics to his own song 'D.i.s.c.o.'

vi

Mum drives the four kids to school in the morning. On the street, the snow is as high as his waist. It's midwinter but his mum is wearing sunglasses so large they cover half her face. They climb into their car and head off, bound for the land of the nuns.

In the back, the boy's legs flap to and fro, dangling from the rear seats. He strains to see from the frost-emblazoned window. He works his fingertips into the skeuomorphic plastic-moulded stitching that borders the seats. As he picks at it, he listens to them speed-praying because it's less than a couple of miles to school. He plunges deep into the prayers' rhythm while only paddling in the shallows of their meaning.

They do a Hail Mary and he is loud and confident in joining in with this one. Next, the Lord's Prayer, where he stumbles on the sibilants of repeated 'tresspasses', never entirely sure of how many syllables the word has. There is another car staple. It has a familiar lexis but doesn't make sense – but then, the others don't either. He knows a bit about being 'into a session' and there is a bit with a cool metaphor for eternity: I will love you 'O Virgin of virgins' and I will love you for all time until 'before the ice stands'. Before the ice stands? It makes him think of a tundra, barren except for a ziggurat constructed of giant blocks of ice.

Many years later, when he is writing a book about it, he will look up the prayer and discovered it begins, 'Never was it known that anyone who fled to thy protection, implored thy help, or sought thy *intercession*, was left unaided'. There is nothing in the Memorare prayer that refers to 'ice' of any kind. The line is not in the least metaphorical. It is a simple cry for help, a daily incantation of hope that someone somewhere might be listening: 'To thee do I come, *before thee I stand*, sinful and sorrowful. O Mother of the Word Incarnate, despise not my petitions, but in thy mercy hear and answer me.'

Perhaps with five voices reciting such an intercession, there was a greater likelihood that the gracious Virgin Mary might hear and answer her before the ice stands.

vii

She takes the kids to church on Sunday. It used to be that they walked round the corner to the local one but they now go to several and have recently begun driving all the way to the back streets of central Manchester to a magical little place called The Hidden Gem. For some reason, his father doesn't come with them to church. He goes out, sometimes to teach a learner driver, sometimes just 'out'.

To the boy, the hour-long services feel like an eternity when they are sat through in the knowledge that games are being missed on the street. The children know it well enough to recognise that the length of the service rides on how long the priest takes to tell his story. This is the only bit of the entire service that his mum doesn't whisper along to in sync with the priest. After the story bit there's Communion, but he's too young for that. Once people have eaten of the body of Christ, it's the closing straight. In the minutes of silence following Communion, the silence in the church is heavy with muted prayers of thanks, pleas of not being worthy. One day during this, his sisters begin to whisper. They are for it, he thinks. Their heads turn to look behind them, more urgent whispers. Then, in a surprise move, one of them whispers something to his mum. This time he catches the hiss of it: 'He's here!' Like a family of meerkats looking for a predator, the five of them glance about. Perhaps a dozen rows back sits his father. He has followed them the six miles into town, not to join them but to watch.

viii

A few weeks later, his mother is hospitalised with head injuries. She's gone for weeks. The kids are scooped up by social services. The boys and girls are separated. In a mansion in the way of institutional gothic, the brothers are shown their beds. They are told to bathe. Father in custody, mother in hospital, sisters gone, strangers and 'bad' kids running wild on the other side of a door with no lock on it. The rest of their stay is a blank in his memory, like he'd run full pelt into a fist.

The Yorkshire Ripper had only a few weeks before attacked a woman with a hammer in a neighbouring suburb, but despite the similarities, the police aren't much interested. They know who did it and could see through his transparent attempt to pass the blame to the notorious murderer. But there's no proof and he won't confess.

The parents of friends volunteer to take the children in. For weeks, they holiday in the lives of other, more settled families. Other parents have normal jobs, which mean they are around evenings and weekends.

She returns from hospital all bandages, like a mummy. She has to wear head scarves to keep all the dressings in place. The boy thinks it is to stop her skull from falling open.

His mum takes a few days off but is back to work as soon as she's upright. When she's out, they're in. They are under strict instructions not to answer the door to anyone. The cars outside the house have gone, but who knows what his dad has been up to? The bailiffs might call any time for anything. There were two parents; now there seem to be none.

ix

One day, she's out on a driving lesson and the children are upstairs doing nothing when their stomachs collectively swoop at the sound of a man's voice, calling to them up the stairs. They freeze like gazelles unsure if they've spied movement in the long grass.

Then the voice starts saying their names. The boy watches as the rest of them scatter, quiet as deer. They pull detritus from under the beds, climb in and pull it back in place. They lie in the dark, unable to hear over the sound of blood thudding in their ears. Nothing.

Then the voice calls up through the house again, louder this time, with a touch more aggression, like it knows they are here, like it recognises their disobedience in not responding. Then again, even louder this time.

'It's Danny,' one of them says in relief. He feels like he's been granted a pardon on the scaffold. Danny! Danny from across the road. Danny, the son of the German-Jewish immigrant Mrs Bernstein, who crossed the Channel on a raft in the war when she was a little girl. Danny who babysits them. Danny, who is so strong he lifts them up on his flexed biceps like the Incredible Hulk. It's just Danny. The children scrabble out into the light and patter down the stairs to greet him.

x

The weeks pass in a blur, or maybe they're months. He wakes one morning to find his mum has gone. It all happened while he was in a thick, dark sleep. His father had arrived in the middle of the night bearing a can of petrol and a shotgun. He smashed his way into the house and made his way upstairs to her bedroom. It was locked, so he proceeded to kick it down. The doors were heavy, though. In time they would give, but not yet. It bought her a little time to come up with a plan. She opened her window, no wider than her waist. As he came through the door, she was seated on the edge and ready to go. She jumped.

When she landed in the front of the house, she crumpled and broke. Then, like some Amazon warrior, she stood. She saw lights across the street and clambered, stumbling towards neighbours already roused by the noise. She fled over the road to a family who gave her sanctuary until the police and ambulance arrived.

The dad was gone. She was hospitalised with a catalogue of injuries including two vertebrae crushed to gravel.

Arrests, courts, sentences, all of it happens in the background. He is aware that his father has gone to prison but is unsure what for or for how long.

xi

I still wonder about that petrol can. What was it for? Did he not need it or did he not get to that part of his plan? It amazes me how quickly it was all forgotten, that a decade later, once he was infirm, some of us shared a house with him. What an insult!

My mum did more than her best for us. In the space of a few weeks, her life suddenly narrowed to providing for four open mouths. She recovered but didn't so much develop scar tissue as armour.

She was self-employed in a precarious job, without sick pay, paid holiday, private health etc., all the while working *around* the 9–5 office hours of her pupils. And this is part of the problem of what we expect of women, that first and foremost they should always be doting and loving mothers. Was she supposed to do this while working precariously, full-time, to feed, clothe and shelter four children? Was it her responsibility to always be kind, indulgent and patient, while doing everything else as well? There were many times in my life when, selfishly, I have felt this way. As I get older, though, I admire her spirit, tenacity and determination more and more.

But none of that made it OK at the time. No amount of making up the difference or filling in can compensate for something that is just missing. Not for a second am I saying they ought to have stayed together. It's more a self-pitying desire, a plea: couldn't we just have had the chess master and the poet, minus the jealousy, deception and violence?

Invariably, when people talk about a seemingly unattractive aspect of someone's personality, you can think about what those things also give them. If one of your friends is tiresome because they always overreact to things, they are also the best people to give good news to. If you know someone who is a bit sensitive, that needs to be managed, they are probably also the most empathetic of people. What did the jealousy and violent temper do for my dad or the people around him except ruin their lives and his?

While many of the things he did, he didn't do to me (or to us), he still cued me up to become the teenager that I became, the one that was nearly lost. He was the one that left us vulnerable to be picked off by paedophiles wheedling their way into family lives with the same dexterity as they undo the drawstrings on a pair of trunks. It was my dad that served us up to these people.

And all of it makes the fact that some of us gravitated towards my dad and later lived in his house all the harder to understand. It certainly wasn't because I forgave him. It was because I was an adolescent. Our house was not easy to be a teenager in and neither was it easy to be a mother in. I went towards my dad because it was easier to be there than at home and I was nothing if not selfish and lazy. Moreover, I went to him because I was greedy and he occasionally gave me a fiver, because he never nagged me about anything, because he was happy to see me, because I misunderstood his lack of concern and interest in my schooling for paternal care. If grief is the latter part of love, then the fact that the world felt odd after his death, rather than empty, speaks volumes.

xii

What if I hadn't have got it back? Where would I be? Still failing to persuade drunks not to punch me? I'm not criticising the status of those jobs; it's not that they aren't worthwhile, just that I was unhappy and frustrated in them and without the faculties necessary to succeed. I am grateful to them, though, because it was those jobs that gave me the grit I needed. I didn't have any particular talent for reading or for literature; I just saw myself in a room one day surrounded by books, swimming in them, and teaching others too. So, I moved towards that.

I think I got it back because I have lucky genes. I might have that high ACE score, but I obviously benefited from other things, too – sufficiently so as to negate the damage. We might not have had much as kids but, for example, I was only around adults that cared deeply and believed fundamentally in the value of education. We may have eaten apple or sugar sandwiches, but that belief in education proved to be a kind of affluence I didn't recognise at the time but was still the beneficiary of. I might have taken a circuitous route, but with the right faculties, and eventually the right environment, I got there at last. Without tenacity, I'd be nowhere.

I might have inherited brains from both parents, but look where my dad's intellectual powers got him. Intelligence is no use unless it's buttressed by other faculties like tenacity. I get my tenacity from my mum. Nobody taught me to keep going like she did. And I never remember her once saying it, just doing it.

xiii

I've thought a great deal about sharing what I have. Some of it is deeply personal and much of it is not known, even to my friends. My motive for sharing is not for a 'hasn't he done well', for I can see any number of ways in which dropping the mask will work against me professionally. For me, though, the scale of what is happening to the humanities and how much it matters to me is worthy trade. I have shared what I have because I wanted to make the strongest possible case, not only for the transformative nature of a humanities education, not just to articulate the tremendous power of reading to change us and the world around us, but also because it grieves me that our privatised and monetised education system is not one that permits second chances or genuinely fosters social mobility.

You might balk at the idea of using something so personal to make a case for the value of English, the arts and all things extra-curricular. But that is the point: what is it if it's not personal? These subjects, just like others, respond to people's differences. Some need science, some computing or maths, others (like the ranting Simon Pegg) less so. You cannot make someone do something they don't want to do. You can push them, but you just make them miserable. What is it if it's not personal? To the 93 per cent of children in the UK that attend a state school, the curriculum is about as personal as you get.

What would happen to people like me coming of age today? If I wanted to study something like English, I'd have to be prepared to take on a minimum of £30,000 of debt. This is assuming that I don't accrue additional debt through study (most students take on an additional £10,000 per year). For my master's degree, that's another £12,000. For my DPhil or doctorate, that's another £36,000. That's £76,000 of fee debt, at which point there are a wealth of university-level jobs that don't even promise any hours. I've excluded the debt accrued for living expenses, which across a minimum of seven years of education would be about the same again. How long would it take someone to repay that debt? And if that amount of money is unimaginable to you, who would do that? They would have to possess Matt Hancock levels of self-confidence in their abilities. The likelihood of ever paying such an amount back seems small, and someone who accrued it would be servicing that debt throughout their professional lives.

My confidence grew slowly. I made decisions year-on-year based on my performance, not my confidence. Others in a similar situation might feel that they had something to prove, but I had no idea how far I'd be able to go. My confidence had to be teased out like a dog kept too long in kennels. Knowing these numbers at the outset would have meant I would never have considered the option of university. Who would?

Books found me. I was privileged enough to have the faculties and the means to pursue them, to build this life. How many people have been lost because of these outrageous fees and debts? How many were not able to do what they might have because they were deterred?

xiv

From the first year in which tuition fees were introduced, the proportion of mature students began to drop.[1] This has been disastrous for institutions that focused specifically on social mobility and widening participation. Those specialising in mature students and teaching people to retrain to become university professors or barristers – places like the Open University and Birkbeck – have been plunged into chaos since about 2010. Like many, those places have had numerous organisational restructures, staff will have taken voluntary redundancies or left, 'unprofitable' departments will have been closed or merged. Bereft degree students sit through courses that are being 'taught out', meaning that no new students are coming in behind them: most of the staff have been sacked but a miserable skeleton crew are retained to finish off the remaining students, then they will be sacked, too. All this while columnists pen articles titled 'We should cheer the decline of humanities degrees'. Never mind that these journalists attended private schools that cost over £30,000 per year before going up to Oxford and think that social mobility is something to do with the availability of e-scooters.

xv

While I was writing this book, I was excited to learn about a new funding stream for higher education about to launch in 2025. Its driver was that it would remove the 'equivalent or lower qualification' restriction from current loans. Previously, someone that had studied anything at degree level could not retrain as a nurse or doctor without self-funding because they already possessed a qualification at that level. This new funding scheme remedied the situation.

I thought, 'At last, someone is doing something to help those who want a second chance.'

Then I read about it.

When it was first announced, the scheme's title was the Lifelong Loan Entitlement. Perhaps the name telegraphed too extensively that government was only interested in money, so it was later changed to the Lifelong Learning Entitlement.

The Lifelong Learning Entitlement provides 'all new learners with a tuition fee loan entitlement to the equivalent of four years of post-18 education to use up to the age of 60. This would be £37,000 in current fees.'[2] 'Repayment terms for these loans are the same as for current higher education undergraduate student loans.'[3]

xvi

There is a strong social aspect in all of this. We are not a particularly happy society at the moment. Young people are disappearing under waves of debt. There has also been a catastrophic decline of trust in democratic institutions. Chucking out the humanities will only worsen this situation. Degrees like English teach students to read closely, to read and to think critically, to do so with honesty and integrity, with faithfulness to the tenor of the source materials. It's often the case that there are no 'right' answers. This matters for democracy because graduates of all kinds are less susceptible to misinformation shared on social media, for example.[4] We live in a world in which false stories travel farther and faster than real ones. A humanities graduate, a trained critical thinker, will want to know where the information came from. Is it a reliable source? What other evidence is there? Is that evidence trustworthy? Can they find evidence of falsehood? In this way, education and specifically a humanities education is of real social value. The line between democracy and the humanities is so yin and yang that their interdependence starts to look like indistinguishability. Critical thinking, civic engagement, ethical awareness, cultural understanding and historical perspective all are essential for a healthy democracy and the humanities contribute to and encourage all of these.

I love the uncertainty that the humanities, and English in particular, foster. Shakespeare is not in the business of delivering certainty. He elevates drama into art by, among other things, presenting a particular situation or philosophical problem and asking us to think about it. It's what I love about literature. The best of it is never done. Once something is decoded and completed, it's dead. Great literature never lets this happen. A play like *Hamlet* is still here because it is part of a conversation that is still ongoing after 400 years. The philosopher Bertrand Russell said, 'One of the painful things about our time is that those who feel certainty are stupid, and those with any imagination and understanding are filled with doubt and indecision.'[5] Russell was writing about the mood in post-war Europe but for me he says something about the innate value of uncertainty. It's like a hunger. An incomplete understanding of something draws you further in to investigate more, whereas certainty invites you to look away because there is nothing more to see. Certainty is the crutch of the inexperienced. A love of literature teaches you that.

As we push ever harder towards STEM, just like sending 40 per cent of eighteen-year-olds to university, there is going to come a point of diminishing returns. Those who are talented at STEM are probably already doing STEM. If you push more and more young people to do those subjects, they are unlikely to be as good, as they won't share the same natural abilities. It's the same as pushing ever-higher percentages of young people through the gates of universities and expecting the same results. At that point, having a population that is curious about the world, that is 'into' something other than having any number of facts at their disposal, is going to be a good thing for everyone. Humanities graduates know how to go and get stuff. They know how to research, to gen up on something and how to deploy what they've learned in persuasive terms. AI is coming for us fast, but at the moment, its prose is still covered in that adjectival lacquer that gives it away. Moreover, the way that the large language models work means they are not going to be reliable research tools for the foreseeable future. We need people with humanities skills.

xvii

But why study something that is not real? Literature has done plenty for people in the past. It has created parallel worlds for us. Try-out places that we can investigate. We can step into the Harlem Renaissance in New York in Toni Morrison's *Jazz* or central Europe gripped by the pathological scientism of the Enlightenment in Mary Shelley's *Frankenstein*. These worlds provide important psychological, physiological, sociological and political functions for us. We need these worlds.

The one thing that drives me crazier than celebrities publishing children's books is when people idly assert 'but fiction isn't real'. How are *The Handmaid's Tale* or *1984* not real when everyone has heard about them? When people read and are shocked by them, then go on to think or argue about them, when they are filmed and then broadcast in over a hundred countries, translated into a hundred languages? When the books sell in their millions, as their iconography becomes part of the cultural landscape, as their metaphors make their way into our language, as they are used to understand the sometimes-dubious motives of our leaders, to make sense of our personal lives, to translate the world for us?

Or when, in the Victorian period, Charles Dickens's *Oliver Twist* or Charles Kingsley's *The Water-Babies* were used to germinate and inform parliamentary debates about the new Poor Laws or child labour laws respectively? Or when Toni Morrison's *The Bluest Eye* is singled out as inspiration to a generation of black writers called to arms by the Black Lives Matter protests?[6]

Or when novels like Angie Thomas's *The Hate U Give* or Chinua Achebe's *Things Fall Apart* are removed from school libraries in the US or when novels like E. M. Forster's *Maurice* or Nella Larsen's *Passing* never make it into them. What about those works of fiction that rewire neural circuitry? How is any of this *NOT* real? When works of fiction were burned in the streets of prewar Germany, it wasn't paper and ink being torched; it was ideas and stories.

On the level of imagination, the existence of fiction is a persistent reminder that for most of us, this world as it is simply isn't enough. The evolutionary depth of storytelling in our species also tells us that it never was. We need regularly to exercise our capacity to move and explore beyond it. Fiction articulates the deep-seated belief that this world can be other than it is. Novels, the best of them, represent a slit in the curtain of reality, and via their pages we can sidle one of our limbs through and tentatively feel our way into those other minds, imaginations and lives. This cultural output is very real and informs key social functions.

xviii

Where are the universities in all this? The economic imperative is having a twofold effect. Firstly, it is having an effect on students and their parents, who see universities as a conduit for securing high-paid employment. Secondly, it is having an effect on the way that universities themselves understand their role in society. Most now see themselves as institutions that are economically driven, as businesses that need to be efficient and marketable rather than simply being good at what they do. The market and survey culture that now dominates has skewed their efforts. Everyone wants to maximise their student survey scores. Some institutions tweak their regulations so that it is almost impossible for students to fail or drop out and do what they can to massage their figures for graduate employment rates. They do this because of pressures from a government with its hand up the sock of the Office for Students. While much of it is well intentioned, there isn't all that much difference between some institutions and those addled primary school teachers prepping their kids for the phonics screening check. Everyone is teaching to the test and how much that has to do with 'quality' is questionable.

It's as if nothing matters unless it's numerical. We live in a world that is increasingly equating value with that which is quantifiable. Experiences, values, ideas and skills that cannot be atomised to fit into our increasingly mathematical reality are written off because they cannot be quantitatively interpreted by a survey. The feelings you derive from a marriage proposal, a Picasso or Schubert's 21st piano sonata in B-flat are not quantifiable and as such are not a) trusted or b) valued. The assignation of numbers to things is so naturalised that we cannot think of a world in which they didn't exist.

In the history of universities, we assume that since their inception, a thousand years ago, students have been having their essays marked and have been departing institutions with grades. This is not so. The very first instance of a student's paper being graded occurred as recently as 1792 at Cambridge University. Keith Hoskin, a professor of accounting, has called this 'the major single step towards a mathematized model of reality'.[7] Quantifiability has become so ingrained in our thoughts around education that it seems impossible to understand what universities did for the 800 years in which essays were not marked.

With the levels of government interference, what universities are reducing themselves to is just another school, another obstacle to be clambered over before the student's 'real life' commences. It's one of the reasons why students pay to go to university, then don't attend class. (This happens more than you think – but it's also because some of them have one, two or three jobs.) Is this what we want our universities to be, something that students are shoved into after sixth form?

Universities are at risk of becoming the seventh form, an extension of formal schooling that continues from A-levels and segues straight into the workplace. But this is disingenuous. Universities cannot be the seventh form because the variety of work they undertake is so much greater than schools. It was a university that co-produced the Covid vaccine. A university worked with stonemasons on the restoration of a rather weather-worn York Minster Cathedral. An engineering lecturer came up with FM radio. Seatbelts in cars, the same. A masters' student at Sussex University worked out that police cars should park diagonally at the scenes of accidents as it improved visibility for oncoming traffic. Universities undertake such a variety of work that it is difficult to explain to someone that only wants to hear the answer to 'but what job can you get' and assessing the value of it accordingly.

That said, universities need to lean in a lot harder to become more accessible to everyone. They could do a much better job of engaging their local communities and educating them in the work it is that they do. But why would they, when they are in receipt of so little public money?

xix

Who are the beneficiaries of a humanities education? The obvious one is the individual. They are the one who is educated; they are the one whose earning potential increases across their lifetime. People with university-level education live longer (as much as ten years longer – analysis also suggests not attending school is as harmful to longevity as smoking).[8] As higher earners, they also contribute a higher proportion of their salary in tax. Tax that once funded the education they are now paying for.

Secondly, universities are an obvious beneficiary. Across the sector, they have expanded hugely in the last two decades as cash has flowed into them. Besuited vice chancellors with sensible haircuts and conservative dress have their pictures taken outside the new buildings that have sprung up on their campuses. Vice chancellor salaries have risen, nay exploded, outpacing both inflation and the pay of their staff, which has fallen hugely in real terms. Meanwhile, herb walls have been erected. Digitised access systems have been put in place. Libraries look more like airport terminals than quiet places for study.

Third, and this might be the biggest beneficiary, are the employers. Industry leaders have the ear of government, and they get to dictate their needs so that university education can be refashioned to their desires.

Finally, society. When English students go on to become English teachers (as many of them do), that benefits society at the most basic level, but even if they enter IT, healthcare, the police, the civil service or even retrain as a heating engineer or a plumber, they are contributing to society. Society is always the winner when it comes to having an educated populace.

While everyone benefits from an educated population, the bill is slipped to the graduate, as they register with horror what a staggeringly expensive meal it was that they were just stuck with.

Employers benefit most from university education, yet contribute nothing. For a group with such political influence, this is surprising. If an employer is profiting from someone's education, couldn't they contribute to their student loan in the same way that they contribute to their employee's pension? Couldn't some of their profits be used in this way? For reference, in 2022 Amazon US earned $225 billion (billion!) in net profit.[9] The total of all (private, federal, even parental) student loans taken out in the US in that year was $94.7 billion.[10] What about using some of that? Instead of, you know, buying a rocket and seeing if you can get into space with it for fun, during a climate crisis.

Currently £20 billion is loaned to around 1.5 million higher education students in England each year.[11] That is a lot of money to find. But we are not trying to find all of it, so let's look for £15 billion. For context, the UK government spent £9.9 billion on unusable PPE during the pandemic. The test and trace system that was put in place to avert a second lockdown, which failed, cost £29 billion. Unthinkable amounts of money for basically nothing. The current estimated economic and social costs of mental health are estimated at £300 billion.[12] The groups most affected are disproportionately women and men aged between sixteen and thirty-four. Relieving the debt burden in this group only needs to claw back a fraction of this for the entire costs of a generation to be met.

My feeling, after all this, is that the individual should contribute to the cost of their education but that what we are doing at the moment to our young people is worse than the Stanford prison experiment, which was at least over eventually. This time, the older folks have been given uniforms and truncheons and have decided to charge the young for something that was always free to them.

Why don't the old folks chip in a bit? Why not add 1–2 per cent to the higher earners' income tax, charge the students a 'European-style' fee, introduce generous caps on numbers and we can forget about the whole thing? It's not hard.

A part of me feels like the government wants some universities to go bankrupt, if only to prove that they were right about them all along. I'm thinking of a city and its university, a fictional one. Skintbridge University does well, with about 50,000 students. The population of the city of Skintbridge is about 200,000. Skintbridge, in recent years, has lost tens of millions after it invested heavily in the overseas-student market. The banks foreclosed and the university is out of business. Now what happens? The teaching staff all lose their jobs, as you'd expect. But what about the students that have already commenced their degrees? They can't go to a neighbouring institution because there wouldn't be space for them. Complex litigation and legal actions would ensue. What about all the professional support staff; what about hospitality, estates, tech support? They would all go too. A minimum of half a billion pounds would disappear from the local economy and Skintbridge is not a large city.[13] Landlords would be without tenants. Shops without customers. And what would the electorate do? If politicians see universities going bust as indicative of a healthy market, then they do so in that same stubborn, mistaken knowledge that universities are just like businesses.

xx

What should we do with the university system? One option is to tear the whole thing down. Universities now bear little relation to what they were conceived as being. Their first purposes in the medieval period were to provide advanced education in theology, law, medicine and what today would be called liberal arts, which attempts to create well-rounded individuals through the cultivation of critical thinking and a broad understanding of various disciplines. They were about the transmission of knowledge in a world where it was possible, in one's lifetime, to read most of all available books. An important part of university was the scholarly community. These were not 'the good old days', though. The university system, until recently, was elitist in the extreme. As the new breed of universities began to sprout in the late nineteenth and early twentieth centuries, these were explicitly for those men (for it was men) who sought to improve themselves. Scholarship and social mobility have run in tandem in the university system ever since, with the latter taking on an expanding purpose and remit within institutions. But the idea of a university as a time and place devoted to advanced study has persisted throughout.

What has changed dramatically in the last thirty years is the level of government interference in universities, in how they are supposed to teach, in what the researchers are supposed to be researching.

Interference in teacherly content has been rife and has got

considerably worse since the Higher Education and Research Act of 2017. The aim of it was to 'create more competition and choice that will promote social mobility', to 'boost productivity in the economy', to 'ensure students receive value for money from their investment in higher education' and to 'strengthen the UK's research and innovation sector'.[14] Skipping over many of the specifics, the act resulted in the creation of the Office for Students (OfS).

The OfS has driven much of the change in recent years that has seen increased focus on employability – a catch-all term for the inculcation of skills, knowledge and attributes that make an individual suitable for the workplace. It encompasses not only technical skills related to a specific job but also soft skills such as communication, teamwork and problem solving. There is nothing wrong with this – such skills acquisition is embedded in every humanities degree. But the OfS always wants more and, as a result, entire lectures are given over to 'employability' events, and the students mostly hate them. I feel for the students, I really do. On the one hand, they are paying big fees and don't want but need a return on their investment. On the other hand, they are also paying to get away from all this, for just a brief interlude before a lifetime of work overwhelms them.

The focus on employability is now so total across degrees that universities are fundamentally different places. Polytechnics might have been granted university status in 1992, but with the focus on vocationalism, today's universities are being turned back into polytechnics in all but name.

The result is that nobody now trusts the OfS. It is supposed to be politically independent, but a recent review by the House of Lords Industry and Regulators Committee found that the OfS

has poor relations with both providers and students, a controlling and arbitrary approach to regulation, and a lack of independence from the Government … The OfS is meant to be an independent regulator and describes itself as such. Yet we found that it lacks both real and perceived independence, with its actions often appearing driven by political priorities. The fact that the OfS Chair continues to take the Conservative Party whip in the House of Lords has not helped.

Furthermore, they concluded that

the Government has also contributed to this situation, by being too prescriptive in the guidance it sends to the OfS. The situation has been worsened by the fact that the OfS has had to work with seven Education Secretaries and six Universities Ministers since 2018.[15]

Burn.

xxi

From interference in teaching to meddling in research.

There was a fairly horrific moment in the 2010s when the then government mandated that the Arts and Humanities Research Council (AHRC) allocate funds to projects promoting the study of the 'big society', a concept championed by Prime Minister David Cameron.[16] It was as if academics were an army of drones who could be set to work upon, and provide depth for, a Tory Party slogan from a campaign brochure. The research money given to the humanities was already a paltry 3 per cent of the entire budget, and now even that was being harnessed for political purposes.

And why is every discussion that is had about universities always about money, value for money, funding, or whether or not they do valuable research that has 'impact'?

It brings to mind the Haldane principle, established over a century ago: that it is researchers themselves who are best at deciding what research needs to be done and whether or not it requires funding. Instead, universities now exist in this hinterland in which nobody is really sure who is making the decisions any more. If academics are being told that they cannot make headway in their careers without research funding (as many of them are) and that research funding is awarded to projects that have demonstrable 'impact' beyond academia, then researchers are going to tailor their projects around things that are likely to have the most impact. This sounds reasonable, until you think about it for about three seconds.

How can a researcher anticipate the impact of their research? If we think about some obvious leaps forward in knowledge and technology, I don't believe that Judith Butler, Alexander Fleming, Mary Wollstonecraft or Einstein would have been able to articulate the impact of their work – even after the fact. Forcing researchers to bend their plans and ideas to fit 'impact' is not good 'value for money'. And why does everything have to be about value for money anyway? One of my old colleagues in an anthropology department was part of a team that discovered that our species, *Homo sapiens*, was not 200,000 years old but 300,000. But what is the 'impact' of that discovery? It didn't benefit local business. Neither did it alter anyone's life for the better. It didn't enhance anyone's wellbeing. The 'impact' is nil, yet I'm at a loss to think of a more important discovery in the last decade. This is what universities should be for: expanding the borders of our knowledge, broadening our worldview. (And while we're at it, my old employer is closing that department, too.

They say it's because they are responding to financial challenges. In such an environment, fees are reshaping what knowledge might exist in the future.)

I'm not going to click my fingers and suggest a fix for this because how we fix it is a discussion that needs to be had. I was particularly diverted by a recent piece in the *Washington Post*, which suggested that the best way to fix universities is to get rid of the academics and then the students – 'the elimination of professors and students would greatly improve most colleges' financial position'.[17] The discussion is unlikely to progress if the focus is only on teaching and cost, if it is overwhelmingly focused on the short term. We are at a moment that counts. It feels as though the university system is teetering on privatisation. The fees are already getting there, though some university leaders are keen for them to be increased.[18] Is this what we want? If so, what next? Should A-level and GCSE students be charged for sitting non-vocational exams? Should they pay for the tuition of them?

John Ruskin, a nineteenth-century art historian and commentator, of whom I am much beloved, said of crumbling Venetian architecture that it is not ours. We cannot go into those buildings and daub over the frescoes, knock out the buttresses and replace them with girders. We cannot do these things because they do not belong to us. Instead, he said, we have been entrusted with their care so that they may be handed on to future trustees. What has happened to the university system over the past decades is like when Cecilia Giménez botched the restoration of García Martínez's *Ecce Homo*, turning the fresco into something now infamously known as the 'monkey Christ'.

If we are not careful, this is the university we will be left with. Instead of world-renowned centres of education, we will have institutions run by bean counters, cheered on by politicians luring students in with their herb walls. The engines of social mobility, the pistons driving our creative economy, all daubed over by inept Education Secretaries who think that painting can't be all that hard. After all, they were privately educated; they can do anything!

xxii

Where is reading in all this? Have Micheal Gove's interventions in the curriculum seen long-term results? In 2009, the overall reading standard for the UK was scored at 494 on the PISA reading scale.[*][19] By 2022, the UK reading score was... still 494.[20] On first glance, this looks bad for the government, but it is important to take into account the scale and level of disruption to children's education caused by the pandemic. In the rankings, the UK had actually risen. There are more downsides, though. The data that was used in the 2022 rankings wasn't ideal. The response rate fell below the OECD's official requirements.

All things considered, the PISA results tell us that reading competency, in terms of the rankings at least, is on the rise. But this is a system in which there has been an all-out push towards prepping children to pass phonics tests. Are these results really enough?

If you speak to teachers, they worry that the current system is not nurturing a love of literature and desire to read for its own sake. The latter is the golden ticket of any kind of education: getting the engine to make itself.

For the decision-makers, this might be the outcome that they

---

[*] The Organisation for Economic Co-operation and Development is a forum in which thirty-seven market-based economies can compare and develop policy standards. The OECD's Programme for International Student Assessment (PISA) compares student attainment in maths, science and reading at the age of fifteen.

desired all along. After all, why do we need a nation of book- and story-loving children? Given the drive towards STEM at every level of education, it's only basic reading competency that matters; only the kind of reading competency that will allow students to 'get by' in other subjects matters. We need children to read so that they can excel in STEM. But it's not like the UK is doing all that well in the science and the maths rankings, either. The UK's science score on the PISA tests has seen a slow but steady decline in the last decade; mathematics has dropped several points over the same period.[21] The drive towards STEM subjects might seem to make sense but only when you deliberately ignore the value of the creative industries in the UK and globally.

As a nation, our best exports, the things we are really good at, are, first and foremost, financial services, which have an estimated export value of £94.9 billion.[22] We are also known throughout the world for our 'defence' exports (this is 'government' for missiles, guns and tanks). The export value there is about £11.5 billion.[23] The push towards STEM makes sense in these contexts. But not when you stop to consider the UK's export value of our creative industries, which is estimated at £45.6 billion.[24] Yet the AHRC is granted 1.4 per cent of government funding.

A government report into creative industries found that the sector 'contributed £109bn to the UK economy in 2021 … equivalent to 5.6% of the UK economy that year'.[25] The report also explained that the creative industries sector of the economy was more resilient than the UK economy as a whole. The sector is growing at twice the rate of the rest of the economy, yet 40 per cent fewer pupils are taking arts GCSEs than in 2010.[26] A government 'vision' for the sector was promised in 2021, then delayed until 2023 and, as of the time of writing, has still not appeared. (If one of my students asked for that kind of extension, I'd slip a disc.) This is why we need a nation of book- and story-loving children, to sustain one of the most significant contributors to our economy.

We know that if we train children to take tests, they get better at taking the tests. What we can be less sure of, though, is what kind of people this is turning them into. We know what Dickens thought of this kind of teaching. Teachers do not like teaching this way, and we know how children feel about it because the number of missed school days is spiralling to pandemic levels. It is being called 'the Gove Effect'.

But does it really matter if children enjoy reading?

Well, there's demonstrative evidence that children who enjoy reading and writing are happier.[27] The National Literacy Trust recently surveyed five- to eighteen-year-olds and drew the conclusion that nearly a million of them don't own a book.[28]

Young people are being deterred from enjoying one of the most life-altering powers available to them via reading and a love of literature. How many children think they are no good at school, just because what they are good at is not valued? Current education policy denies a basic genetic truth: that within any given population there is variation, a broad spectrum of it. When you try to make artsy kids do only STEM, it's like forcing left-handers to write with their right hands.

In political climates so beloved of results, tables and facts, we seem, where the humanities are concerned, to be in a world beyond them. Facts matter to Education Secretaries but only when it suits them. Once the data starts pointing one way, they look in the other. As E. M. Forster said, we truly are in a world 'beyond facts'.

xxiii

Meanwhile, I should have been cosily ensconced in my ivory tower. But instead of working our way through the year, welcome weeks, first assessments, end of term, Christmas break, more courses to teach, Easter, then the final assessments and exam boards, everything was in chaos. All of that steady rhythm was gone and it now felt as comfortable as heading straight down a black run while being struck and tossed by every mogul on the way.

As everyone else was emerging from the disruptions of Covid, there was talk of closing the English department at the university I worked at, maybe some of the arts subjects, too. We were told this was 'because of the data' – as oft-repeated and vague a phrase as 'we are following the science'. Redundancy rounds opened and closed and every time they did, the mood across the institution sank deeper and deeper. News arrived that this was happening very quietly elsewhere, too. Professors – not necessarily 'old' ones – were being leant on to take early retirement. Everyone I spoke to felt this was the endgame. I started looking at other jobs I could do. Perhaps I'd work in a bookshop. I even went so far as to do a bookselling course. Anything, anything to get out of the grind my work had become.

I concluded it was all over for me. I had calculated my redundancy pay, how much I would have to pay in tax and how long I could string out the remaining money. *Far from the Madding Crowd* was ticked off the list. I'd been in that role nearly eighteen years, so it was a good pay-out, but mortgages and bills would have ripped through it all in less than a year. By which time, I would be in my mid-fifties looking for work. Everywhere I looked were news stories like 'Over-fifties at work: "You feel your usefulness has passed"' or 'Broke, unemployed and "useless": how the over-55s are struggling to find post-pandemic work'.

Inevitably, I sunk into a depression, the like of which I've never known. I was living in a fog. All the things that I was supposed to do to help my mental health (exercise, go outside, mindfulness) seemed suddenly ridiculous. People tried to help and said things like, 'You need to get another job.' But the idea of rocking up at an interview somewhere, bounding through the door and singing 'Take meeeeeee!' seemed far from likely.

The depression lasted for months. When people asked how I was, I told them. And I learned, then, just how many of my friends in higher education were already on medication for depression or anxiety. I entertained the notion of antidepressants but refused to be prescribed them on principle. I wasn't medicating because of my job.

The light that pierced the curtain arrived when I resolved to leave. Although I had been able to hold on through eight rounds of voluntary severance or redundancy over several years, it was now at too high a price. Despite my strength of belief in the value of what I was doing, it was becoming impossible to actually do any of it. I had accepted defeat and would surrender what I'd worked for. At the next opportunity, I would give up and do something else. I would take some time to recover, then make a plan. The main thing was to get out. My head cleared a little. Some days there was only a light mist instead of heavy fog. All I had to do was sit it out and wait for the next round of redundancies. Meanwhile, my employer was announcing further restructures and changes in governance. Academics would be asked to teach for three terms instead of two. A fourth term would also be put on the books but the staff were reassured that this could mostly be used as vacation or research time. None of it mattered to me; I had already mentally resigned.

I knew I was reaching another crisis. I found myself rereading A. S. Byatt's *Possession* for a third time. I dug around for my old copy and found it among the piles of books in my office. When I opened it, a visitor pass from 2004 fell out – it was from when I had gone to meet the 'famous author' agent in that year and the discovery made all the hope, optimism and energy of that time resurface.

The first time I'd read *Possession*, I was through the book in five days flat, but things were very different now. This time, while I was re-rereading the novel – one which revels in the romance of academic labour, in the love of books, of poetry, of language – a job was advertised. They wouldn't take me. I'm not qualified. Why would they take someone like me? I hesitated in submitting the application because it would only lead to the humiliation of not being shortlisted. Worse, being shortlisted and having to submit to presentations and attend panel interviews while depressed. No. But I'd made the mistake of telling my husband about the vacancy and he only encouraged me, so there was now no way out of applying. I had no armour; I couldn't possibly slay the dragon and rescue the prince. They would see it – they would see how incapable I'd become.

Nonetheless, I felt strongly that I wasn't finished with academia even though it seemed to be finishing with me. I still felt passionately that I wanted to help people, especially those students who needed it most, and I felt I was somebody who might understand what they were coming from and how far they might be able to go.

Once I was invited for interview, I went full Leslie Knope in preparing. I had folders, binders, slews of notes. I had Post-its, highlighters and even a maths set to help me draw shapes to link notes together. I wrote and rewrote answers to generic interview questions, over and over and over. I practised saying a few out loud. I refined the notes into a single notebook, but there were still so many, I actually had to create a contents page and an index. I made infographics as mnemonics so I could remember long sections of dialogue, like you do for a TED Talk.

When the day arrived, instead of the 550-mile commute that I usually had to do for work, I strolled less than a couple of miles across the city. In the room were four members of staff who introduced themselves and began.

'So, Vybarr. Why York?'

They had pronounced my name correctly.

Notes

Chapter 1

1   *The Scientific Century: securing our future prosperity* (London: The Royal Society, 2010), p. 14.

2   'Annual net sales revenue of Amazon from 2004 to 2023', Statistica.com, 1 February 2024, https://is.gd/oJEsVF accessed 10 May 2024

3   Mayank Tiwari, 'Stay home, stay well-read: Pandemic drives book sales in twin cities', *New India Express*, 11 April 2021, https://is.gd/8i76V9, accessed 21 December 2023; Tauseef Shahidi, 'Pandemic a boon for books, bane for bookstores', *Mint*, 16 September 2020, https://is.gd/7CEyFn accessed 21 December 2023.

4   'Publishing in 2020', *Publisher's Association*, 27 April 2021, https://is.gd/DxWj3a accessed 10 May 2024

5   '"Projects", Australia's creative industries: valuation', *SGS Economics and Planning*, December 2013, https://is.gd/UXtSbL accessed 21 December 2023; 'Creative Economy Contributes over $1.1 trillion to the US Economy', *National Assembly of State Arts Agencies*, 25 March 2024, https://is.gd/PryIRM accessed 10 May 2024.

6   Angus Fletcher and John Monterosso, 'The Science of Free-Indirect Discourse: An Alternate Cognitive Effect', *Narrative*, 24:1, January 2016, pp. 82–103.

7   Mary Oliver, 'The World I Live In', in *Devotions: The selected poems of Mary Oliver* (New York: Corsair, 2019), p. 5.

8   Caitlin Cassidy, 'Students choose arts degrees in droves despite huge rise in fees under Morrison government', *The Guardian*, 13 April 2024, https://is.gd/a3eXNw accessed 9 May 2024.

9   Daniel Kurt, 'What Harvard Actually Costs', *Investopedia*, 7 August 2023, https://is.gd/aUvQeF accessed 10 May 2024.

10   'Teacher Salary by Country 2024', *World Population Review*, https://is.gd/F1BDSq accessed 10 May 2024.

11   Will Hazell, 'University courses: number of students taking humanities subjects is down 40,000 in 10 years', *The i*, 23 September 2021, https://is.gd/GNugRu accessed 10 May 2024

12   David Laurence, 'The Decline in Humanities Majors', *The Trend – Research and Analysis from the MLA Office of Programs*, 26 June 2017, https://is.gd/ORrlHo accessed 21 December 2023; Benjamin Schmidt, 'The Humanities Are in Crisis', *The Atlantic*, 23 August 2018, https://is.gd/aXarqA accessed 10 May 2024.

13   Eleanor Hopkins et al., 'English Studies Provision in UK Higher Education', *The British Academy*, June 2023, p. 27, https://is.gd/AClzxT accessed 10 May 2024.

14   Oxford Learning College, 'The UK Degrees With the Best Earning Potential', https://is.gd/OdfzYZ accessed 21 December 2023.

15   'Employment Outcomes of Bachelor's Degree Holders', The Condition of Education 2020, *National Center for Education Statistics*, https://is.gd/d3wBI7 accessed 10 May 2024.

16   Ibid.

17   The AHRC gives £110 million of funding to projects each year. The total UKRI funds are in excess of £8 billion. See 'Who AHRC is', *UK Research and Innovation*, 28 November 2023, https://is.gd/oKsG4a accessed 10 May 2024; 'Geographical Distribution of UKRI Spend FY 2019–20 and FY 2020–21', *UK Research and Innovation*, p. 7, https://is.gd/4ayTWH accessed 10 May 2024

18 Sophie Thomas, 'Prime Minister's Questions: Rishi Sunak says it is "absolutely right" Gavin Williamson resigned – and admits "regret" over appointment', Sky News, 9 November 2022, https://is.gd/ndomc1 accessed 21 December 2023.

19 Aubrey Allegretti, 'Gavin Williamson apparently confuses Maro Itoje with Marcus Rashford', *The Guardian*, 8 September 2021, https://is.gd/se7mio accessed 21 December 2023; Sally Weale, 'Funding cuts to go ahead for university arts courses in England despite opposition', *The Guardian*, 8 September 2021, https://is.gd/isk51s accessed 10 May 2024.

20 Anna Isaac, 'Nadhim Zahawi "agreed on penalty" to settle tax bill worth millions', *The Guardian*, 20 January 2023, https://is.gd/sUElv6 accessed 21 December 2023.

21 Andrew Woodcock, 'Gavin Williamson knighted six months after losing cabinet job following exams fiasco', *The Independent*, 3 March 2022, https://is.gd/se7mio accessed 10 May 2024.

22 John Milton, 'Areopagitica', in *Areopagitica & Other Writings*, edited by William Poole (London: Penguin, 2014).

23 Stephen King, *On Writing: A memoir of the craft* (New York: Scribner, 2000), p. 104.

Chapter 2

1 Vincent J. Felitti, 'The Relation Between Adverse Childhood Experiences and Adult Health: Turning Gold into Lead', *The Permanente Journal*, 6(1), Winter 2002, pp. 44–47.

2 Amber Dance, 'Survival of the Littlest', *Nature*, 582(7810), June 2020, pp. 20–3.

3 M. D. R. Evans, Jonathan Kelley, Joanna Sikora et al., 'Family scholarly culture and educational success: Books and schooling in 27 nations', *Research in Social Stratification and Mobility*, 28(2), June 2010, pp. 171–97.

4 Board of Education, *The Teaching of English in Secondary Schools* (London: HMSO, 1910).

5 Nowell Smith, 'The Place of Literature in Education', in *Cambridge Essays on Education*, edited by A. C. Benson (Cambridge: Cambridge University Press, 1918), pp. 107–8.

6 James Callaghan, 'A rational debate based on the facts', Ruskin College Oxford, 18 October 1976, https://is.gd/xbvWoH

7 Raymond A. Mar, Keith Oatley, Jacob Hirsh et al., 'Bookworms versus nerds: Exposure to fiction versus non-fiction, divergent associations with social ability, and the simulation of fictional social worlds', *Journal of Research in Personality*, 40(5), October 2006, pp. 694–712. See also R. A. Mar and K. Oatley, 'The function of fiction is the abstraction and simulation of social experience', *Perspectives on Psychological Science*, 3(3), 2008, pp. 173–192.

8 See also Keith Oatley, *Such Stuff as Dreams: The Psychology of Fiction* (Oxford: Blackwell, 2011); Keith Oatley, 'Why Fiction May Be Twice as True as Fact: Fiction as Cognitive and Emotional Simulation', *Review of General Psychology*, 3(2), June 1999, pp. 101–17.

9 NSPCC, 'Statistics briefing: child sexual abuse', March 2021, https://is.gd/6TH4cQ accessed 16 May 2023.

10 For some moving and hair-raising accounts of conversion therapies and an exploration of the relationship between diagnosis and homosexuality, see the excellent Jules Montague, *The Imaginary Patient: How Diagnosis Gets Us Wrong* (London: Granta, 2022).

11 *The Sun*, 20 August 1983; *The Sun*, 14 October 1985; *Daily Telegraph*, 15 November 1985; *The Sun*, 12 December 1987.

12 *Daily Express*, 13 December 1987.

13 *Private Eye*, August 1985.

14 Kim Pilling, 'No-nonsense "God's copper" James Anderton dies aged 89', *The Independent*, 6 May 2022, https://is.gd/B8wwDq accessed 18 May 2023.

15 Hansard, HC Deb, 18 May 1982.

16 See Claire Monk's wonderful *Heritage Film Audiences: Period Films and Contemporary Audiences in the UK* (Edinburgh: Edinburgh University Press, 2012).

17 Margaret Thatcher, speech to the Conservative Party Conference, Winter Gardens, Blackpool, 9 October 1987, https://is.gd/Vxbwfc accessed 22 May 2023.

18 Local Government Act 1988, https://is.gd/Kc6QLl accessed 9 June 2023.

19 'The 10 least and most trusted professions in the UK', *CV Library*, 10 June 2019, https://is.gd/czlHie accessed 6 February 2024.

20 Rahil Sheikh, 'Crumbling schools plagued by leaks and cold, BBC finds', BBC News, 22 January 2024, https://is.gd/SUUETs accessed 8 February 2024.

21 Gill Plimmer, 'UK's HS2 railway offers "very poor value for money", MPs warn', *Financial Times*, 7 February 2024, https://is.gd/Bc37Nh accessed 8 February 2024.

Chapter 3

1   Stonewall, *LGBT in Britain: Health Report*, 2018, https://is.gd/Ci2OTj accessed 20 June 2023.

2   E. M. Forster, *Where Angels Fear to Tread* (Harmondsworth: Penguin, 1985), p. 146

3   Ibid., p. 157.

4   Oliver Stallybrass, 'Introduction' in E. M. Forster, *The Life to Come and Other Stories* (London: Edward Arnold, 1972), p. iv.

5   John S. Lofty, 'News from England: Coming Home to the National Curriculum', *English Education*, 22(4), December 1990, pp. 241–64, p. 241.

6   Patrick Parrinder, 'Nationalising English', review of *The Great Betrayal: Memoirs of a Life in Education* by Brian Cox, *London Review of Books*, 15(2), 28 January 1993, https://is.gd/ZxmhuN accessed 12 June 2023.

7   'Mathematics programmes of study: Key Stage 3', *National curriculum in England* (Department for Education, September 2013).

8   'Science programmes of study: Key Stage 3', *National curriculum in England* (Department for Education, September 2013).

9   'English programmes of study: Key Stage 3', *National curriculum in England* (Department for Education, September 2013).

10 Department for Education, *The Cox Report: English for ages 5 to 16* (London: HMSO, 1989), https://is.gd/B3qJCO accessed 24 March 2024.

11 Ibid.

12 See Jonnie Robinson, 'Grammatical variation across the UK', British Library, https://is.gd/edfDa7 accessed 12 June 2023.

13 Richard Hudson and John Walmsley, 'The English Patient: English Grammar and teaching in the twentieth century', *Journal of Linguistics*, 41(3), November 2005, pp. 593–622.

14 Kitt Carpenter, 'Gay Men Used to Earn Less than Straight Men; Now They Earn More', *Harvard Business Review*, 4 December 2017, https://is.gd/dNB1iq accessed 22 June 2023; see also Marieka Klawitter, 'Meta-Analysis of the Effects of Sexual Orientation on Earnings', *Industrial Relations*, 54(1), January 2015, pp. 4–32.

15 Matthew Whysall, 'Ian McEwan: watch the interview in full – video', *The Guardian*, 3 April 2012, https://is.gd/I5aK25 accessed 24 June 2023.

16 N. Landi et al., 'Neurobiological bases of reading comprehension: Insights from neuroimaging studies of word level and text level processing in skilled and impaired readers', *Reading and Writing Quarterly*, 29(2), April 2013, pp. 145–67.

17 'Facts and Figures', *The Open University*, https://is.gd/uKCXlw accessed 27 June 2023.

18 'Brian Walden Interview with Margaret Thatcher', Margaret Thatcher Foundation, LWT transcript, https://is.gd/JAYnWE accessed 28 June 2023.

19 Keith Oatley, 'A Feeling for Fiction', *The Greater Good Magazine*, 1 September 2005, https://is.gd/zJhLJv accessed 19 October 2023.

20 David Comer Kidd and Emanuele Castano, 'Reading Literary Fiction Improves Theory of Mind', *Science*, 342(6156), 3 October 2013, pp. 377–80, https://is.gd/N28oQq accessed 19 October 2023.

21 G. S. Berns et al., 'Short- and long-term effects of a novel on connectivity in the brain', *Brain Connectivity* 3(6), 2013, pp. 590–600.

22 Carmen Aguilar García, Pamela Duncan, Paul Torpey et al., 'This year's A-level results in England explained in five charts', *The Guardian*, 18 August 2022, https://is.gd/shrEHq accessed 3 July 2023.

23 'Pupil absence in schools in England – Autumn term 2022/23', National Statistics, 18 May 2023, https://is.gd/3Fvdc2 accessed 3 July 2023.

24 NHS Digital, 'Mental Health of Children and Young People in England 2021 – wave 2 follow up to the 2017 survey', NHS England, 30 September 2021, https://is.gd/7lE0YF accessed 3 July 2023.

25 Maeve Thornton, Merike Darmody and Selina McCoy, 'Persistent Absenteeism among Irish Primary School Pupils', *Education Review*, 65(4), 2013, pp. 488–501; Gary W. Ladd, Eric S. Buhs and Michael Seid, 'Children's Initial Sentiments About Kindergarten: Is School Liking an Antecedent of Early Classroom Participation and Achievement?', *Merrill-Palmer Quarterly*, 46(2), April 2000, pp. 255–79; Lucy Riglin, Norah Frederickson, Katherine H. Shelton et al., 'A longitudinal study of psychological functioning and academic attainment at the transition to secondary school', *Journal of Adolescence*, 36(3), June 2013, pp. 507–17.

26 'Simon Pegg says "f*** the Tories" in scathing Rishi Sunak criticism', YouTube, https://is.gd/wOOsFI accessed 3 July 2023.

27 Eleanor Busby, 'Bradford primary school Feversham Primary Academy transformed by love of music in running for £40,000 global prize', *Yorkshire Post*, 15 June 2023, https://is.gd/wf6zk2 accessed 14 December 2023.

Chapter 4

1 Press release by the Department for Education, 'Crackdown on rip-off university degrees', 17 July 2023, https://is.gd/13LMGk accessed 20 February 2024.

2 Andrew Frobisher, 'Degree Dropouts', *Debut*, 30 January 2020, https://is.gd/KdaYmd accessed 17 July 2023.

3 Figures adapted from Sabrina Collier, 'How Much Does it Cost to Study in Europe?', QS Top Universities, 15 September 2022, https://is.gd/OBzds2 accessed 21 February 2024.

4 'Elegy Written in a Country Churchyard', The Thomas Gray Archive, https://is.gd/iytEUQ accessed 17 July 2023.

5 'Take Up Figures 1991–2005', Student Loans Company, https://is.gd/Ta5A59 accessed 17 July 23.

6 Department for Education, *The Dearing Report: Higher Education in the learning society* (London: HMSO, 1997), https://is.gd/8W6iXC accessed 21 July 2023.

7 Ibid.

8 Ibid.

9 Hansard, HC Debs, 29 October 1997, cols. 891–9, https://is.gd/J9CdGn accessed 21 July 2023.

10 Hansard, HC Debs, 4 November 1997, cols. 118–75, https://is.gd/Prvl2L accessed 21 July 2023.

11 Sue Littlemore, 'Student tuition fees: costly changes', BBC News, 19 May 1998, https://is.gd/2FKBHL accessed 25 July 2023.

12 Paul Bolton and Joe Lewis, 'Equality of access and outcomes in higher education in England', *House of Commons Library*, 31 January 2023, https://is.gd/pgmpSf accessed 20 July 2023; Nicole Stephens and Sarah Townsend, 'The unseen reason working-class students drop out', *Politico*, 16 January 2019, https://is.gd/5zCpRR accessed 24 March 2024; Rachel Hall, 'Disadvantaged graduates earn half as much as privileged peers in first job', *The Guardian*, 12 November 2021, https://is.gd/ytZOz2 accessed 11 May 2024; Harriet Coombs, 'First-in-Family Students', *Higher Education Policy Institute*, HEPI Report 146, 2021, p. 9. See also Victoria Yuen, 'New Insights into Attainment for Low-Income Students', *Center for American Progress*, https://is.gd/gxA9qH accessed 20 July 2023.

13 Committee on Higher Education, *The Robbins Report: Higher Education* (London: HMSO, 1963), https://is.gd/4N5lya accessed 20 July 2023.

14 Laura Peek, 'Medieval history is bunk, says Clarke', *The Times*, 9 May 2003, https://is.gd/fVDMb0 accessed 12 May 2024.

15 'Clarke questions study as "adornment"', BBC News, 9 May 2003, https://is.gd/xyQ312 accessed 8 September 2023.

16 Will Woodward and Rebecca Smithers, 'Clarke dismisses medieval historians', *The Guardian*, 9 May 2003, https://is.gd/DwOZ2w accessed 3 June 2024.

17 Jeevan Vasagar and Rebecca Smithers, 'Will Charles Clarke have his place in history?', *The Guardian*, 10 May 2003, https://is.gd/1H3XIE accessed 12 May 2024.

18 'Charles Clarke: You Ask The Questions', *The Independent*, 31 March 2008, https://is.gd/x93Ze4 accessed 12 May 2024.

19 George Eliot, 'The Natural History of German Life', *Westminster Review*, vol. LXVI, July 1856, p. 54.

20 D. C. Kidd and E. Castano, 'Reading literary fiction improves theory of mind', *Science*, 342(6156), 2013, pp. 377–80, https://is.gd/x7ZHvc accessed 2 March 2024.

21 Bruno Dubuc, 'Broca's Area, Wernicke's Area and Other Language-Processing Areas in the Brain', *The Brain from Top to Bottom*, McGill, https://is.gd/hKdIl4 accessed 12 May 2024.

22 Labour Party, *2001 Labour Party General Election Manifesto*, https://is.gd/cvhqG8 accessed 18 September 2023.

Chapter 5

1 Pati Hill, 'Truman Capote, The Art of Fiction No. 17', *The Paris Review*, 16, spring–summer 1957, https://is.gd/86LEOZ accessed 3 October 2023.

2 Conservative Party, *The Conservative Manifesto 2010*, https://is.gd/sOCAJ9 accessed 19 September 2023.

3 Liberal Democrats, *Liberal Democrat Manifesto 2010*, https://is.gd/sOCAJ9 accessed 19 September 2023.

4 Greg Hands, 'Nick Clegg's Tory Past', *Conservative Home*, 15 April 2008, https://is.gd/w35zNK accessed 1 September 2023.

5 Department for Education, *Securing a Sustainable Future for Higher Education: An Independent Review of Higher Education Funding & Student Finance*, https://is.gd/VrGgJ2 accessed 19 September 2023.

6 John Morgan, 'Now that's research impact: "paradigm-shifting" Browne drew on a single opinion survey', *Times Higher Education*, 6 January 2011, https://is.gd/Cq2TLG accessed 19 September 2023. See also Richard Taylor, 'Browne Opinion Survey', What Do They Know, 10 March 2011, https://is.gd/LZCuVi accessed 19 September 2023.

7 Paul Bolton, 'Student loan statistics', *House of Commons Library*, 1 December 2023, https://is.gd/W8exuH accessed 5 March 2024.

8 Azara Lantra, 'How Much Does College Tuition Cost for US Universities?', Shorelight, 9 August 2023, https://is.gd/dv9E4Y accessed 3 June 2024.

9 Mohammad Nurunnabi and Abdelhakim Abdelhadi, 'Student satisfaction in the Russell Group and Non-Russell Group Universities in UK', *Data in Brief*, 22, February 2019, pp. 76–82; Richard Adams, 'Is the Russell Group Still Relevant?', *The Guardian*, 10 September 2023, https://is.gd/EkOfqH accessed 12 May 2024.

10 Richard Adams, 'Is the Russell Group Still Relevant?'.

11 Ibid.

12 *London Economics*, 'The Exchequer costs and benefits of student loan forgiveness for nurses: Report for the Royal College of Nursing, May 2022', https://is.gd/K2t3gR accessed 12 October 2023.

13 Anna Fazackerley, 'Schools across England face unprecedented struggle to hire English teachers as recruitment crisis grows', *The Guardian*, 17 June 2023, https://is.gd/tfmrer accessed 12 October 2023.

14 Chihiro Udagawa and Christine Whitehead, 'Private sector rents and rates of return, 1996/97 to 2000/01', Dataspring, September 2006, https://is.gd/3MRKMp accessed 12 October 2023.

15 Ellie Isaac, 'The beginner's guide to renting costs', Zoopla, 8 February 2024, https://is.gd/OR1ppS accessed 12 May 2024.

16 Alison Flood, 'Thousands call for Michael Gove to go in wake of GCSE English literature row', *The Guardian*, 5 June 2014, https://is.gd/rARKMH accessed 12 October 2023.

17 Holly Bancroft, 'Revealed: Michael Gove's sexist jibes, racist jokes and homophobic slurs', *The Independent*, 13 September 2021, https://is.gd/nh1V7O accessed 12 May 2024.

18 'Michael Gove Talking Passionately on Education in October 2010', YouTube, https://is.gd/fJp2Wn accessed 23 May 2024.

19 'Gove's education speech to Conservative conference', Local Government Information Unit – the local democracy blog, 5 October 2010, https://is.gd/rixrks accessed 12 May 2024.

20 Mike Baker, 'Tory school reform: Autonomy v tradition', BBC News, 6 October 2010, https://is.gd/SMdflV accessed 12 May 2024.

21 Ibid.

22 Jessica Shepherd, 'NUT passes unanimous vote of no confidence in Michael Gove', *The Guardian*, 2 April 2013, https://is.gd/ID7hIK accessed 17 October 2023.

23 'ITV News – Changes to National Curriculum', ITV News, 8 July 2013, YouTube, https://is.gd/oGEfM5 accessed 16 October 2023.

24 Department for Education, 'National Curriculum: Sue Wilkinson on Physical Education', YouTube, 3 June 2014, https://is.gd/Y0VAE9 accessed 16 October 2023.

25 'Michael Gove on BBCQT – The National Curriculum 21/03/2013', YouTube, https://is.gd/jP7IIj accessed 16 October 2023.

26 Standards Testing Agency, 'Phonics screening check: 2023 materials', 26 June 2023, https://is.gd/bBUjED accessed 17 October 2023.

27 Aletha Adu, 'Nearly 7,000 ambulance workers in England left job in past year, figures show', *The Guardian*, 22 August 2023, https://is.gd/82rSaA, accessed 21 October 2022; '"Alarming" numbers of recruits leaving police before completing their probation', *Suffolk Police Federation*, 17 March 2022, https://is.gd/BgIllW accessed 21 October 2022; Amy Walker, 'Record rate of teacher departures as 40,000 quit sector last year', Schools Week, 8 June 2023, https://is.gd/O5hVwE accessed 12 May 2024.

28 Sally Weale, 'Focus on phonics to teach reading is "failing children", says landmark study', *The Guardian*, 19 January 2022, https://is.gd/3NizWH accessed 17 October 2023.

29 National Literacy Trust, 'Children and young people's reading in 2023', 4 September 2023, https://is.gd/3WOb4m accessed 6 March 2024.

30 National Literacy Trust, 'New research reveals only 1 in 3 children enjoy writing in their free time', 1 June 2023, https://is.gd/3WOb4m accessed 6 March 2024.

31 Standards and Testing Agency, 'Key stage 2 tests: 2022 English grammar, punctuation and spelling test materials', 20 May 2022, https://is.gd/CQm7Av accessed 17 October 2023.

32 'English programmes of study: Key Stage 3', *National curriculum in England* (Department for Education, September 2013), https://is.gd/xPcyE9 accessed 18 October 2023.

33 Ibid.

34 Lynsey McCulloch and Matthew Collins, 'Time to Act', Royal Shakespeare Company, 2024, https://is.gd/EdLN5U accessed 6 March 2024.

35 Raymond A. Mar, Keith Oatley et al., 'Emotion and narrative fiction: Interactive influences before, during, and after reading', *Cognition & Emotion*, 25(5), May 2024, pp. 818–33, https://is.gd/nc77oz accessed 19 October 2023.

36 Thalia Goldstein, 'The Pleasure of Unadulterated Sadness: Experiencing Sorrow in Fiction, Nonfiction, and

'In Person"', *Psychology of Aesthetics, Creativity, and the Arts*, 3(4), November 2009, pp. 232–7, https://is.gd/H6D5H2 accessed 19 October 2023.

37 National Literacy Trust, 'Children and young people's reading engagement in 2021', 12 October 2021, https://shorturl.at/hnJLO accessed 19 October 2023.

38 Megan Mansworth and Marcello Giovanelli, 'The significance of emotion in English literature teaching', in *The New Newbolt Report*, edited by Andrew Green (Routledge: London, 2021).

39 'English programmes of study: Key Stage 4', *National curriculum in England* (Department for Education, July 2014), https://is.gd/6daIT3 accessed 23 October 2023.

40 'Survey into A Level recruitment: summary report', English and Media Centre, 9 December 2019, https://is.gd/TsStwT accessed 23 October 2023.

41 Ibid.

42 Ibid.

43 'Set text selector: English Literature A', AQA, https://is.gd/YroyDb accessed 29 March 2024

44 Richard Adams, 'Warnings of economic damage to UK as international student numbers fall by a third', *The Guardian*, 29 February 2024, https://is.gd/aoq2Wy accessed 29 March 2024

45 Claire Shaw, 'Lifting the cap on student numbers: five lessons learned from Australia', *The Guardian*, 7 August 2014, https://is.gd/xjGHTS accessed 24 October 2023. See also Andrew Norton, 'Unleashing student demand by ending number controls in Australia: An incomplete experiment?', *HEPI Report 68*, Higher Education Policy Institute, April 2014, https://is.gd/5Qml2K accessed 24 October 2023.

46 William Annandale, 'Mid-ranking universities will feel squeeze when student numbers cap ends', *The Guardian*, 3 July 2014, https://is.gd/hGaxP0 accessed 24 October 2023.

47 Charles Morgan, *The House of Macmillan* (London: Macmillan, 1944), p. 88.

48 Michael Millgate, *Thomas Hardy: A Biography Revisited* (Oxford: Oxford University Press, 2004), p. 104.

49 Unsigned review, *The Spectator*, 22 April 1871, pp. 481–3.

50 Thomas Hardy, *The Woodlanders*, edited by Patricia Ingham (London: Penguin, 1998), pp. 6–7.

51 'Media Advisory: Pen America Experts on Book Bans Available, Ahead of Senate Hearing 9/12', *Pen America*, 11 September 2023, https://is.gd/e8BGL4 accessed 15 November 2023.

52 Kiara Alfonseca, 'More than 40,000 people killed in gun violence so far in 2023', ABC News, 7 December 2023, https://is.gd/Wkgpfr accessed 12 May 2024.

Chapter 6

1 Sue Littlemore, 'Student tuition fees: costly changes', BBC News, 19 May 1998, https://is.gd/2FKBHL accessed 25 July 2023.

2 Joe Lewis and Paul Bolton, 'The Lifelong Learning Entitlement', House of Commons Library, 12 March 2024, https://is.gd/GJyDZC accessed 5 December 2023.

3 Ibid.

4 David M. J. Lazer, Matthew A. Baum, Yochai Benkler et al., 'The science of fake news', *Science*, 359(6380), 9 March 2018, pp. 1094–6, https://is.gd/l2683z; Allesandro Siani and Imogen Green, 'Scientific Misinformation and Mistrust of COVID-19 Preventive Measures among the UK Population: A Pilot Study', *Vaccines*, 11(2), 30 January 2023, https://is.gd/VGnexJ accessed 28 March 2024.

5 Bertrand Russell, *New Hopes for a Changing World* (London: George Allen & Unwin, 1960), pp. 10–11.

6 'Top 10 Banned Books That Changed the Face of Black History', National Coalition Against Censorship, 5 February 2015, https://tinyurl.com/yeb32kxo accessed 12 May 2024.

7 Keith Hoskin, 'The Examination, Disciplinary Power and Rational Schooling', *History of Education*, 8(2), 1979, pp. 135–46, p. 144.

8 R. A. Hummer and E. M. Hernandez, 'The Effect of Educational Attainment on Adult Mortality in the United States', *Population Bulletin*, 68(1), June 2013, pp. 1–16, https://is.gd/QxLTso accessed 13 December 2023.

9 Brian Connolly, 'How Much Does Amazon Make Every Year?', Jungle Scout, 27 October 2023, https://is.gd/HGrNp2 accessed 13 December 2023.

10 Matt Schultz, 'Student Loan Debt Statistics', Lending Tree, 10 August 2023, https://is.gd/ovLE7E accessed 12 May 2024.

11 Paul Bolton, 'Student loan statistics', House of Commons Library, 1 December 2023, https://is.gd/o6qgee accessed 28 March 2024.

12 Frederico Cardoso and Zoë McHayle, 'The Economic and Social Costs of Mental Ill Health – Review of Methodology and Update of Calculations', Centre for Mental Health, 27 March 2024, https://is.gd/NhQ3Id accessed 12 May 2024.

13 'The Economic Contributions of the Higher Education Sector in England: Summary report prepared for

Universities UK', Frontier Economics, 27 September 2021, https://tinyurl.com/np69y948 accessed 29 March 2024.

14 Department for Education, 'Higher Education and Research Bill', 19 May 2016, https://is.gd/ms7G6T accessed 19 March 2024.

15 House of Lords Industry and Regulators Committee, 'The Office for Students is not trusted by students or universities', 13 September 2023, https://is.gd/y8J1hD accessed 19 March 2024.

16 Daniel Boffey, 'Academic fury over order to study the big society', *The Guardian*, 27 March 2011, https://is.gd/M7HJub accessed 14 December 2023.

17 Gary Smith, 'How to fix college finances? Eliminate faculty, then students', *The Washington Post*, 23 April 2024, https://is.gd/h7ZtKH accessed 16 May 2024.

18 Patrick Jack, 'Increase tuition fees "really quickly" after election, says Stern', *Times Higher Education*, 29 February 2024, https://is.gd/i2I2Fl accessed 12 May 2024.

19 OECD, *PISA 2009 Results: Executive Summary*, https://is.gd/9NuRbE accessed 14 December 2023.

20 OECD, 'PISA 2022 Results Factsheets: United Kingdom', 5 December 2023, https://is.gd/ZK6MOz accessed 14 December 2023.

21 OECD, 'PISA 2022 Results: Factsheets, United Kingdom', 5 December 2023, https://is.gd/fNTJNW accessed 12 May 2024.

22 'UK generates world-leading financial services trade surplus', TheCityUK, 18 January 2024, https://is.gd/ZIbDEp accessed 13 May 2024.

23 Hamish Morrison, 'How much does Britain make from arms sales?', *The National*, 22 April 2024, https://is.gd/8bjKPK accessed 13 May 2024.

24 'Creative Industries Add Almost £25bn To UK Trade Balance', Creative Industries Council, 27 September 2023, https://is.gd/cPVTcJ accessed 13 May 2024.

25 Edward Scott, 'Arts and creative industries: The case for a strategy', House of Lords Library, 1 December 2022, https://is.gd/BHsoSE accessed 14 December 2023.

26 Cultural Learning Alliance, 'Arts GCSE and A Level entries 2022', 25 August 2022, https://is.gd/oS2uLz accessed 14 December 2023.

27 'Children who enjoy reading and writing have significantly better mental wellbeing than their peers', National Literary Trust, 25 September 2018, https://is.gd/aWC2ym accessed 12 May 2024; National Literacy Trust, 'Mental wellbeing, reading and writing', 26 September 2018, https://is.gd/Q2dO7g accessed 14 December 2023.

28 National Literacy Trust, 'What is Literacy?', https://is.gd/8eSNFM accessed 14 December 2023.

Acknowledgements

T hanks to the many teachers with whom I spoke and who wished to remain anonymous. Thanks to Olivia Beattie for liking the book. Thanks also to Catriona Allon for liking it (despite having done a fine job of editing it too) and to everyone at Biteback. I'd like to thank the *Literary Review* for publishing essays that became parts of Chapters 1 and 5 as 'Pages for the Ages' (September 2016) and 'One Book, Thirty-Six Years' (September 2021). Thanks also to Olivia Marlow; Professor Abi Curtis and Dr Anne-Marie Evans; my agent, Jane Graham-Maw, for believing it was worthwhile; to Dr Sara Lyons, Dr Lars Atkin, Dr Bashir Abu-Manneh and also to Dr Florian Stadtler for checking my German; to Amy Sackville for support in so many ways; Siân Prime for always listening; my siblings Rebecca, Erika and John for putting up with their little brother that learned and performed all the dance moves to Brotherhood of Man's 'Save Your Kisses for Me' and many more; to Helen Pleasance for taking the time and to Helen Walker, Dr Clive Johnson and Aylla MacPhail for the same; to Catherine Brereton; and to Sheelagh O'Farrell for practically daring me; to Lynne Truss for encouraging me; to my mum, Johanna, for all she did for me and for all of us; but most of all to my husband Adam for making me laugh twenty times a day, as well as everything else, basically all the time.